Walter Lippmann

SPIRITUAL LIVES

General Editor
Timothy Larsen

The *Spiritual Lives* series features biographies of prominent men and women whose eminence is not primarily based on a specifically religious contribution. Each volume provides a general account of the figure's life and thought, while giving special attention to his or her religious contexts, convictions, doubts, objections, ideas, and actions. Many leading politicians, writers, musicians, philosophers, and scientists have engaged deeply with religion in significant and resonant ways that have often been overlooked or underexplored. Some of the volumes will even focus on men and women who were lifelong unbelievers, attending to how they navigated and resisted religious questions, assumptions, and settings. The books in this series will therefore recast important figures in fresh and thought-provoking ways.

Walter Lippmann

American Skeptic, American Pastor

MARK THOMAS EDWARDS

OXFORD
UNIVERSITY PRESS

Great Clarendon Street, Oxford, OX2 6DP,
United Kingdom

Oxford University Press is a department of the University of Oxford.
It furthers the University's objective of excellence in research, scholarship,
and education by publishing worldwide. Oxford is a registered trade mark of
Oxford University Press in the UK and in certain other countries

© Mark Thomas Edwards 2023

The moral rights of the author have been asserted

All rights reserved. No part of this publication may be reproduced, stored in
a retrieval system, or transmitted, in any form or by any means, without the
prior permission in writing of Oxford University Press, or as expressly permitted
by law, by licence or under terms agreed with the appropriate reprographics
rights organization. Enquiries concerning reproduction outside the scope of the
above should be sent to the Rights Department, Oxford University Press, at the
address above

You must not circulate this work in any other form
and you must impose this same condition on any acquirer

Published in the United States of America by Oxford University Press
198 Madison Avenue, New York, NY 10016, United States of America

British Library Cataloguing in Publication Data

Data available

Library of Congress Control Number: 2023930671

ISBN 978–0–19–289516–5

DOI: 10.1093/oso/9780192895165.001.0001

Printed and bound by
CPI Group (UK) Ltd, Croydon, CR0 4YY

Links to third party websites are provided by Oxford in good faith and
for information only. Oxford disclaims any responsibility for the materials
contained in any third party website referenced in this work.

Contents

Preface — vii
Acknowledgments — xi

   Introduction — 1

Part I: The Younger Lippmann

1. The Disciple, 1889–1913 — 19
2. The Theologian, 1913–1930 — 39
3. The Priest, 1913–1930 — 62

Part II: The Older Lippmann

4. The Evangelist, 1930–1939 — 99
5. The Prophet, 1939–1949 — 130
6. The Shepherd, 1949–1960 — 162
7. The Heretic, 1960–1974 — 188
   Epilogue: Saint Walter — 204

Selected Bibliography — 213
Index — 221

Preface

The columnist and his wife were just settling into their seats aboard the plane when they received the letter: Nikita Khrushchev, the Premier of the Soviet Union, was delayed at the Black Sea. He would not be free for their meeting in Moscow until a week later. Their interview was intended to serve as an icebreaker before Khrushchev's summit with President John F. Kennedy in Vienna in April 1961. The couple had been preparing for weeks through meetings with Soviet officials, the CIA, and even Kennedy himself. Furthermore, any delay threatened their narrow travel window, which included a private consultation with Pope John XXIII and then some alone time in Paris. Rescheduling simply would not do. The newsman wrote "impossible" on a note intended for a Soviet ambassador. By the time they had landed in Rome, the conference was back on. Khrushchev greeted his guests on time with a bear hug, more food and vodka than they could manage, badminton at his posh villa, and hours of conversation about world affairs. The correspondent went home a few pounds heavier and ready to pen what would become his second Pulitzer-prize-winning series—thanks to his partner, notetaker, and translator Helen who had spent six months learning Russian.[1]

That columnist who made the second most powerful man in the world rearrange his calendar was the political commentator and philosopher Walter Lippmann (1889–1974). Lippmann was one of the most widely read and respected print media personalities of the twentieth century. His work for the *New Republic*, the New York *World*, the *New York Herald Tribune*, and the *Washington Post* established his reputation as the godfather of modern journalism. His syndicated column, "Today and Tomorrow" (1931–1967), garnered a weekly audience of 10–12 million nationwide and overseas. Unofficially, Lippmann served as counsellor and confidant to U.S. bureaucrats, administrators, and politicians including Woodrow Wilson, the Roosevelts, the Kennedys, and Lyndon Johnson. Lippmann traveled frequently to Europe to grill persons of world interest, most famously

Khrushchev in 1958 and 1961. Besides Lippmann's thousands of articles and editorials, he also authored over twenty books, including the hit sensations *A Preface to Morals* (1929) and *U.S. Foreign Policy* (1943). His *Public Opinion* (1922) is regarded as the founding text of American media studies. Lippmann either coined or stole several of the twentieth century's keywords, including "stereotype," the "manufacture of consent," "totalitarianism," the "Atlantic Community," "national security," the "Cold War," and the "Great Society." His towering quiet influence was dramatized in the film *Thirteen Days* (2000) about the Cuban missile crisis that Lippmann both escalated and helped to disarm.

Despite his global prominence, Lippmann has been the subject of only a few comprehensive biographies. The best of them, Ronald Steel's *Walter Lippmann and the American Century* (1980), offers the most fascinating insider portrait. Yet Steel sidestepped one of the central questions about Lippmann: Why did someone who seemed so indifferent toward religions spend so much time writing about them? Lippmann rarely talked about the subject with friends except to deny that he was spiritual in any conventional sense. Between the 1910s and the 1970s, however, Lippmann could not shut up about America's changing religious landscape—and what everyone should do about it. To remember him is to confront the paradox of Lippmann the private skeptic and public pastor.

Ultimately, Lippmann's religious and political labor cannot be separated. His lifetime of reflections on national and world affairs must be read in light of his conviction that the United States and the rest of the West had entered a "post-Christian" era. To highlight that fact, the introduction begins in the middle of things with Lippmann's critical series on America's anticommunist foreign policy. The articles and book reveal Lippmann's chief legacy for readers then and now: His ambivalent attachment to civil religions, or what he called "ideological crusades." Lippmann rarely if ever lived up to his criticism of others, notably in the areas of race, sex, and class privilege. Yet he worked hard to transform cynicism into a positive democratic philosophy of life. Lippmann's story has the potential to challenge our hubris, our laziness, and our despair.

Note

1. This story comes from Ronald Steel, *Walter Lippmann and the American Century* (Boston: Little, Brown, 1980), 526–7. Steel was given unrivaled access to Walter and Helen Lippmann and also granted total reign over Walter's papers. Steel took about thirteen years to complete his book. It contains stories and information about the Lippmanns found nowhere else—most likely derived from conversations Steel had with the couple. The biography deservedly won several awards, including the Bancroft prize for the best book in American history. Steel's work was completed at Yale University, which now houses The Walter Lippmann Papers (MS 326), Manuscripts and Archives, Sterling Memorial Library, Yale University (hereafter WLP); and The Robert O. Anthony Collection of Walter Lippmann (MS 766), Manuscripts and Archives, Sterling Memorial Library, Yale University (hereafter RAC), a complete microfilmed collection of Lippmann's thousands of editorials, opinion pieces, essays, and addresses.

Acknowledgments

I would like to thank Spring Arbor University for generous research funds and release time to complete this project. A shout out to Robbie Bolton, Karen Parsons, and Kami Moyer for invaluable support in navigating Lippmann's thousands of columns and many other sources. Michael Frost and the archivists and staff in the Sterling Memorial Library at Yale were an immense help in getting me into and through Lippmann's papers.

I could not be more grateful to everyone at Oxford University Press for their time and assistance, especially Jamie Mortimer and Theo Calderara. Timothy Larsen, the Spiritual Lives series editor, has been an incredible mentor and encourager from start to finish. Thanks as well to the anonymous reviewers whose comments significantly framed this biography.

Many colleagues have made this a better book than I ever could. Thanks to Daniel Bessner, Elesha Coffman, D. G. Hart, Kathryn Lofton, Daniel Steinmetz-Jenkins, Jonathan Rinck, Chris Schaefer, Lauren Turek, Margo Wang, John Wilsey, Gene Zubovich, and the members of the Cold War liberalism workshop for the conversations and comments on drafts. If I forgot anyone, please send me an angry email and know that I owe you a Pepsi. The following deserve a superhero's tribute for reading the entire manuscript at least once and sometimes more: Tom Arnold-Forster, Susan Curtis, Janine Giordano Drake, Ethan Goodnight, Dan Hummel, Amy Kittelstrom, David Kohns, Aaron Pattillo-Lunt, and Emily West. A special thanks to Julia Mayer for her work on the bibliography.

I am blessed with a wonderful circle of friends and family. Thanks as always to my humility partners Aaron, Brad, Jeremy, Josh, Mark, Matt, Steve, and Tom. Godspeed to the Catch the Fire support group for the enlightenment, distraction, rage-venting, and joy. My parents Gerry and Whitey, in-laws Carol and Terry, brother Matt, and sister Cathy have always been there for me and my family.

I cannot love them enough. You're a good boy, Mackey. We miss you, Moe—thanks for keeping me company while I wrote this. To Kristi, thank you, thank you, thank you for everything you are and do. This book is dedicated to my son Matthew, my buddy in laughter at this upside-down world.

Introduction

> Personally, being by temperament a skeptic and having very little faith in the power of any formula to encompass the enormous variety of real things I am an incurable eclectic.
>
> Walter Lippmann, 1933[1]

People who love being close to power usually do not risk angering the President of the United States. But Walter Lippmann was no sycophant. Flattery had not made him the highest paid opinion columnist in America with over ten million weekly readers. His books had not become bestsellers because he said what everyone wanted to hear. The State Department was not looking for validation when it began policy planning sessions with a discussion of his "Today and Tomorrow" editorials. So when Lippmann sensed that his country was about to give away the worldmaking authority it had gained through the blood and sacrifice of World War II, he did what he always did in times of crisis: He wrote. Lippmann's essays would be collected under the title, *The Cold War* (1947). He had used the phrase "Cold War" before, but this time it would stick. America's fifty-year showdown with the Soviet Union was branded by someone who thought it was a fool's errand.[2]

The context of Lippmann's series was President Harry Truman's declaration of U.S. leadership of the "free world" in 1947. The Truman Doctrine pitted the world's democracies against autocratic "totalitarian" regimes in a struggle for dominance over the developing Third World (or "Majority World"). During the war, the Roosevelt and Truman administrations had worried about the lengths that the Soviet Union might go to obstruct American designs for international peace and prosperity. Would they follow in the footsteps of Nazi Germany and risk World War III? In his "long telegram" to Truman in February 1946, Russian expert George Kennan answered yes. However, if the United States challenged Soviet aggression, Kennan predicted that Stalin would stand down. Kennan then published his "containment theory" in *Foreign Affairs*, the most important foreign policy journal in America—and a publication that Lippmann had frequented before he had stolen the senior editor's wife. Lippmann wrote *The Cold War* specifically in response to Kennan's article and Truman's endorsement of it. Several years later, Kennan would agree that Lippmann had been right all along.

To Lippmann, the Truman Doctrine was straight out of a horror film. The Americans had won World War II because they had followed Lippmann's advice, or so he believed. They had respected the limits of their power while maximizing their military and diplomatic strengths. Now it looked like they were ready to go chasing communists all over the planet on behalf of a "half-baked" theory. To Lippmann, Kennan's "unalterable counterforce" against the Kremlin was a "strategic monstrosity." No country, let alone the United States, had enough weapons, wisdom, or will to fight the Soviets and their satellites everywhere. The U.S. army was not built to occupy foreign territory indefinitely, and the American people were not patient enough to wait forever on the communists' next move. A superpower should be proactively restrained in pursuing its national interests.[3]

Lippmann suggested that Americans invest their time, energy, and resources in resolving the last world war. He challenged readers and policymakers to preserve what he called the "Atlantic community." Robust regional alliances like the United States, Great Britain, and their allies had recently built would be essential to any enduring world peace of the future. From a situation of strength, the United States might then focus on the construction of a united Europe through the "evacuation" of both the Russians and the Americans from the continent. The Truman administration needed to move the Soviet Army out of Germany and preferably all Eastern Europe. It should not trouble itself with conditions in Asia and the Middle East. They were "secondary."[4]

For Lippmann, the buzzword of the 1940s, "globalism," was not only unwise, it was un-American. He still thought his country might manifest a date with destiny so long as it lowered its expectations. If the United States could orchestrate a Soviet withdrawal, "we shall have written off the liabilities of the Truman Doctrine which must in practice mean inexorably an unending intervention in all the countries that are supposed to 'contain' the Soviet Union," Lippmann concluded.

> We shall be acting once more in the great American tradition which is to foster the independence of other countries, not to use other countries as the satellites of our own power, however beneficent, and as the instruments of our own policy, however well meant. Our aim will not be to organize an ideological crusade. It will not be to make Jeffersonian democrats out of the peasants of Eastern Europe, the tribal chieftains, the feudal lords, the pashas, and the warlords of the Middle East and Asia, but to settle the war and to restore the independence of the nations of Europe by removing the alien armies—all of them, our own included.

Lippmann's critique combined principled anti-imperialism with the isolationism of the xenophobe. Americans must not exploit weaker states because it was wrong. They also should not expect too much of people who were not ready for self-government. Democracy was hard, and Lippmann did not think everybody deserved it.[5]

Lippmann cast himself as the prophet of limitation for what he perceived to be an extravagant American Century. The irony was that he would support almost every Cold War intervention of the next three presidencies. So then what was his problem with containment? That could be summed up in one word: ideology. Ideology, in Lippmann's lexicon, meant any pattern of thought or course of action that was presumed to be absolute, complete, and unequivocal. To him, no idea or value should enjoy Doctrinal status. Politics and diplomacy were the arts of the possible at any given moment.

Lippmann believed Americans were overestimating the Kremlin's threat to world peace and free market expansion. They were also misreading communism's appeal, which Lippmann thought could make some gains among "backward" nations but was "irrelevant" to Western Europe and the United States. There simply was no warrant for an "ideological crusade" of "unending intervention" such as the Truman administration assumed. Frank, rational analyses of the balances of power in Europe and elsewhere were imperative.[6]

Too few chroniclers have appreciated how Lippmann's refutation of Cold War ideology was actually an indictment of American civil religion. Throughout this study, "civil religion" refers to any nationalism that relies upon figures, ideals, and images traditionally deemed to be religious. The term was coined by Jean-Jacques Rousseau in the 1760s. What it describes, the invocation of the sacred to imagine or reimagine a public's life, has been around for millennia. Civil religion in the United States had long been bound up with efforts to remember and remake the country as, in some way, a Protestant Christian nation. Lippmann's struggle with "ideological crusades," beginning during World War I and continuing well after, transpired amidst the rise and fall of rival civil religions. To be sure, most countries invoke a "God" in to justify their war machines. Lippmann's point was that they should not. He mocked Kennan for pretending to know the "mind of Providence." Lippmann was never an advocate for Christian Americanism or the many Red Scares it produced during his lifetime.[7]

Or was he? On the use of religious assets to foster national unity, Lippmann appeared to be a physician needing to heal himself. He feared the political consequences of Christian fundamentalism yet presumed that peoples required a fighting faith. "Among the nations that are indisputably members of the Atlantic community," Lippmann boasted in *The Cold War*, "there exists a vital connection founded upon their military and political geography, the common traditions of Western Christendom, and their economic, political, legal, and moral institutions which, with all of their variations and differences, have a common origin and have been shaped by much the same experience." Lippmann had helped initiate the "Atlantic community" imaginary during World War I. His allusion to "the common traditions of Western Christendom" to rationalize it now piled abstraction upon abstraction.[8]

Lippmann knew that wedding theology and nationality complicated the administration of a pluralist democracy. He had written his Cold War articles to divorce the two. Nevertheless, Lippmann had already decided by 1938, "a civilization must have a religion." This paradox—a good society must have and yet could not have a fixed set of first principles—had surfaced around the time of Lippmann's best-selling manifesto, *A Preface to Morals* (1929). It had and would free and constrain him whenever he faced down forces of disruption.[9]

*

What follows is a spiritual biography of Walter Lippmann. I argue that Lippmann's sixty years of commentary on personal, public, and world order were pastoral. His panopticon of print proceeded from and integrated sacred texts and philosophies. Lippmann offered theology as therapy, and vice versa. He habitually transgressed separated spheres of the religious and the secular. As one *New York Times* writer concluded his eulogy, Lippmann had been "the dean of American political journalism" but also a "public schoolmaster who obliged his readers to think of the transient in terms of the everlasting." To Lippmann, the "news" only made sense in the light of the "olds."[10]

It might seem strange to begin Lippmann's saga well past the middle of his life and career. Yet *The Cold War* essays demonstrate something essential about the man, namely, his deep-seated skepticism toward absolutes in any form. Lippmann served as the nation's leading contrarian over the course of his career in letters. Few private citizens did more to direct public attention toward critical, bipartisan reviews of U.S. foreign and domestic policy. Lippmann's core message was that nothing was immutable, everything and everyone (except perhaps himself) should be subject to scrutiny. Akin to our recent "Reinhold Niebuhr revival," Lippmann's work stands as a corrective to America's imperial overreach since 2001—but really since 1979 and Lippmann would say after 1945 yet maybe 1823.[11]

The Cold War reveals another Lippmann legacy: He was both a friend to and foe of organized religions. By "religions," I mean historically conditioned constellations of ideas, institutions, and practices like Christianity and Islam. Religions are not stable categories of experience, they are what Lippmann called "stereotypes," drifting compilations of prejudices and imaginings shaped by culture and desire as much as by reality. That elasticity also helps explain why they so easily take on civic-political forms. Most biographers either ignore or marginalize the role of religions in Lippmann's self-making. He would have wanted it that way. He did not like sharing privately about his own religious views and rarely confessed to being spiritual. He censored everyone from talking about his religion of birth, Judaism. He was a staunch anti-Zionist and only a few times mentioned Jewish contributions to Western cultures. From early on, Lippmann felt the compulsion, but never the freedom, to be religiously nonaligned (to be what we would call today a "None").[12]

To understand why, we need fresh reporting on the man and his times. For too long, American history was the documenting of what persons like Lippmann said and did. It seemed that money, polity, and war—the intrigue of states—were all that mattered to scholars. The exclusion of historical subjects reinforced the neglect of historical actors. A wealthy son from a religious and ethnic minority family, Lippmann pursued the privileges of class, race, and sex bestowed by American governments. Over the duration of his life he responded to threats to straight white male authority, often by not responding at all. Lippmann was a pioneering theorist of "positionality" but drew little attention to his own. Positionality means that ideologies cannot be abstracted from the political, cultural, and socioeconomic positions of power their perpetrators hold. To put it another way, in the words of one of Lippmann's early heroes and later villains, "every great philosophy up till now has consisted of... involuntary and unconscious autobiography." Lippmann worked hard to achieve his place in American media, and he labored harshly to maintain it. He must be judged by what he did publicize and by what he did not, especially his views regarding women.[13]

Yet throughout his adventures as a columnist, scholar, and adviser to America's elite, Lippmann presupposed that philosophy, religion, and statecraft were of one piece. His younger life was spent in search of a maverick spirituality to sustain liberal democracy. The opposite was true of his adulthood. Lippmann's signature policy stances emanated from as well as shaped his cynicism. His story is a perfect place to recognize and lay to rest some of our most cherished binaries: public versus individual and private; secular versus religious and spiritual; politics versus religion and culture; and intellectual versus social and political history. By doing so, we can understand how the ideas Lippmann expressed intersected with the positions he wanted to occupy, or wanted others to occupy, in American and world society.

*

Upending binaries is vital to discovering how and why Lippmann, a forerunner of today's Nones, ranked among the premier post-Christian thinkers of the twentieth century. He never committed to any religions, but he did choose to affiliate with and amalgamate them.[14] Lippmann was a nonpracticing Jewish intellectual who adapted Protestant and Catholic ideals to realize a principally secular vision of self and society. That conflux was evident in *The Cold War*, where Lippmann positively appraised Western Christendom while lobbying against civil religions. It could be seen even earlier in Lippmann's *A Preface to Morals* (to be discussed at length in Chapter 2). Through those works and others, Lippmann offered himself as a model of and for post-Christianity.

Much like the term postmodernism, "post-Christian" indicates an invention that began in the nineteenth century but was not named until later. It was both wanted and worried over by many. Lippmann never uttered the word himself, but he did come of age during its evolution from a clinical to a critical concept. "Post-Christian" was used by church historians in the 1800s to denote the historical period after Jesus Christ. Its modern meaning—regarding some sort of crackup in Christendom, or the waning social controls of Christian ideas, morals, and institutions in Europe and the United States—did not arise in earnest in America until the 1960s with the "Death of God" theologians (see the epilogue). Yet Right-wing European thinkers started using "post-Christian" in its contemporary sense during the 1930s, notably the National Socialist pastor Hans Ehrenberg and Otto Petras, an educator, ex-clergy, and author of *Post Christum* (1935). One of the initial English mentions occurred in Arnold Toynbee's lecture, "Christianity and Civilization" (1940), where the famed British historian cautioned about "our post-Christian Western secular civilization." Toynbee's influence on Lippmann would be significant.[15]

It is doubtful that Lippmann ever crossed paths with Anglican Bishop Stephen Bayne on the streets of New York where both grew up, but Lippmann had long embodied Bayne's reflections on post-Christianity in *The Optional God* (1953). According to Bayne, railing against the evils of "secularism," as many Western churchmen and Lippmann himself had been doing, missed the point, for "our secularism is a post-Christian secularism." A "post-Christian age" was one in which belief in God is "a helpful supplement to the real dynamics of life," theology is divorced from ethics, religion is made a "means" of mental health and good works, and civil society is organized "as if it made no difference whether there be a God or no." Nevertheless, Jesus-speak permeated a post-Christian society, meaning that "the moral habits, the ethical questions, the political improvisations are still, in general terms, those nourished by Christian faith." (Perhaps Bayne had in mind President Dwight D. Eisenhower's 1952 reflection on the Declaration of Independence: "Our form of government has no sense unless it is founded in a deeply felt religious faith, and I don't care what it is. With us of course it is the Judeo-Christian concept, but it must be a religion with all men are created equal.") Bayne did not speculate on the causes of post-Christianity, but his description implied that certain conditions had to align to bring it forth. If that was the case, was it possible that "post-Christian" was a historical sensibility, appearing and disappearing in times and places, rather than an inexorable, irreversible age? Bayne supported that view when he held up Abraham Lincoln as an example of the "myth of optionalism"—meaning someone who did not think that belief in a God was necessary.[16]

In words Lippmann would appreciate, consider this book a "preface" to post-Christianity. Bayne is a good starting point. Like Toynbee, Bayne recognized that the unbelief and secularism of their day was a Christian-inflected unbelief and secularism. A post-Christian project, such as Lippmann served on, represented a revolution in what Charles Taylor, in *A Secular Age* (2007), termed the "conditions of belief." All religions should be evaluated on functional terms. It did not matter if Christianity was true or false in the customary meaning of those words. Was it useful for human flourishing, however that might be defined? In thinking about Lippmann and his situation, post-Christian could be considered a type of secularization, and secularism a form of post-Christianity.[17]

Toynbee, Bayne, and successors intended "post-Christian" in a pejorative sense to signal a fall from "true" Christianity. Its value as an academic resource is debatable. At the same time, scholars need a term to describe the affirmative-yet-dismissive attitude toward religions that Lippmann and others of his generation adopted, and post-Christian is an excellent contender. Post-Christianity was a big tent, enveloping Lippmann's do-it-yourself "agnosticism," "humanism," the "higher law," and "traditions of civility," among other notions. For him, the post-Christian was a hope-fear manufactured through his many, many, many words.

In fact, an instrumentalist approach to religions had gained movement status during the Progressive era after 1880. That was especially the case among the brain trust of Progressivism, the Chicago and New England pragmatists like John Dewey and William James, the latter of whom was Lippmann's most beloved life coach. The pragmatists did not use the term "post-Christian" either. Still, they looked forward to living in a world that nurtured authentic spirituality by releasing it from the trappings of Christianity and Judaism. With the help of other fellow travelers living and dead—Alexander Hamilton, Edmund Burke, Friedrich von Hayek, Reinhold Niebuhr, Friedrich Nietzsche, John Maynard Keynes, and more—Lippmann applied his pragmatic outlook to a variety of subjects. So many topics, in fact, that it has been easy to forget Lippmann's predominant interest: How to get along in a world where it seemed like belief in a God had become an option. That sense of spiritual indeterminacy animated everything Lippmann wrote, including his landmark contributions to democratic theory and foreign policy.

*

Lippmann provided political and diplomatic answers to theological and philosophical quandaries. His decades of moralizing highlighted the post-Christian parentage of the twentieth-century liberalism that he worked so hard to articulate column after column. Liberalism, associated with the two Roosevelts, Theodore ("Teddy") and Franklin, will be designated "strong-state" liberalism to distinguish it from its "classical" variant exemplified by theorists like John Locke, Adam Smith, and John Stuart Mill. Strong-state liberalism has also been called New Deal liberalism and Cold War liberalism to demark its time period, although its genesis was in Progressivism. Lippmann's career spanned strong-state liberalism's halcyon days, from its emergence in the Teddy Roosevelt years to its fracturing during Richard Nixon's tenure (fun fact: Lippmann would live long enough to endorse both men for president twice). Lippmann was also part of strong-state liberalism's failure to live up to its radical racialized and gendered potential.[18]

But Lippmann's aim as a public philosopher was never to advance civil rights for women and marginalized communities. It was to prove that gods help those who help themselves. Lippmann carried forward the Progressive conviction that nation-states do not form naturally. They are made through strenuous effort. Whatever cosmic entities might be on our side, it was up to us to become what James called "tough-minded." We must fashion meaningful lives out of the immutable creativity and chaos of human existence. That message, more than any other, was how Lippmann earned the mantle of liberalism's "Moses" during and following World War I. By Lippmann's own admission, his crusade to humanize what another friend and mentor, Graham Wallas, called the "Great Society" was a pastoral mission from its start. Lippmann believed newsmen must serve be modern-day clergy, shepherding their flocks through many trials, temptations, and tribulations.[19]

A Lippmann biography is relevant for more than reimagining American liberalism (and conservativism and socialism), however. Both in his person and pen, Lippmann reconciled two seemingly incompatible post-Christian persuasions: The "Spiritual but Not Religious" (SBNR) and the "Religious but Not Spiritual" (RBNS). Granted, those are academic classifications more than they are popular self-identifications, but that does not make them any less real or fruitful as means of analysis. Both the SBNR and the RBNS problematize portrayals of secularization as a linear march toward no faith. A goal of this book is to show that they have a much older history than has often been remembered—and Lippmann was central to each. His ambivalence toward civil religions is best understood within and among this terminology.

The SBNR became an archetype around 2000 and 2001, yet the term dates to the 1960s and what it represents even earlier. Many consider William James to have been its exemplar. The SBNR style is post-Christian. The "Religious" it rejects is centered around churches and creeds, not mosques, synagogues, or temples. The "Spiritual" it embraces are nominally Christian ideas and practices. The SBNR arises from and encourages an anti-institutionalism that spans boundaries of class, culture, and politics. In James's terms, the SBNR type understands personal mystical experience to be "primordial" and theology, ethics, and congregations to be "second-hand." The pathway to beatitude runs through liberation from false authority—through the Nietzschean realization that the "God" of Christendom is dead. "In my Father's house are many mansions," James counselled, "and each of us must discover for himself the kind of religion and the amount of saintship which best comport with what he believes to be his powers and feels to be his truest mission and vocation."[20]

But with the branding of the SBNR complete, it was inevitable that our polarized age would produce a rival, the RBNS. There is no systematic study of the RBNS to date, yet evidence for it is everywhere. One expression is the Christian nationalism which mobilizes the politics of millions of churched and unchurched alike. For those communities and their leaders, robust Christian American institutions and outward displays of piety are crucial to preserving order in a free society. Respect for tradition, not self-actualization, is the pressing need of the day. But for all their upset with the SBNR, the Christian nationalists, too, are post-Christian. The RBNS and the SBNR alike treat tenets of Christianity as optional. Both care more about the utility of religions than they do about their ability to render the cosmos legible in any particular way.[21]

Lippmann occupied the SBNR and the RBNS simultaneously. His greatest impact as a post-Christian aspirant-critic was to show how they might fit together. Obviously, Lippmann never used those terms himself, but he did reveal their long origins in the United States. The SBNR and the RBNS types were latent in what Lippmann saw as the dialectic ("marriage") between "freedom" and "authority." He once elaborated, "the conflict of the two principles can be resolved only by uniting them. Neither can live alone. Alone, that is without the other, each is excessive and soon intolerable. Freedom, the faith in man's perfectibility, has always and will always in itself lead through anarchy to despotism. Authority, the conviction that men have to be governed and not merely let loose, will in itself always lead through arbitrariness and corruption to rebellion and chaos. Only in their union are they fruitful. Only freedom which is under strong law, only strong law to which men consent because it preserves freedom, can endure." For Lippmann the conflict-consensus between freedom and authority was personified in the undying bromance-battle between Thomas Jefferson and Alexander Hamilton. They were the original SBNR and RBNS combatants respectively.[22]

It is tempting to say that Lippmann began as a spokesperson of the SBNR and ended up siding with the RBNS. He spent his younger years heralding and yet lamenting the demise of organized religion.

Later, he trumpeted Christian rights when warning that the country needed a moral majority to survive secularism. Yet Lippmann was constantly traversing the types. He recognized that our present culture war between the SBNR and RBNS concerns one of the most basic questions in American history: Does a free society depend more upon strong institutions or upon strong people? Lippmann's remarkable, terrible life was one answer to that question.

*

This story of how Walter Lippmann tried to save American democracy from itself is told thematically as well as chronologically. Chapters 2 and 3 will play and then replay parts of Lippmann's maturation. But overall, the narrative will proceed from the beginning to the end of his adventures in ideas. Many of Lippmann's contemporaries carved him up using the "Tired Radical" trope. I prefer to think in terms of the "younger" and "older" Lippmann. Chapters 1 through 3 cover Lippmann's younger self (1889–1931). We will see him choose his intellectual postures and role models, craft a personal and professional identity beyond Judaism, and work out the political and diplomatic implications of his religious and philosophical inheritances. He will express for the first time his thoughts about the necessity and impossibility of civil religions. Chapters 4 through 7 will show how the older Lippmann (1931–1974) was the result of national and global politics reshaping but not mangling his original outlook. Lippmann's affiliation with Christianity deepened during these years, but he became even less of a joiner. He would proffer multiple public philosophies only to be undone by his own disbelief.

Lippmann coveted an ordered self and society against a backdrop of world war, depression, and still more world war. Coming to final judgments about the man is challenging. Readers will find a lot to dislike. Lippmann encapsulated some of the worst elements of twentieth-century American patricians. At the same time, few men did more to contest that elite from the inside. When at his best, Lippmann turned his will to power into a pastoral career of calling countrymen to live up to their most humane values. If he remains a hard man to know, on one point we can be certain: His skepticism made him an incurable post-Christian eclectic.

Notes

1. Walter Lippmann, to Robert E. Wood, Aug. 1, 1933, in WLP, Reel 99.
2. On Lippmann and the origins of "Cold War" phraseology, see Anders Stephanson, "Cold War Degree Zero," in *Uncertain Empire: American History and the Idea of the Cold War*, ed. Joel Isaac and Duncan Bell (New York: Oxford University Press, 2012), 19–50.
3. Walter Lippmann, *The Cold War: A Study in U. S. Foreign Policy* (New York: Harper and Brothers, 1947), 12–14, 18–20.
4. Lippmann, *Cold War*, 24–30, 38–9, 55–7.
5. Lippmann, *Cold War*, 44–5.
6. Lippmann, *Cold War*, 30–34, 52–4.
7. For an overview, see Philip Gorski, *American Covenant: A History of Civil Religion from the Puritans to the Present* (Princeton: Princeton University Press, 2019); and Rhys H. Williams, Raymond Haberski, Jr., and Philip Goff, eds., *Civil Religion Today: Religion and the American Nation in the Twenty-First Century* (New York: New York University Press, 2021).
8. Lippmann, *Cold War*, 13, 25.
9. Walter Lippmann, "Men and Ideas," Notes made in Europe, 1938, in WLP, Box 235, Folder 592.
10. Alden Whitman, "Walter Lippmann, Political Analyst, Dead at 85," *New York Times*, Dec. 15, 1974, A1.
11. Lippmann and Niebuhr became closely aligned on several political issues, as will be evident throughout this book. On the "Niebuhr revival," see K. Healan Gaston, "Then as Now, Why Niebuhr?" *Modern Intellectual History* 11 (Nov. 2014): 761–71.
12. Ryan P. Burge, *The Nones: Where They Came From, Who They Are, and Where They Are Going* (Minneapolis: Fortress Press, 2021). Steel, *Walter Lippmann*, remains the sole comprehensive biography. Steel addresses Lippmann's religious views at points, especially his Judaism, but overall he accepts his subject's argument that religion never mattered to him. Along the same lines, see Barry D. Riccio, *Walter Lippmann: Odyssey of a Liberal* (New Brunswick, N.J.: Transaction, 1994); and Craufurd D. Goodwin, *Walter Lippmann: Public Economist* (Cambridge: Harvard University Press, 2014). The exception is Charles Wellborn, *Twentieth Century Pilgrimage: Walter Lippmann and the Public Philosophy* (Baton Rouge: Louisiana State University Press, 1969), which analyzes some of Lippmann's religious writings with an eye to determining whether Lippmann was or was not a Christian. See also Tom Arnold-Forster, *Walter Lippmann: An Intellectual Biography* (Princeton: Princeton University Press, forthcoming).
13. Friedrich Nietzsche, quoted in Walter Lippmann, *A Preface to Politics* (New York: Mitchell Kennerley, 1913 [Reprint: University of Michigan Press, 1962]), 177. See Walter Lippmann, *Public Opinion* (New York: Harcourt, Brace, 1922 [Reprint: Pantianos Classics, 2019]), 51, on positionality.

14. My notion of "affiliation" is drawn from Linford D. Fisher, *The Indian Great Awakening: Religion and the Shaping of Native Cultures in Early America* (New York: Oxford University Press, 2012).
15. Arnold Toynbee, *Civilization on Trial* (New York: Oxford University Press, 1948), 230. On European uses of "post-Christian," see Paul Herman, "'Our Post-Christian Age': Historicist-Inspired Diagnoses of Modernity, 1935–1970," in *Post-Everything: An Intellectual History of Post Concepts* ed. Paul Herman and Adrian van Veldhuizen (Manchester: Manchester University Press, 2021), 17–39. See Brooke Foss Westcott, *The Gospel of the Resurrection: Thoughts on Its Relation to Reason and History* (London: Macmillan, 1884), 3, 98, 106, 147, for an example of nineteenth-century uses of "post-Christian." The term obviously overlaps with concepts tied to secularization studies, including "post-Protestant," "dechristianization," and "Protestant secularism." For an overview, see David Hollinger, *Christianity's American Fate: How Religion Became More Conservative and Society More Secular* (Princeton: Princeton University Press, 2022). See also Amy Kittelstrom, *The Religion of Democracy: Seven Liberals and the American Moral Tradition* (New York: Penguin, 2016), who uses "post-Christian" in reference to this era.
16. Stephen F. Bayne, *The Optional God* (New York: Oxford University Press, 1953 [Reprint: Morehouse-Barlow, 1980]), xiii, 8, 11–14, 18–20, 25. See Patrick Henry, "'And I Don't Care What It Is': The Tradition-History of a Civil Religion Proof-Text," *Journal of the American Academy of Religion* 49 (Mar. 1981): 35–47.
17. Charles Taylor, *A Secular Age* (Cambridge: Belknap Press, 2007), 3. See also Hollinger, *Christianity's American Fate*, and James Turner, *Without God, Without Creed: The Origins of Unbelief in America* (Baltimore: John Hopkins University Press, 1986).
18. On strong-state liberalism and its racial and gender limitations, see Gary Gerstle, *American Crucible: Race and Nation in the Twentieth Century*, Reprint ed. (Princeton: Princeton University Press, 2017).
19. *Time* magazine called Lippmann a "Moses" to liberals in 1931. See Steel, *Walter Lippmann*, 276.
20. William James, *The Varieties of Religious Experience* (New York: Longmans, Green, 1902 [Reprint: Signet Classic, 1983]), 45, 316. See Sven Erlandson, *Spiritual but Not Religious: A Call to Religious Revolution in America* (Bloomington: IUniverse, 2000); and Robert C. Fuller, *Spiritual, but Not Religious: Understanding Unchurched America* (New York: Oxford University Press, 2001), for early uses. See also William B. Parsons, ed., *Being Spiritual but Not Religious: Past, Present, Future(s)* (New York: Routledge, 2018).
21. See Craig Luekens, "4 Reasons Why I'm Religious, But Not Spiritual," *Huffpost*, Feb. 16, 2016, at https://www.huffpost.com/entry/4-reasons-why-im-religiou_b_9240166 (last accessed 2/20/23); and Andrew L. Whitehead and Samuel L. Perry, *Taking America Back for God: Christian Nationalism in the United States* (New York: Oxford University Press, 2020).

See also J. Aaron Simmons, "Religious, but Not Spiritual: A Constructive Proposal," *Religions* 12 (June 2021), at https://www.mdpi.com/2077-1444/12/6/433 (last accessed 9/5/22), for illuminating reflections on both categories.

22. Walter Lippmann, "Today and Tomorrow: The Living Past," *Washington Post*, Apr. 13, 1943, 15.

PART I

The Younger Lippmann

Part I covers the years 1889 to 1930. Chapter 1 looks at Lippmann's youth and chief influences, including his Harvard years, his first friends and careers, and his complicated relationship with Judaism. The post-Christian revolution is also discussed, especially as it pertained to the Progressive and pragmatist movements that Lippmann inhabited. Chapter 2 examines religions in Lippmann's early writings between 1914 and 1929. It begins with an examination of his best seller, *A Preface to Morals* (1929). The chapter then tracks that book's long origin story. The same years are considered in Chapter 3, but with an eye to Lippmann's military service and political thought. The goal is to recognize Lippmann's religious and philosophical outlook as interdependent with his political and diplomatic counsel. Lippmann's ambivalence toward civil religions will be highlighted throughout these early chapters.

1
The Disciple, 1889–1913

"I was really an agnostic.... For me there was no struggle of any kind." That was how Walter Lippmann described his religious orientation—or lack thereof—in 1950 when he was sixty-one years old. Lippmann was being interviewed by his friend and longtime promoter, the historian Allan Nevins. Nevins had worked with Lippmann at the New York *World* during the 1920s. He had turned hundreds of Lippmann's editorials into books during the Great Depression. The Lippmann–Nevins conversation is the closest thing we have to an autobiography of the famed journalist, since Lippmann never got very far in producing a memoir. He would say it was because he did not trust his memory, which begs the question of why we should either.[1]

Lippmann's confession was sincere to an extent. He never did settle for any organized theological expression. It was also false. By the time of his interview, Lippmann had been wrestling with the place of religions in society for nearly half a century. He had chosen "humanist" to describe his spiritual orientation, but even that would be misleading. A survey of Lippmann's earliest years and influences will show how he came to prize, in his words, an "open mind." His worries about such an orientation will also be plain to see. The younger Lippmann was a cheerleader of the SBNR, yet his RBNS self was faithfully emergent.

*

Lippmann was born in 1889, the only child of German-Jewish parents in the Upper East Side of New York City. He enjoyed a freethinking, materially comfortable life, including yearly excursions to Europe where his love of art and nature first took root. Lippmann's father, a landlord who had inherited his wealth, "always let him do whatever he wanted to do." Lippmann would receive emotional and financial support from his parents well past his college years.[2]

Both his mother and father were agnostics, Lippmann told Nevins. Still, the family attended the center of Reform Judaism in America, Temple Emanu-El. Walter was confirmed there in place of a Bar Mitzvah. As a young man, Lippmann recalled his childhood fear of "the impending wrath of God," which the Lippmanns' housekeeper had instilled in him after he had thrown cakes around the house during a birthday party. "For years God was the terror of my twilight," Lippmann admitted. But that anxiety did not affect his youthful rage to persuade in any noticeable way. Lippmann excelled at the prestigious Dr. Julius Sachs's School, where privileged German-Jewish boys attended alongside wealthy Catholics. During these years, he fell in love with a fellow New Yorker: the "Jane-Dandy"-turned-"Rough Rider" soldier-statesman Teddy Roosevelt. It would be the longest romance of his life, even after Roosevelt rejected him personally (to be discussed in Chapter 3). Lippmann served on Sachs's debate team with his friend Carl Binger, where they defended the Chinese Exclusion Act (1882) among other national policies. The two also co-edited the school newspaper.[3]

The younger Lippmann once confided that he "never cared for an upholstered life." Roosevelt's "strenuous life" ideal—the call to men to dare great conquests—weighed heavily upon him. But Lippmann did not advocate taking the Philippines like his muscular Christian hero. The strenuous life to Lippmann meant occupying (with Binger) one of the most esteemed campuses around, Harvard University. The two were part of a small wave of Jewish admissions into elite East Coast schools. They would have to make their own melting pots once they arrived.[4]

Like many other institutions of higher learning, Harvard was coming to terms with its Protestant past when Lippmann entered in 1906. The school had long served as a training ground for ministers and missionaries. Attendance at daily and Sunday chapel services had been mandatory just twenty years earlier. Yet Harvard had been theologically cosmopolitan for over a century—a hothouse of Calvinist and Unitarian thought. Following the Darwinian revolution, the school joined other educational centers around the country in promoting scientific over sectarian worldviews. Religious and intellectual change was furthermore driven by social and cultural contests within the universities, as more women had entered higher education after the Civil War. The professionalization push did not reflect the egalitarian potential of the evolutionary sciences, however. Instead, it generated new separate and unequal spheres for male and female experts. Lippmann's fields of study—philosophy foremost, followed by languages, literature, economics, and art—remained the province of cozy men.[5]

Harvard's overhaul was also part of a great transformation within the United States. The "Progressive Movement," associated with Roosevelt's Progressive Party, affected all sectors of American society after 1880. While never a coherent nationalist program, settlement and social workers (women like Jane Addams, the founder of Hull House in Chicago), investigative journalists, social scientists, Northeastern and Midwestern politicians, and church leaders sought the moral and material progress of society through scientific reform. Progressives looked back to the republicanism of the founding fathers, with its preference for "public" over "private" interests. They leaned forward toward government regulation of economic injustices and inefficiencies. Progressives argued that increased mobility, communication, industrialization, and urbanization had made America "interdependent." Assumptions about human nature and society from prairie days could no longer go unquestioned. Progressives constructed networks of public–private partnerships to address problems stemming from the new immigration from Southern and Eastern Europe, the rise of a new corporate economy and working class, and the growth of the country's largest cities.[6]

Progressives conjured post-Christianity amidst and as critical to their socio-economic passions. They were not the first to do so in American history, and they would not be the last. But they were the most intentional and creative. The term "post-Christian" had been used commonly among nineteenth-century church historians as a chronological tool. Progressivism prefigured post-Christian's contemporary meaning as signaling a break in the ideals, practices, and authorities of Western Christian societies.

Many Progressive reformers had been raised in Christian homes or had adopted some version of Christianity while in college. Yet most replaced supernaturalism with new ways of understanding the world, especially drawn from the social sciences. Few Progressives became atheists—most remained agnostics like Lippmann would say he had always been. (Aside: "agnosticism" was a term that had just entered general usage around the 1880s.) Progressives were not social gospelers, the explicitly Protestant and Catholic wings of the Progressive movement that believed God was concerned about social justice. Nor were they theologically liberal or "Modernist" Christians, some of whom were adopting labels such as "Christian agnostics." Like the Modernists, though, Progressives harnessed the productive power of doubt and the saving grace of uncertainty.[7]

Progressives were "post-Christian" in that they found Christianity verifiable only in being beneficial in this world. For instance, in his 1907 essay, "New Varieties of Sin," Edward Ross repurposed Christian theology in the service of sociological analysis. "Interdependence puts us, as it were, at one another's mercy, and so ushers in a multitude of new forms of wrongdoing," he observed. If Ross could convince readers that not paying railroad workers a living wage was just as "sinful" as drunkenness or murder, he could mobilize Christian readers to support Progressive reforms. What mattered to Ross and other post-Christian Progressives was not whether Christianity or any institution was true in a supernatural sense. Rather, were so-called religions demonstrably helpful for personal and group wellbeing?[8]

Of course, the rulers of empires, monarchies, and nation-states had long embraced such utilitarian conceptions of religions. (One thinks of George Washington's Farewell Address, where he maintained that religion promoted virtue which, in turn, was essential to republican government.) What was novel in Lippmann's time was the rupture of a long peace between philosophy, science, and Christianity. Protestant and Catholic revelation could no longer count upon the cooperation of rational, empirical investigation. Historians have given that cultural falling-out many names, including the "crisis of faith," the "crisis of authority," and the "triumph of uncertainty." I am calling it the popularization of a post-Christian persuasion.

But how might religions be useful if they were, in Lippmann's later words, only "pictures in our heads?" First, recognize that Progressivism was always a contested ideal. Its adherents fought amongst themselves over increasing or decreasing rights for industrial workers, women, and minorities. For some Progressives, religions still had a role to play in advancing social justice and mental health. For others, religions were about better social control, whether of a statist or antistatist variety.

Social scientists such as Ross and Albion Small aided Presidents Roosevelt and Woodrow Wilson in that latter endeavor. After considering several "bonds" of nation-making (language, family life), Small deduced that a "convincing religion" was the best "fusing agent" available. Small's civil religion partook of the message of social gospelers that Protestantism was foundational to republican government. Small lobbied for an "American Religion" to tie his fractured people together. He concluded,

> The Jew, the Catholic, and the Protestant might graft this religion each on the trunk of his peculiar faith, and each might contribute to his rendering of religion all the spiritual force there is in his distinctive beliefs. The documents of this religion are every scripture, canonical or uncanonical, in which a seeker after God or an avoider of God has set down an authentic truth encountered in the experience of either. Its ceremonial is not a single prescribed ritual. It is every outward form of worship by means of which anyone feels himself brought nearer to God and to his fellow-men. Its polity is the concerted purpose of every American, from Eastport to San Diego, to join in a perpetual league for finding out the quality and program of life which gives sincerest heed to the spiritual possibilities in every one of us.... I do not know of anything short of *the American Religion* which can be more than a settlement of preliminaries to the genuinizing of our lives.

Small's tri-faith American Religion offended nativists who favored immigrant restriction. It was post-Christian in that Small was asking religions to bend the knee in service to an imagined community devoted to sanctity for life. Progressives like Small wanted all religions to shed their sectarian parts and aspire to a positive moral whole.[9]

Others closer to Lippmann spoke to post-Christian nationalism as well. "The American system stands for the highest hope of an excellent worldly life that mankind has yet ventured," Progressive theorist Herbert Croly exclaimed, "the hope that men can be improved without being fettered, that they can be saved without vicariously being nailed to the cross." Croly's parents had raised him in the "Religion of Humanity." His book, *The Promise of American Life* (1909), synthesized many reformers' concerns and served as an inspiration for Roosevelt's "New Nationalism" and for the Progressive Party platform. A fellow Harvard man, Croly would also become Lippmann's co-laborer in crafting a new liberal republic for an age of interdependence.[10]

Lippmann's response to Croly's and Small's civil religion of Americanism was always a yes/no. He would be critical of most of the ideologies that he was aware of—of the attempts to invest transient ideas and customs with the divine weight of glory. At the same time, Lippmann worried about the problem of effectual social control— even to the point, from 1935 onwards, of recommending loyalty to Christian-infused "higher laws" and "traditions of civility." He would become one with both Croly and Small in post-Christian awareness.

*

Lippmann's love–hate dalliance with civil religions was the legacy of his Harvard years. He could thank his mentors for that. His first guide, the philosopher George Santayana, stole Lippmann away from the law and art history and brought him before the queen of the sciences. "I thought I was heading for a life of scholarship in the fine arts," Lippmann would report at age eighty. Instead, he took more classes with Santayana than any other instructor. After finishing his graduation requirements in three years, Lippmann served as Santayana's teaching assistant during his fourth. Santayana's books were often quickly forgotten, but he mentored many of the greatest intellectuals and activists of the twentieth century, from T. S. Eliot to W. E. B. Du Bois. Under Santayana, Lippmann honed his aestheticism—the conviction that love of beauty was vital to human flourishing beyond the brutal drabness of the Megalopolis. Lippmann would later tell friends he was glad Santayana had showed him the importance of having a constructive philosophy of life. But Lippmann rarely revealed his appreciation for art and nature in print. Instead, Santayana's vision of a "socialistic aristocracy" had a more immediate and lasting impact on the young pupil.[11]

By his own recounting, Lippmann's greatest love was the Harvard psychologist William James, one of the founders of New England pragmatism. Building upon Darwinism, the comparative study of religions, and new views of the Bible as a historical, not divinely inspired, text, the pragmatists argued that the "truth" of beliefs and practices rested in their ability to help human beings make better adjustments to and of their environments. Pragmatists' instrumental view of knowledge was welcomed by many, including Santayana, as a liberation from philosophical idealism—with its emphasis on conformity to transcendent and unchanging ideas and values. The pragmatists led other post-Christian Progressives in seeing the end of the Christian era as an opportunity to find out what Christianity and other religions were good for.[12]

No one would do more to promote a functional understanding of Christianity's value than James. He was a complex mixture of acceptance, empathy, elitism, and cruelty (he once told Lippmann that his colleague, the idealist thinker Josiah Royce, looked like "an unborn fetus"). Like other pragmatists, James stressed that intelligence was a matter of achieving harmony or "satisfaction" between belief and environment. Because our material, social, and even metaphysical worlds were in flux, so too was our experience, the stuff of intelligence. For James, there were absolutely no fixed, universal standards, just rest stops on the endless pilgrimage of validating how well our ideas put us into touch with reality for however long they could.[13]

James's pragmatism led him to embrace multicultural democracy (in theory but not in practice) and anti-imperialism (in theory and in practice). In 1906, James proposed a "moral equivalent" for war to unleash manly energies in a disciplined way—something akin to the future Peace Corps. America needed a "socialistic equilibrium," but it also had to decide how to conserve the "martial virtues" of yore. Like Roosevelt's strenuous life, James called his adherents to become "tough-minded," by which he meant "Empiricist (going by facts), Sensationalistic, Materialistic, Pessimistic, Irreligious, Fatalistic, Pluralistic, Skeptical."[14]

Yet like his father and the liberal Protestants at Harvard before him, James preferred to cross-examine pastors, not politicians. He wanted to see what remained of Christianity once its superstructure had been deconstructed. In *The Varieties of Religious Experience* (1902), a landmark work in the comparative scientific study of religions, James summed up his years of analysis of religious texts, interviews, introspection, and personal drug use by concluding that a "MORE" or "wider self" existed beyond the "over-beliefs" of organized religion. James's post-Christianity shone forth in his edict that persons were free to keep or to discard as much of orthodoxy as they wanted to. He asked, "who knows whether the faithfulness of individuals, here below to their over-beliefs, may not actually help God in turn to be more effectively faithful to his own greater tasks?" James defended a person's "will to believe" things that could not be corroborated empirically. It was impossible to know anything with certainty, but we could still fake it until we make it—whatever "it" meant.[15]

James was capable of great generosity toward people who thought like him. That included the time he knocked on Lippmann's dorm room door to commend the young man for an article he had written about how America's destiny lay in her own hands. So began a beautiful if all too brief friendship over Thursday morning teas—James passed away in 1910 when Lippmann was only twenty-one years old.

In one of his first professional publications, Lippmann remembered James as an unmatched "open mind." He regarded him as "the most tolerant man of our generation." James manifested the "democratic attitude of mind" through his insistence that all perspectives should be brought to the public square for testing—none could claim special privilege. Lippmann was most impressed with his mentor's devotions to doubt in the realm of the spirit. "I think he would have listened with an open mind to the devil's account of heaven," Lippmann mused of James, "and I'm sure he would have heard him out on hell." James's will to believe should have been called "The Right to Believe," Lippmann said, asserting that "until the evidence is complete men have a right to believe what they most need."[16]

Like James, the young Lippmann was unafraid of radical subjectivity. In his first major work on politics, Lippmann would praise *Varieties of Religious Experience* for humanizing religion—making it a tool for rather than a master of troubled souls. Lippmann would forge a career out of applying James's post-Christian insights about religion to statecraft, especially to democratic and diplomatic theory. To Lippmann, as to James, religious and political questions were inseparable.[17]

*

During and after Harvard, Lippmann funneled his secondary influences through his primary ones. Lippmann was drawn to Freudian psychology and would even have a chance to meet the celebrity doctor and his counterparts, Alfred Adler and Carl Jung. Freudianism promised to make the cosmos legible as just so many secret wish fulfillments of the ravenous human heart. In other words, everything had a natural explanation, including religions. Lippmann believed psychoanalysis was as revolutionary as anything Darwin had brought forth. He also thought it was being wasted on bored socialites. Lippmann would apply psychoanalysis to politics where it belonged, especially Freud's emphasis on the limits of reason to civilize unconscious destructive impulses. But that just brought Lippmann back to James. To him, Freud's theory of "sublimation"—substituting acceptable for illicit desires—was James's technique of moral equivalency.[18]

Something similar happened in Lippmann's handling of the philosopher Friedrich Nietzsche, the forerunner of contemporary postmodernism. Through his fictional soothsayer Zarathustra, Nietzsche had proclaimed the death of Western cultural conceptions of God (1883). Lippmann welcomed Nietzsche's skepticism and relativism even as he Americanized the German thinker. "Any philosophy will justify anything," Lippmann heard him saying. Lippmann read Nietzsche through Santayana as calling for a creative life instead of one lived in loyalty to timeless truths. In his younger years, Lippmann invoked Nietzsche as a Jamesian warning about the imperial nature of thought. His older self would say that he was not that into postmodern rejections of verities, but nor could he ever truly quit them, as we shall see.[19]

Nietzsche, James, Freud, Roosevelt—the pattern is clear: Lippmann was drawn to strong men. He would emulate those contrarians and iconoclasts in his own way. He, too, would demand men (and a few women) wrestle meaning out of the chaos of existence. But Lippmann's life aim would be to tear down. He would never be very good at building up philosophies or people. His compassion was always cold and his coolness always humane. "You and I, Walter do not suffer from the same things," one Harvard friend noted to him. "Your pain is rarely personal.... When your flesh has been scourged you become taut, Spartan and rebellious." Lippmann's future spouses could confirm that.[20]

*

Lippmann's post-Christian rebellion was front and center in a number of his Harvard term papers. In an ode to Santayana, Lippmann rejected the notion of "art for art's sake." Art was the quest for beauty and so should not be segregated from science, morality, and religion. Rather, art was their founder and master. "The craving for beauty is basic," Lippmann explained. "The aesthetical duty creates religion that it may harmonize man and the infinite; creates morality that it may harmonize man and his social environment; creates science that it may harmonize man and his world." In other words, beauty not deity was the "synthesizing element" of existence.[21]

Lippmann's aestheticism would be suffocated by his tough-minded policy advocacy during and after World War I. But it was forever there in his SBNR moments. "The people are too busy and too much blinded to care about the beauty of nature or the works of the masterbuilders," Lippmann complained to "Lucy" Elsas, one of his closest confidants during his college years. Americans failed to understand that "morality is not respectability, that the Life Force is above marriage laws, that society is against the individual." City folk needed to be enraptured by a comprehensive philosophy of beauty, just as Lippmann had advanced in his art paper. "This is our ideal of happiness everlasting," he told Lucy. "To build a citadel of human joy upon the slum of misery—to raise the heads bowed in degradation to the blue and gold of God's sunshine—to give human hearts their heritage of happiness—to raise upon the ruins of infamy the purity of the hearth—to give to the world not a doctrine but a fact—to give to the words 'the brotherhood of man' a meaning."[22]

If only the younger Lippmann could have heeded his own prescription for happiness. A year later, he confided to Lucy, "a religion which doesn't make life richer, fuller, more splendid than it now is, which doesn't touch life at every point, thus creating a harmony between the soul of man and the stars in heaven, is no religion at all. The only religion is one of joy—we worship when we are happy and when we are beautiful. Joy and Beauty are God's inner consciousness—we live in God when we realize His nature." Evidently, Lippmann had tamed his twilight terrors through the romancing of all things—except Lucy. He made every profession to her except personal affection. Still, he was wounded when she chose another man over him.[23]

Lippmann's almost-love letters to Lucy highlight his desire to bring religion, philosophy, and science to bear upon public policy. He used another essay to work out a new spiritual culture for democracy. Evolutionary biology had confirmed the "Brotherhood" (or at least "Cousinhood") of all living things. However, Westerners following Rousseau had added to that "organic view" of democracy a false gospel of egalitarian, libertarian individualism—the "right to live as [one] wishes to live." Lippmann unleashed a barrage of adjectives to discredit that belief, including "eccentricity," "license," "petty," "amateur," "selfishness," and "freakishness." The younger Lippmann never sounded more like his older self than on this point. Both versions could agree that self-government should not mean a race to the ethical bottom.[24]

But how to reconcile aristocracy and democracy? Lippmann saw one solution in professionalization, including Harvard's just-opened Graduate School of Business Administration. He believed government needed to learn the way of scientific management. Yet in training for better social service, elected officials would have to assume clerical robes. "The State of the future," Lippmann foresaw, "will teach a new conception of the State as a religion. That religion will have as its core the organic unity of the Species, and it will make its fundamental teaching the entire responsibility of each individual. That will mean that for all men the interests of their life will be centered in that State.... It will have as its necessary corollary the conception of an impersonal immortality. Such a conception will bring unity into the State, for it means all that a real Democracy means—the eternal importance of each smallest thing in a large, necessary scheme." Lippmann shared the fears of other Progressives that America was not ready for interdependence—that it needed a State not a state to fulfill its destiny as the world's Democracy. Like Small and Croly, Lippmann also thought organized religions might play a social ordering role after they had lost their luster as private beatitudes.[25]

A visiting professor supplied the missing piece of Lippmann's public intellectual puzzle. Among Lippmann's earliest political influences had been the British socialist Fabian Society, including the novelist H. G. Wells. One of their ex-members, Graham Wallas, would have the greatest impact. Wallas arrived at Harvard in 1910, just as

Lippmann was leaving. A mentor–student relationship quickly developed, but one rooted in mutual interest, admiration, and respect for William James. It was James who had led Wallas to apply pragmatic psychology to political theory, as Wallas acknowledged in *Human Nature in Politics* (1908). Wallas's point in that book was that an effective statecraft had to take into consideration humankind's irrational as well as its rational side. In Wallas's work, Lippmann found the practical application of James's insight that all politics starts with anthropology—and thus with philosophy and religion. Wallas would grow and sustain Lippmann's Jamesian worldview through twenty years of correspondence. Lippmann, meanwhile, would merge both of their life's work. He was a "disciple of William James and Graham Wallas," he would write in his unfinished memoirs.[26]

*

After Harvard, Lippmann found himself torn between two places, two peoples, and two ways of life. Part of him wanted to live in New York. And he did: a few years on his own and then several with his parents (who provided for him financially up and through World War I). But belonging was much harder, especially when Lippmann was an Upsider wanting to run downtown with the bohemians of Greenwich Village. The bohemians were artists and activists who pursued experimentalism in personal and social living. They shared Progressives' concerns to advance worker rights. They also feared what Lippmann, referencing the Catholic distributists G. K. Chesterton and Hilaire Belloc, called the "bureaucratic tyranny" of the "Servile State." When they were not anarchists, most bohemians embraced a holistic grassroots socialism inclusive of feminism, anti-imperialism, but rarely antiracism.[27]

At times, Lippmann seemed a good fit. He had come to socialism not only intellectually through the Fabians but also by the experience of working at Hale House, a settlement home for children, and by helping the victims of a fire in one of Cambridge's neighboring cities. Lippmann went on to start the Socialist Club at Harvard and assist New York's first socialist mayor in Schenectady. During and after college, Lippmann frequented the house of Ralph Albertson, a Christian socialist minister, and eventually married his daughter Faye. Friends warned that it was a bad match, but Lippmann confided to

Wallas that "so far as a man can be happy with the world as it is, I am happy." When in Greenwich Village, the happy Lippmann frequented the "salon" meetings of wealthy socialite Mabel Dodge, where he exchanged ideas with the globetrotting journalist-adventurer, Bolshevik, and Harvard rival John "Jack" Reed; the socialist editor and activist Max Eastman; the anarchist freethinker Emma Goldman; birth control advocate Margaret Sanger; and veteran muckraker Lincoln Steffens. Steffens gave Lippmann his first writing job investigating Manhattan's "Money Power."[28]

Try as he might, though, Lippmann remained a "Puritan in Babylon," in the words of a future friend. He lost his taste for socialism in name if not in practice (to be explored in Chapters 2 and 3). Despite having an affair later in life, Lippmann was never one for open marriage, homosexuality, or feminism. "Agitation isn't my job," he decided firmly to the celebrity socialist Upton Sinclair—no doubt thinking of his Village friends Jack and Max. Lippmann held the former in contempt and envy. "I can't think of a form of disaster which John Reed hasn't tried and enjoyed," Lippmann would grumble. "In common with a whole regiment of his friends I have been brooding over his soul for years, and often I feel like saying to him what one of them said when Reed was explaining Utopia, 'If I were establishing it, I'd hang you first, my dear Jack.' But it would be a lonely Utopia."[29]

Much like James, Lippmann could tolerate intellectual chaos to a degree that he never would private and public disorder. He often wished it was the other way around. Though Lippmann never took a college math class, at age eighty-three he would tell his biographer Ronald Steel that he would have enjoyed "the precision, the elegance" of the mathematician. "There's something about it that attracts me aesthetically," Lippmann would confide. In fact, he had brought extraordinary rigor to bear upon the art of writing, having become one of the most efficient and prolific editorialists of his generation. But I am getting ahead of the story.[30]

Professional and personal satisfaction came for Lippmann outside the Village. He scolded Dodge to get her salon under control. Nevertheless, she persisted. So, around 1912, Lippmann began frequenting the "House of Truth" in Washington, D.C.'s, Dupont Circle. There he found the friendships and vocational connections he was pining for: his roommate Felix Frankfurter, the government lawyer, later Harvard Law professor, and eventual Supreme Court Justice; Associate Justices of the Supreme Court Oliver Wendell Holmes, Jr., and Louis Brandeis; whiz kid, wartime administrator, and future U.S. President Herbert Hoover; and many more. Roosevelt's Progressive Party campaign had been the originating force behind the House of Truth. Yet members quickly moved to larger questions about reconciling Stars Hollow values with twentieth-century urban-industrialism.[31]

Lippmann eventually joined forces with Progressive sages and House of Truth regulars Croly and Walter Weyl, a like-minded skeptic of German-Jewish descent. Together, the three rough-riding public philosophers launched the *New Republic*, which in turn became one of the generators of strong-state American liberalism. The upstart journal was based in New York but obsessed with Washington. Of the *New Republic* Progressives-turned-liberals, Lippmann would say, "they wished to distinguish their own general aspirations in politics from those of the chronic partisans and the social revolutionists. They had no other bond of unity. They were not a political movement. There was no established body of doctrine." But that was not entirely true: A classist, gendered, and racialized anti-radicalism was a creed that self-professed liberals would uphold well into the 1960s and even into the twenty-first century.[32]

The bohemians felt betrayed by Lippmann's sell-out to middle-class paternalism. "I always wanted the sky to fall on Walter Lippmann and make him suffer," Eastman wrote after Lippmann kissed socialism goodbye. Another friend lamented to Dodge, "if you will sometimes go down to the Bowery and see the Booze victims, you will see another way in which God manifests himself. God does not manifest himself *at all* in Walter Lippmann."[33]

*

Lippmann would have preferred that an opening chapter on his life end there. He would not like us to talk about his Jewish heritage. He never mentioned it and did not allow friends to do so either. Some acquaintances did not even know he was Jewish. Lippmann found ethnic fellowship at the House of Truth but refused to support his associates' Zionism. He never joined or spoke at any Jewish organizations, and he refused all the awards they granted him. It was as if, by 1930, "Judaism does not exist for Mr. Lippmann."[34]

The opposite could not have been truer, though. Lippmann was ultra-sensitive to his cultural background—he had to be to suppress it so ruthlessly. Lippmann's "gilded Jewish ghetto" where he had grown up had practiced what Steel called "Jewish anti-Semitism" toward newly arrived Jews from Russia and Poland. Those immigrants were still "Oriental," said Emanu-El's rabbi on one occasion. He went on to praise his congregation for their strenuous lives of assimilation. Lippmann followed suit when he married a Protestant minister's daughter. Walter had always had a "predilection for Nordic blondes," according to Dodge (who also prophesied to Lippmann's future mother-in-law that the union would not last).[35]

But integration was not enough for the younger Lippmann. The occasion of his declaring a religion of "Joy and Beauty" to Lucy had been his disgust with his childhood faith community. "Can we tell them that the Temple Emanu-El exhibition is a piece of blatant hypocrisy," he had asked her in 1908. "That its mechanical service, its bromide interpretation, its drawing room atmosphere of gentility, its underlying snobbishness, which makes it an exclusive organization for the wealthy, strangle all the religion that is in us?" Lippmann's words tempt us to think that his repudiation of Judaism was an intellectual exercise—a byproduct of his aesthetic pragmatism and socialism. But what if the reverse was true: That Lippmann's refusal to live openly as a member of a maligned minority in a white Northern European Protestant country was an answer in search of an excuse? One evidence of the power of American anti-Semitism was the extreme measures Lippmann would take to mask his ancestry (although he would never change his last name as many others did).[36]

Ultimately, we do not need to decide about Lippmann. It is enough to appreciate that he rejected organized religions for himself if not for others. "The devoutest people are not church-going," he continued to lecture Lucy. "The truly religious man needs only the bright sun, the gossamer tints of the twilight and the blue beyond blue of the clear night to make him happy and worshipful. The beauty of our friends, in full meaning of the word beauty, works of art, and music those are the things that make life still more devout. Add to this religion a passion for deed... expressed in Socialism, Pragmatism and poetry, and you have a 'Theory of Life,' which the young will never outgrow." Lippmann's Theory was to find spiritual life everywhere except in Judaism or any other orthodoxy, religious or political. He would never really outgrow the post-Christian, SBNR impulse he boasted to Lucy.[37]

For whatever reasons Lippmann may have forgone his birthright, his country would not let him. No matter how many sports Lippmann played or medals and ribbons he earned—"the Harvard symbol of having arrived," according to Binger—no Jews were admitted to Harvard's social clubs, the gateways to post-graduate greatness. That rebuff played no small part in Lippmann's formation of Harvard's Socialist Club as well as his participation in the Intercollegiate Socialist Society and New York's Socialist Party. College made him aware of the precarious position of Jews and other minorities in America and around the world.[38]

In one of his most insightful early works, Lippmann used the occasion of German American persecution during World War I to meditate on the "pains of denationalization."

> What is called pride of race is the sense that our origins are worthy of respect.... Man must be at peace with the sources of his life. If he is ashamed of them, if he is at war with them, they will haunt him forever. They will rob him of the basis of assurance, leave him an interloper in the world. When we speak of thwarted nationality like that of the Irish, the Jews, the Poles, the Negroes, we mean something more intimate than political subjection. We mean a kind of homelessness which houses of brick can obscure but never remedy. We mean that the origins upon which strength feeds and from which loyalty rises—that the origins of these denationalized people have been hurt. They are the children of a broken household, and they are never altogether free. They are never quite sure of themselves.

Was that an admission that Lippmann was at "war" with his ethnicity—that he, too, felt a "kind of homelessness" and was "never quite sure" of himself? Or was this Lippmann the dispassionate observer and reporter? Perhaps it was both. We should guard against making too much of Lippmann's hostility toward Judaism. There are many good reasons to disbelieve in the supernatural. But nor should we accept his argument that his ethnicity did not factor into his thoroughgoing skepticism.[39]

Eventually, Lippmann would find peace in monotheism. Not Judaism or Islam, but Christianity. He would tell his second wife Helen in 1938 that the "classical and Christian heritage" was where he had always felt most comfortable. Conversely, he had a hard time understanding Binger who reportedly suffered from the "rather common Jewish feeling of not belonging to the world he belongs to." Lippmann (almost fifty years old) said that he had "never been oppressed by" or felt "disqualified" by his Jewishness. "To be oppressed by that sort of thing is a sign of not having learned to care about those things which anyone can have if he is able to care about them."[40]

That was Lippmann's "rags-to-riches" fairy tale—easier to believe if your parents had sent you to Sachs and Harvard. In the battle between multiculturalism and Americanism, Lippmann erred on the side of the latter. That meant an affiliation with Christianity for the same reasons that he had dabbled in socialism and bohemianism: Not because they were true—that was impossible to know—but because they were the MORE he chose to make life meaningful. They were the moral equivalents of the "pride of race" which Lippmann never thought he could express himself nor tolerate in others. In his groundbreaking study of caste in America, *The Protestant Establishment* (1964), E. Digby Baltzell would situate Lippmann both as a member of the Christian American power elite and as one of its keenest critics.[41]

Lippmann's self-described agnosticism was an amalgam of his post-Christian influences, his personal temperament, and his felt need to disengage from his Jewish heritage. It had been and would be tested again and again through struggle. Sometimes that brawl was private. Usually, it was before an attentive public. Skepticism was never a compartmentalized issue for Lippmann. It touched the core of his pursuit of happiness, his careers in journalism and politics, and his management of ethnic bigotry. It was a manifestation of as well as a source of his incurable eclecticism. Thus, a Lippmann biography should start with a discussion of his attachments to religions, not end with it. We might find that there was a God in Lippmann after all.

Notes

1. Walter Lippmann, "Interview," Columbia Oral History Project, conducted by Allan Nevins and Dean Albertson, Apr. 3–8, 1950, 39, in WLP, Reel 111.

2. On Lippmann's father, see Steel, *Walter Lippmann*, 5.
3. For Lippmann's maid story, see Walter Lippmann, *Drift and Mastery* (New York: Mitchell Kennerley, 1914), 241–2. On Lippmann's time at the Sachs's school, see Carl Binger, "A Child of the Enlightenment," in *Walter Lippmann and His Times*, ed. Marquis Childs and James Reston (New York: Harcourt, Brace, 1959), 26–8. Roosevelt was considered effete and over-civilized—a "Jane Dandy"—when he first entered politics. See Sarah Watts, *Rough Rider in the White House: Theodore Roosevelt and the Politics of Desire* (Chicago: University of Chicago Press, 2003).
4. Walter Lippmann, to Hazel Albertson, Sept. 18, 1912, in *Public Philosopher: Selected Letters of Walter Lippmann*, ed. John Morton Blum (New York: Ticknor and Fields, 1985), 12.
5. Binger, "Child of the Enlightenment," 29. On Harvard and transformations in higher education, see Andrea L. Turpin, *A New Moral Vision: Gender, Religion, and the Changing Purposes of Higher Education, 1837–1917* (Ithaca: Cornell University Press, 2016).
6. Studies of Progressivism are legion. For an excellent survey, see Eldon J. Eisenach, *The Lost Promise of Progressivism* (University Press of Kansas, 1994).
7. On ties between Christianity and the social sciences, see Dorothy Ross, *The Origins of American Social Science* (New York: Cambridge University Press, 1992). On the social gospel, see Susan Curtis, *A Consuming Faith: The Social Gospel and Modern American Culture* (Baltimore: Johns Hopkins University Press, 1991). See also David Mislin, *Saving Faith: Making Religious Pluralism an American Value at the Dawn of the Secular Age* (Ithaca: Cornell University Press, 2015).
8. Edward A. Ross, *Sin and Society: An Analysis of Latter-Day Iniquity* (Boston: Houghton, Mifflin, 1907), 4.
9. Albion Small, "The Bonds of Nationality," *American Journal of Sociology* 20 (1915): 667–8, 682–3, italics original.
10. Herbert Croly, *The Promise of American Life* (New York: Macmillan, 1909), 13.
11. George Santayana, *Reason in Society* (New York: Charles Scribner, 1905), 136. On Santayana's influence, see Steel, *Walter Lippmann*, 19–22. On "fine arts," see Mary Blume, "Walter Lippmann at 80: The Hopeful Skeptic," *Washington Post*, May 31, 1970, B3.
12. Lippmann, "Interview," 27. On pragmatism and its ties to Progressivism, see James T. Kloppenberg, *Uncertain Victory: Social Democracy and Progressivism in European and American Thought, 1870–1920* (New York: Oxford University Press, 1988).
13. George Cotkin, *William James: Public Philosopher* (Baltimore: Johns Hopkins University Press, 1990).
14. William James, "The Moral Equivalent of War," *McClure's* (Aug. 1910), in *The Moral Equivalent of War and Other Essays*, ed. John K. Roth (New York: Harper, 1971), 4–14, which was based on an address from 1906.

For "tough-minded," see William James, *Pragmatism: A New Name for Some Old Ways of Thinking* (New York: Longmans, Green, 1907 [Reprint: Dover, 1995]), 4. See Christopher McKnight Nichols, *Promise and Peril: America at the Dawn of a Global Age* (Cambridge: Harvard University Press, 2011), on James's politics.

15. James, *Varieties of Religious Experience*, 359, 418–27.
16. Walter Lippmann, "An Open Mind: William James," manuscript, 1910, in WLP, Box 19, Folder 6.
17. Lippmann, *Preface to Politics*, 89–90.
18. Walter Lippmann, to Graham Wallis, Oct. 30, 1912, in WLP, Reel 32.
19. Walter Lippmann, "Nietzsche," undated reading notes, in WLP, Box 20, Folder 117; and Walter Lippmann, to Herbert Croly, July 10, 1919, in WLP, Reel 7.
20. David Carb, to Walter Lippmann, Jan. 11, 1913, in WLP, Reel 1.
21. Walter Lippmann, "A Philosophy of Beauty," term paper for Philosophy E, May 15, 1908, 9–10, in WLP, Reel 170.
22. Walter Lippmann, to Lucile Elsas, n.d. (1907); Walter Lippmann, to Lucile Elsas, n.d. (1908), in *Public Philosopher*, ed. Blum, 3.
23. Walter Lippmann, to Lucile Elsas, n.d. (1908), both in *Public Philosopher*, ed. Blum, 5.
24. Walter Lippmann, "The Possible Development of Democracy in the Future," term paper for Philosophy 10, Nov. 2, 1908, 3–7, in WLP, Reel 170.
25. Lippmann, "Possible Development," 8–10.
26. Walter Lippmann, "Memoirs," unpublished, n.d. (between 1939–1955), in WLP, Box 217, Folder 294; Walter Lippmann, to Audrey Wallas, Aug. 16, 1932, in *Public Philosopher*, ed. Blum, 295.
27. Lippmann, *Preface to Politics*, 201. See Christine Stansell, *American Moderns: Bohemian New York and the Creation of a New Century*, rev. ed. (Princeton: Princeton University Press, 2009).
28. Walter Lippmann, to Graham Wallas, Apr. 23, 1919, in WLP, Reel 32. See Binger, "Child of the Enlightenment," 32, on Faye. On Lippmann's Greenwich Village years, see Jeremy McCarter, *Young Radicals: In the War for American Ideals* (New York: Random House, 2017).
29. Walter Lippmann, "Legendary John Reed," *New Republic*, Dec. 26, 1914, in *Force and Ideas: The Early Writings*, ed. Arthur Schlesinger, Jr. (New Brunswick: Transaction, 1970), 295–6. On "Puritan," see Marquis Childs, "Introduction: The Conscience of a Critic," in *Walter Lippmann*, ed. Childs and Reston, 10. See Walter Lippmann, to Upton Sinclair, May 6, 1914, in WLP, Reel 91, for "agitation."
30. "Walter Lippmann at 83: An Interview with Ronald Steel," *Washington Post*, Mar. 25, 1973, C4.
31. Brad Snyder, *The House of Truth: A Washington Political Salon and the Foundations of American Liberalism* (New York: Oxford University Press, 2017).

32. Walter Lippmann, "Liberalism in America," *New Republic*, Dec. 31, 1919, 150. See Charles Forcey, *The Crossroads of Liberalism: Croly, Weyl, Lippmann, and the Progressive Era, 1900–1925* (New York: Oxford University Press, 1961).
33. Max Eastman, quoted in McCarter, *Young Radicals*, 77. Hutchins Hapgood, quoted in Mabel Dodge Luhan, *Movers and Shakers* (New York: Harcourt, Brace, 1936), 487, italics original.
34. Felix Morrow, "Religion and the Good Life," *Menorah Journal* 18 (Feb. 1930): 86–7.
35. Steel, *Walter Lippmann*, 7, 9. For Dodge's thoughts on Walter and Fay, see Steel, *Walter Lippmann*, 118–19.
36. Lippmann, to Elsas, n.d. (1908).
37. Lippmann, to Elsas, n.d. (1908).
38. Binger, "Child of the Enlightenment," 31.
39. Walter Lippmann, *The Stakes of Diplomacy* (New York: Henry Holt, 1915), 62–3.
40. Walter Lippmann, to Helen Armstrong, Feb. 12, 1938, in WLP, Reel 111.
41. E. Digby Baltzell, *The Protestant Establishment: Aristocracy and Caste in America* (New York: Random House, 1964). See also Richard L. Zweigenhaft and G. William Domhoff, *Jews in the Protestant Establishment* (New York: Praeger, 1982), 7, who exclude Lippmann from their understanding of Jewish identity.

2
The Theologian, 1913–1930

Walter Lippmann was unhappy at home, so he decided to write an international bestseller about the death of God. *A Preface to Morals* (1929) went through six printings in its first year, became a Book-of-the-Month Club selection, and would be translated into twelve different languages. Of the several books Lippmann penned over the course of his life, it would rank second in sales (the first would head to press during World War II). Lippmann later confessed to Helen, his lover and then second wife, that *A Preface to Morals* showed a discontentment with Faye that had been there from the beginning. The text also betrayed Lippmann's upset at the impending marriage of their ward, Jane Mather. Lippmann had grown uncharacteristically close to Jane during the five years that she had lived with the couple, even seeing her as an emotional substitute for Faye. For Jane's own good, he said, he had sent her to Oxford so that they would feel "truly separated." He did not relish the prospect of "losing Jane" to another man—and an economist at that.[1]

Still, Lippmann had been thinking about religion as a personal, professional, and social problem all his younger life (recall his Harvard papers and letters to Lucy). Lippmann's manifesto secured his place among the most famous public intellectuals of the era like H. L. Mencken and Sinclair Lewis. For them, secularism—a life lived free from conformity to divine mandates—was America's only responsible choice. Mencken had a different name for themselves, however: "we theologians."[2]

A Preface to Morals was an act of self-care disguised a search for a new creed that could never be. "The modern world is haunted by a realization," Lippmann announced, "that it is impossible to reconstruct an enduring orthodoxy, and impossible to live well without the satisfactions which an orthodoxy would provide." He advanced a

Walter Lippmann: American Skeptic, American Pastor. Mark Thomas Edwards, Oxford University Press.
© Mark Thomas Edwards 2023. DOI: 10.1093/oso/9780192895165.003.0003

homespun secularization theory, an explanation for the evaporating influence of organized religions reflective of post-Christian aspirations. Summoning James, Santayana, and Freud, Lippmann suggested that religions were "a grandiose fiction projected by human needs and desires." They were human creations destined to demolition when no longer useful. Though no friend of 1920s "Fundamentalism," Lippmann saved his worst salvos for "Modernist" Protestants who wanted to bring Christianity into alignment with contemporary thought and culture. Lippmann called out Harry Emerson Fosdick, the most popular Modernist of the era, as a traitor to the pastor's calling to make plain the ways of God. To Lippmann, American Christianity was rotting from within and from without. Unlike other skeptics, he was not sure that was a good thing.[3]

Lippmann argued that "acids of modernity" were causing the "dissolution of the ancestral order"—both catchphrases he would repeat over the next forty years. The corrosive agents included the natural and social sciences as well as extravagant material comforts. But the greatest solvent (per Wallas) was urban industrialism. "The modern man is an emigrant who lives in a revolutionary society and inherits a protestant tradition," Lippmann observed.

> He must be guided by his conscience. But when he searches his conscience, he finds no fixed point outside of it by which he can take his bearings. He does not really believe that there is such a point, because he himself has moved about too fast to fix any point long enough in his mind. For the sense of authority is not established by argument. It is acquired by deep familiarity and indurated association. The ancient authorities were blended with the ancient landmarks, with fields and vineyards and patriarchal trees, with ancient houses and chests full of heirlooms, with churchyards near at hand and their ancestral graves, with old men who remembered wise sayings they had heard from wise old men. In that kind of setting it is natural to believe that the great truths are known and the big questions settled, and to feel that the dead themselves are still alive and are watching over the ancient faith.

Lippmann the pragmatist assumed there was an organic relationship between belief and environment. As one changed, so must the other. Lippmann's lament for "countryside" piety would be comical if it were not also wrong—many of the leading Fundamentalists were fellow urbanites (including New York's John Roach Straton who Lippmann reported on regularly). Lippmann's loss of place might have reflected his great divorce from ethnic pride and domestic bliss. All the same, his publicizing of private homelessness resonated with a lot of people.[4]

For Lippmann's readers, too, felt they needed MORE in a Jamesian sense. It was at this point that *A Preface to Morals* was most paradoxical: Lippmann assumed that individuals must have and yet could not have an intimate, reciprocal relationship with the divine. Trust and love for a "God," or any absolute being, was necessary to bring human desire into accord with facts. Absent vital affections, persons could never enjoy the fullness of personality. "When they find that they no longer believe seriously and deeply that they are governed from heaven," Lippmann opined of modern men, "there is anarchy in their souls until by conscious effort they find ways of governing themselves." Lippmann's complaints about "immature and unregenerate desire" betrayed his alienation from the Jazz Age and anticipated his conservative cultural criticism of the 1930s and after. But those grievances also highlighted Lippmann's conviction that a Great Society required strong persons to lead it. Moderns had to figure out how to remain spiritual—or at least integral—even if they could no longer be religious in a customary sense.[5]

In post-Christian fashion, Lippmann bid the new Nones look to Jesus for salvation. As one of many "sages" throughout the ages, Lippmann's Christ was an exemplar of the "religion of the spirit" or the "high religion" of "disinterestedness." Disinterestedness was a public philosophy deeply reflective of Lippmann's private disillusionments. It was an amalgam of scientific method and Greek philosophy (strangely, Lippmann did not list the Stoics and Epicureans as role models, but they did surface secondhand through his mentions of Santayana). To be sure, Lippmann was not falling in with social gospel Christians like his in-laws when referencing Jesus. He was repurposing the messiah as a star of secular modernity. Lippmann also invoked the Book of Job—one of the few times he mentioned a Jewish source positively—when he counseled getting over the problems of pain and evil. "To be able to observe our own feelings as if they were objective facts, to detach ourselves from our own fears, hates, and lusts, to examine them, name them, identify them, understand their origin, and finally to judge them, is somehow to rob them of their imperiousness," he assured followers. Lippmann's encouragement to exchange hope of permanent satisfaction for a temporary ranking of needs was meant to help "civilize the passions" without recourse to obeying a deity made in archaic images.[6]

According to Lippmann, "the mature man would take the world as it comes, and within himself remain quite unperturbed.... Since nothing gnawed at his vitals, neither doubt nor ambition, nor frustration, nor fear, he would move easily through life. And so whether he saw the thing as comedy, or high tragedy, or plain farce, he would affirm that it is what it is, and that the wise man can enjoy it." Lippmann thought it might be wise to let go of Faye and Jane. Yet like his references to "modern man," Lippmann's "mature man" was a snob. Mature man was a critique of the "acquisitive instinct" of the 1920s and a plea to lay up treasures in heaven—the realm of the spirit—rather than on earth. At the same time, *A Preface to Morals* was crafted by a Jane Dandy. The metrosexual Lippmann, called "Buddha" by friends for his chubby cheeks, constantly worked out, played tennis and squash, and obsessed over his tailored clothes and appearance. His book was consumed by America's new urban leisure classes who had the extra time and money to ponder Lippmann's portent of religious demise. Lippmann was in but not of a middlebrow culture which was prototypical of today's SBNR, searching for a cosmopolitan piety beyond common Christian expressions.[7]

Lippmann's mature man was gendered and racialized in more subtle ways. He was an extension of Lippmann's belief that Jewish Americans needed to abandon their theological and ethnic exceptionalism (to be discussed later). Lippmann suggested that feminism, in terms of women's increasing economic independence and access to birth control, was one reason that monotheism was in decline, since the child that learns that "there are at least two persons who can give him orders... does not educate him to believe that there is one certain guide to conduct in the universe." All that said, Lippmann introduced the modern man with the best of intentions. He believed that he was not alone in his unhappiness and that some sort of moral equivalent for orthodoxy could help maybe. His bestseller was a "preface," far from a final word.[8]

A Preface to Morals was not Lippmann's first book, it would not be his last, and it is not his most enduring. It was, however, the most revelatory of Lippmann himself. It contained everything: his liberalism, his conservativism, his agnosticism, his pluralism, his sexism, his essentialism, his elitism, his racism, but above all his Jamesian awareness of the potentialities and limits of being human. The book was foundational despite falling within the middle of his major works. Religion was always an obsession for Lippmann, as much as any political or intellectual test he would ever take on. The wall between theology and politics that characterized much of twentieth-century historical scholarship did not exist for him. "God" was forever in the machine, even if that day's machine was tariff reform, polling data, or (remember *The Cold War* essays) geopolitics.

*

Let us now step back to Lippmann's post-graduate years. Understand that the ambivalent secularism of *A Preface to Morals* had been a long time coming. Lippmann had rejected Judaism early in life, as has been discussed. His functional appreciation of Christianity as a useful fiction had stemmed from his college influences. It was soon after Harvard that Lippmann began advertising his transgressive thoughts and feelings. He announced that detachment, calculation, and resignation—not love, joy, and peace—were the spiritual fruit of a post-Christian age. The younger Lippmann wanted something from religions that he did not (and never would) think they could provide.

He was in good company. The early decades of the twentieth century heralded a "Christian century" for some, but for others it marked a culmination of centuries of erosion of Western Christian culture. Emile Durkheim, Max Weber, Oswald Spengler, and other European thinkers (Lippmann included Nietzsche and Karl Marx) drafted the first secularization theories to make legible their rapidly changing social worlds. Closer to home, Progressives began subjecting their childhood Christianities to novel criticism. One of Lippmann's future collaborators, the Columbia University historian James T. Shotwell, offered his secularism scheme around the time that Lippmann was starting his. Shotwell observed that "the history of civilization itself is a history of secularization." He boasted that "no other society is or has been so secular as ours; nowhere else is the tendency so consistently away from religious control." Shotwell understood secularization as "circumscribed" Christian authority and privatization of faith and morals, which might also be called dechristianization. Whatever they termed it, secularists like Shotwell believed irreligion essential to the triumph of "intelligence" in public life. They looked forward to a "scientia scientiarum"—a "great science of living"—to replace religious "emotion" and "prejudice." Unlike James, Lippmann, and social gospelers, Shotwell would not try to recover a "real" Jesus to undergird Progressive moral and social reform.[9]

Lippmann's open mind reveled in secularism's promise of freedom from close-minded religious authorities. Yet his Spartan self feared the consequences. Lippmann's post-Christianity was always a mixture of hopes and worries. His contention with religions was sharpened while a member of the Albertson household. Though Ralph Albertson had been a social gospel pastor, he led Walter and Faye in ridiculing what they saw as the frantic piety of evangelical preachers. Billy Sunday "is the dying gasp of a sick religious system," one of them claimed of the baseball player turned celebrity evangelist. "His God is an object of insult and easy exploitation," they complained. The passionate revivalism of a George Whitefield and D. L. Moody simply would not do in a modern age. Urbanites were "too free and intelligent, too intelligent and free." Why city dwellers walked the sawdust trail with Sunday by the thousands well into the 1920s, Lippmann and the Albertsons never said.[10]

Beneath their laughter at Sunday lay concern that an emaciated Christian culture could not produce lasting happiness. "There is a deep sadness in things," Lippmann wrote Hazel Albertson in 1912. To survive that realization, his generation needed to "lay aside this dream" of human perfection. "In laying that hope aside, in a willingness to love life as a finite gift, skepticism enters into your soul. The great faiths are built on absolutism, and when they are gone men have merely their own courage to beat off loneliness. An odyssey that never ends—it's not an unmixed joy." Little did young Lippmann know then that his own odyssey would take him through Wilsonianism, Stoicism, Catholicism, Edmund Burke, Charles de Gaulle, and Richard Nixon. *A Preface to Morals* would embody the Albertsons' middlebrow cynicism—set against Christian populism—even as Lippmann preached bravery in the face of an uncaring cosmos.[11]

For reasons to be discussed in the next chapter, Lippmann's hit book would have much less to say about the socialism he had once shared with the Albertson household. "I have come around to socialism as a creed," he had written Lucy in 1908. "I do believe in it passionately and fearlessly—not that all men are created equal, for that is a misapplication of democracy—I believe that the people must express themselves in an organized society where religion is the dynamic." This was the collectivism of the State religion Lippmann had written about at Harvard. It was an anti-authoritarian ideal in that Lippmann believed individuals found true freedom only through shared experiences and cooperative group actions.[12]

That is not to say Lippmann ever embraced the Albertsons' Christian socialism. Lippmann rather saw in socialism a critique of urban-industrial conformity and a call to creative, aesthetic individualism. "We turn to religion and find orthodoxy in so feeble a condition," he observed. He added, "I am opposed to public regulation of private morals" such as blue laws and bans on smoking. Lippmann believed socialism could afford Americans liberation from clerical authority, middle-class uplift suasion, and Christian supremacy. It could also provide a home for Jews trying to survive anti-Semitism. But what if anything should replace the social controls of Western Christian mores? That was the defining question of Lippmann's philosophical and journalistic career. He just needed to learn how to ask it.[13]

*

Lippmann's faith in socialism as a constructive religious solution was declining even as his skepticism was growing in his first books, editorials, and wartime reflections. Lippmann's critically acclaimed *A Preface to Politics* (1913) might as well have been entitled "Life after Christian Culture." Most of it was hastily assembled, scattershot advice about how to get along in a world where the old gods/Gods were expired—where "the Christian dream is dead," as Lippmann put it. Reflecting on social Christian anti-intellectualism, Lippmann charged, "when churches cease to paint the background of our lives to nourish a Weltanschauung, strengthen men's ultimate purposes and reaffirm the deepest values of life, then churches have ceased to meet the needs for which they exist." Theology mattered, in other words. Lippmann was particularly harsh on the "decadence" of the Catholic church, charging that it was the responsibility of government to achieve the catholicity that Rome could not. Old Christianities were too tender to supply the tough-mindedness needed to conquer untamed material, mental, and moral territory.[14]

Most readers preferred to read Lippmann's book as an application of Freud to statecraft, which of course it was and something MORE. Good policymaking must begin with a realistic appraisal of human nature, Lippmann argued, including its propensity to violence and unreason alongside intelligence and good will. Yet the real hero of *A Preface to Politics* was Nietzsche, the first Westerner to have proclaimed the death of God. Lippmann had read Nietzsche through James's message that there were no eternally fixed doctrines that should command our allegiance. "Whenever we accept an idea as authority instead of as instrument," Lippmann concurred, "an idol is set up." Try as we might to locate a true truth free from prejudice, "autobiography creeps in anyway." There really was no reason to despair of subjectivity, though:

> The men like Nietzsche and James who show us the willful origin of creeds are in reality the best watchers of the citadel of truth. For there is nothing disastrous in the temporary nature of our ideas. They are always that. But there may very easily be a train of evil in the self-deception which regards them as final. I think God will forgive us our skepticism sooner than our Inquisitions.

For his part, Lippmann was all in for the "iconoclasm that is constantly necessary to avoid the distraction that comes of idolizing our own methods of thought." He was ready to tear down the decaying order to make way for what his bohemian friend and *New Republic* partner, Randolph Bourne, called the "Beloved Community."[15]

To Lippmann, an effective politics must redirect, not eradicate, natural human impulses. It should find moral equivalents to undesirable activities, for "only by supplying our passions with civilized interests can we escape their destructive force." Under its façade of Greenwich Village secularism, feminism, and socialism, *A Preface to Politics* hinted at Lippmann's latent conservativism regarding unchecked craving—notably when those desires were expressed by women, African Americans, and immigrant working classes. At the same time, the book was an innovative muckraking of the harms of nationalism, imperialism, and capitalism, especially when justified in any God's name. It also set into motion Lippmann's wartime critiques of civil religions. "For there is nothing so bad but it can masquerade as moral," he warned.[16]

Lippmann's follow-up treatise, *Drift and Mastery* (1914) was his first attempt at a secularization theory. This is where he originally suggested that Christianity and big cities were incompatible. "It isn't indifference to the great problems that leaves the churches empty," he claimed. "It is the intellectual failure of the churches to meet a sudden change." Still, the "secular spirit," which Lippmann equated with the "scientific spirit," had first triumphed in the nineteenth century, the protean age of demythologization. For Lippmann, the result of ceaseless intellectual and social upheavals was that "all of us are immigrants spiritually." Prefiguring the paradox at the heart of *A Preface to Morals*, *Drift and Mastery* outlined how the crisis of Christian authority left persons as well as civilizations without necessary tools of survival. Lippmann cautioned, "the loss of something outside ourselves which we can obey is a revolutionary break with our habits."

But no matter. The destroyer would become the creator. Lippmann's devotion to science as a cure for all private and public ills was nearing its brief zenith. As he explained, "science is the irreconcilable foe of bogeys, and therefore a method for allaying the conflicts of the soul." Lippmann broke from Freud's determinism and embraced James's radical empiricism enthusiastically. Conservative laments about America's "undisciplined man" were easily crowded out by statements on the liberating power of doubt. "Merely to realize that your way of living is not the only way is to free yourself from its authority," Lippmann resolved. *Drift and Mastery* bore witness to Lippmann's strategy for fitting in—finding a home—through establishing a reputation as a constant contrarian. It also furthered the SBNR sensibility expressed in his first book, as Lippmann challenged readers to seek soul satisfaction outside of traditional religious institutions.[17]

Lippmann's heralding of a fortunate fall from orthodoxy continued in the post-Christian pages of the *New Republic*. Though intently focused on practical politics, from time to time the journal betrayed the heterodox religious and philosophical sensibilities of its Progressive sires. Weyl was a lapsed Jew like Lippmann, while Croly espoused an anti-sectarian "Religion of Humanity," the source of his "American system." Together, the three men pioneered the post-Christian conviction, central to modern American liberalism, that humankind must make their own happiness. "If there is any word to cover our ideal," Lippmann wrote a friend of *New Republic*'s mission, "I suppose it is humanist, somewhat sharply distinguished... from humanitarianism. Humanism, I believe, means this real sense of the relation between the abstract and the concrete, between the noble dream and the actual limitations of life." Humanism would remain Lippmann's preferred (though not only) word to describe his outlook for several years, including in *A Preface to Morals*. There, as in the *New Republic*, humanism meant the quest for the good life minus trust in absolutes. Science, understood in Lippmann's pragmatist sense of an open-minded approach toward everyday life, was humanity's last best hope.[18]

World War I became one occasion for the *New Republic* to practice the deconstruction they preached. Like Woodrow Wilson and other Progressives, Lippmann and the editors came around to believing that the United States should enter World War I as a geopolitically and morally transformative force. Still, they resisted popular representations of a "holy war" between Christian and pagan forces. Lippmann was especially disturbed by propaganda on behalf of universal American nationalism. "Americanism is cheapened and debased when it is put forth as the compelling reason for somebody's notion about military legislation, industrial control, or foreign policy," Lippmann lamented in 1919. "People who flaunt Americanism on all occasions do not inspire respect, and if the aristocratic virtues are to be preserved even in the most democratic society, the huckster and the shyster must be rigorously suppressed.... It is a cheap soul that is continually braying about the eternal verities. For thou shalt not take the name of the Lord thy God in vain." Here was Lippmann's "high religion" of disinterestedness juxtaposed to the Christian Americanism of "hucksters" like Billy Sunday. Lippmann's disdain for civil religions ("patriotic swindles") was noteworthy. It would be a repeated theme of his World War II and Cold War writings.[19]

Lippmann offered more explicit renunciations of wartime crusading in private. "Lord knows, I don't feel a bit neutral between the Western Powers and Germany," he told Holmes. "But I can't believe that Germany is the last and most elaborate effort of Satan to destroy God." Lippmann believed that the Christianizing of the war effort nurtured the demons of inquisition. He and the *New Republic* were troubled by increases in censorship, state surveillance, and many other violations of civil liberties (as will be discussed in Chapter 3). Lippmann had learned from James that the best way to safeguard a pluralistic society was to preserve freethinking and thereby disarm ideological crusades. Given organized religions' historic tendency to become fanatical, the younger Lippmann was a secularist who believed religions should be kept out of the public square if not evicted from society altogether. The older Lippmann would rethink the political value of religious consensus even while he never surrendered his conviction that religions should remain primarily private affairs.[20]

*

Lippmann fashioned an editorial career out of complaining about the "Roaring Twenties," no matter how good they were to him. Lippmann had found it hard to return to the *New Republic* following his wartime service. When he was granted a larger platform in 1922 as a writer for the Progressive flagship, the New York *World* owned by the Pulitzer family, it was an offer too good to refuse. He would eventually become the *World*'s editor.

Lippmann chaffed at the daily demands of the journalist and often yearned to be free of its rigors. Yet he also coveted explaining the ways of God to humankind. The newspaper was the "bible of democracy," Lippmann suggested, and journalism was "one of the truly sacred and priestly offices." That was less secularization than sublimation of Christian practice. As Lippmann explained, "the power to determine each day what shall seem important and what shall be neglected is a power unlike any that has been exercised since the Pope lost his hold on the secular mind." Lippmann never made any claims to infallibility, but he also never minded the fame and fortune of leading the new clergy. Before buying their own home in the city, Faye and Walter lived large: Their apartment on East 63rd had a large garden, a large bar area, a large bed with a mirrored ceiling, a large circulation of guests, and a large Chevrolet for escaping most weekends to their country home at Wading River in the Hamptons.[21]

Postwar America appeared poised to accept the younger Lippmann's edict of release from bad faith. Wartime enthusiasm for a Christian America and Christian world order quickly dissipated. Church leaders instead grumbled about empty pews, declining funds, and loss of public morality. One statistical study of American churches and seminaries, conducted selectively by an "honest agnostic," found that "orthodoxy in the old sense of the term simply does not exist." Religious enthusiasm was redirected into alternative spiritual practices, pop psychology, jazz, baseball, chain stores, and Hollywood. Sinclair Lewis's *Elmer Gantry* (1927), a fictional bestseller about the destructive hypocrisy of a conservative Methodist minister, popularized anti-clericalism. In the highbrow skeptics' manifesto, *The Modern Temper* (1929), Joseph Wood Krutch charged that "weak and uninstructed intellects take refuge in the monotonous repetition of once living creeds." Krutch was speaking on behalf of the "New Humanists" who were taking command of the country's literary culture at that moment. Lippmann's *A Preface to Morals* would add fuel to the New Humanist fire that same year, yet Lippmann looked to blaze a different path forward.[22]

Lippmann knew that the rumors of God's demise were greatly exaggerated. His secular city never came to be, as a new cadre of church growth experts drew upon corporate models to supersize the old-time religion—bigger sanctuaries, bigger spectacles, and bigger personalities. Membership in the established denominations grew throughout the New Era. The "Fundamentalist-Modernist Controversy" might have discouraged Protestant leaders. Yet all camps felt emboldened to enact their versions of Christian America. The Fundamentalists maneuvered against their detractors. They blamed theological moderates for tolerating Modernism and challenged them for control of denominational machinery. Under assault, the liberal and moderate mainline leadership expanded support for the social gospel, grew existing ecumenical networks like the Federal Council of Churches (FCC), and launched new interfaith initiatives such as the National Conference on Christians and Jews (NCCJ). Fundamentalists lost most bureaucratic battles but took their apocalyptic gospel home to form new Bible colleges, church networks, and radio programming. In *A Preface to Morals*, Lippmann sided with the Fundamentalist critique of Modernism. However, he was always closer to liberal Protestants in longing for "abiding experiences" within "changing categories" (Fosdick's words). "Those are the true conservatives and the truly hopeful who argue that a living and growing truth can be followed by men who remain within a living and growing church," Lippmann assured *World* readers.[23]

Like Fosdick, Lippmann was emerging as spokesman for a new religious orientation that one day would be called SBNR. He favored the openness of scientific democracy over clerical and ideological compliance. With that in mind, Fundamentalist political organizing was a danger to Lippmann. Their antievolution campaign had gone public in 1923 with the passage of a state law in Tennessee banning the teaching of evolution in public schools. The law was defended by the populist hero, Democratic Party veteran William Jennings Bryan, at the Scopes trial in 1925. Mencken and others mercilessly roasted Bryan and followers for refusing to enter the modern world. Yet those who laughed off the antievolutionists missed the point. Following the Tennessee model, Fundamentalists launched antievolution campaigns in eighteen different states between 1925 and 1928. Even when Fundamentalists postponed legislative organizing during the 1930s, having failed to secure nationwide antievolution legislation, they had changed the way biology textbooks would be written for the next forty years.[24]

Lippmann was among the secularists who took Bryan and antievolutionism seriously. So did Chicago pragmatist John Dewey, who is often (wrongly) remembered as Lippmann's chief foil. Dewey used the occasion of the movement to assess the state of the American mind. He laid the sin of anti-intellectualism squarely at Protestant Christianity's feet, writing,

> We are not Puritans in our intellectual heritage, but we are evangelical because of our fear of ourselves and our latent frontier disorderliness. The depressing effect upon the free life of inquiry and criticism is the greater because of the element of soundness in frontier fear, and because of the impulses of good will and social aspiration which have become entangled with its creeds.... This is the illiberalism which is deep-rooted in our liberalism. No account of the decay of the idealism of the progressive movement in politics of the failure to develop an intelligent and enduring idealism out of the fervor of the war, is adequate unless it reckons with this fixed limit to thought. No future liberal movement, when active liberalism revives, will be permanent unless it goes deep enough to affect it. Otherwise we shall have in the future what we have had in the past, revivalists like Bryan, Roosevelt and Wilson, movements which embody moral emotions rather than insight and policy of intelligence.

Notice that Dewey's complaint encompassed both conservative (Bryan) and liberal (Wilson) Protestants. Intelligence—empirical reflection upon experience to make better adjustments of and to one's environment—was Dewey's salvation from the "fixed limit to thought" typical of religious authority. He prayed and strived for that transfiguration. Out of it would arise the holistic philosophy of life that he and Lippmann found Christendom had been unable to produce.[25]

Like Dewey, Lippmann believed antievolutionism was revelatory on many levels. Lippmann's thoughts on Bryan's democratic theory will be considered later. More important for us here, Lippmann's compilation of essays on the trial, *American Inquisitors* (1928), debuted new directions in his thinking about the place of religion in public life. Lippmann like Mencken had harsh words for the antievolutionists. "The campaign in certain localities to forbid the teaching of 'Darwinism'," Lippmann summarized, "is an attempt to stem the tide of the metropolitan spirit, to erect a spiritual tariff against an alien rationalism which threatens to dissolve the mores of the village civilization." Lippmann believed it was a good thing that the "great diversity" of thought arising from urbanization, immigration, and internationalism was destroying the "like-mindedness" of prewar America. He encouraged schools and cities in their fight for freedom from the "inquisitions" being conducted by Bryan's "ignoramuses."[26]

Besides Mencken, Lippmann was also friends with Clarence Darrow, the famous trial lawyer who had confronted Bryan during the Scopes trial. Darrow worked with Lippmann through the *World* to fight Fundamentalism more generally. Frankfurter commended Lippmann for exposing the "assininity" of the antievolutionists yet added that "Bryan's simple faith is intrinsically no more ridiculous than any ideas of Christian supernaturalism." The two did not agree on much, but they could at least coalesce around Lippmann's confession in *American Inquisitors* that the "only true and final allegiance" of humankind should be to the scientific method. The Fundamentalists' notion of an essential bond between Christianity and civilization was absurd, Lippmann argued. Rather, progress in science "requires more integrity of mind, more purity of heart, more unselfishness, more devotion, more unworldliness" than could ever be found in organized religions.[27]

And yet Lippmann lashed out at those who accused him of idolizing science. Much of the Socratic dialogues in *American Inquisitors* exposed the limits of the "scientific temper," including its Christian companion

Modernism. Lippmann wanted to laugh with Mencken at the Fundamentalists. With Dewey, he wanted to get over the individualism and moral crusading of America's evangelical past. Still, Lippmann knew with James that his audiences needed a MORE. The Scopes trial had revealed that many Americans remained untouched by the "vast disturbance of modernity." Lippmann understood that "the dissolution proceeds—inexorably, I think—until at last the whole community is uprooted and modernized. But these moderns, though they are uprooted from the ancient foundations, retain many of the expectations of the ancient order of life. They crave certainty, they need guidance, they want compensations." Lippmann portrayed a mass of lost "plain" people looking for satisfaction in the worship of authoritarian personalities, material largesse, perverse nationalism, and "the miracles of machinery and the messianic mission of science."[28]

For Lippmann, the real problem of Fundamentalism was that it was fundamentally anti-Christian. Bryan, the antievolutionists, and the Prohibitionists had committed the mortal sin of forgetting that Christianity was a "living faith" that, over the centuries, had proven tough enough to adapt to progress in science. "Political churches" represented a corruption of public life and were an admission of defeat for a once-great religion. "Free churches" could exist only where there were "free states." But it was just as true that states could remain free only as their churches stayed independent from politics. Lippmann went so far as to ban Americans from thinking about political questions as Protestants, Catholics, or Jews.[29]

Lippmann's commentary on antievolutionism was secularist in its desire to keep religions out of politics. It was post-Christian in its affirmation that traditional religions should still have a place in the modern world. But Lippmann's spiritual posture was self-serving as well. His homelessness from Judaism and tribal identification with "modern man"—his siding with those who had "ceased to ask guaranties" but continued "serene"—betrayed his classist-racist pride in having thrown off the supposed primitivism of popular religion. When not entertaining at their apartment, Walter and Faye frequented the company of Gotham's well-to-do and few people of color. Skepticism was not an abstract intellectual position for the Lippmanns. It was their imagined ticket into a world of upscale white privilege.[30]

*

The metropole Lippmann kept prefacing *A Preface to Morals* in a variety of publications. He used one meditation on the South to drive home his thesis that modernization and secularization proceeded hand-in-hand. He was so committed to a narrative of absolute religious decline, though, that he barely referenced Southern conditions. "There exists today no authoritative and organized body of knowledge which it is possible for any living man to absorb," Lippmann declared. Nor should anyone expect a new Aristotle or Aquinas to put the pieces back together again. Like other secularization theorists, Lippmann used words to conjure the "post" future (post-sectarian, post-Judaic, post-Christian) that he had been imagining at least since 1908 in his Lucy letters.

Yet for reasons both personal and professional, Lippmann was anxious about the religious revolution Nietzsche and James had identified. "The situation of the modern man is unique," he argued, "because in regard to the world in which he has daily to act there no longer exists an authoritative body of morals in which he can find guidance for his conduct." Lippmann even tempered his own secularism a bit: "I do not wish to deny that there are still great general principles of morality to which people sincerely adhere. I do wish to point out that in the application of these principles to the concrete situations of today, whether in industry, in politics, or in family life, there is great disagreement, and there is no authoritative interpretation." Again, here was the paradox that a people should have but could not have a satisfying civil religion.[31]

So Lippmann's closest friends, critics, and readers should not have been surprised at the arrival of his bestseller. He had been working toward it for all his young life. "It is not the intention of 'A Preface to Morals' to tear down anything that people believe in," Lippmann chided one reviewer. The book was rather "a description of the causes and results of the process of tearing down beliefs which has been going on in the history of the world during the last four or five centuries." Lippmann insisted his book was constructive. It was "an attempt to find some slight thing that remains in spite of all this destruction." Beneath its somber tone lay its author's sense that moderns still needed a clear and present faith. As one friend understood Lippmann, "you are sympathetic with those who once believed, and the many who still believe in a God with a long, white beard and arms and legs.

You try to give them something fine and satisfying to take the place of their old beliefs."[32]

That "something fine and satisfying" was what Lippmann had started calling humanism. Lippmann saw his work in agreement with Krutch and the New Humanists, although he admitted that "I do not qualify, nor desire to qualify, as one of the strictly orthodox members of the inner cult"—especially after some of them criticized Lippmann in a published symposium, *Humanism in America* (1930). Lippmann's humanism would always be a moral equivalent to orthodoxy instead of a new dogma. "If the principle of a theocratic culture is dependence, obedience, conformity in the presence of a superhuman power which administers reality," Lippmann had written in *A Preface to Morals*, "the principle of humanism is detachment, understanding, and disinterestedness in the presence of reality itself." In a 1930 essay, Lippmann further explained that, while "there never has been a strict doctrine of humanism," the word signified "the intention of men to concern themselves with the discovery of a good life on this planet by the use of human faculties." Lippmann would be listed as a "Naturalistic Humanist," and friends would laud him as "a great humanist," well into the 1940s and 1950s.[33]

Others found Lippmann's humanism confusing at best. Santayana and the Marxist Annette Rubinstein accused Lippmann of misappropriating disinterestedness. Jewish editors felt burned by Lippmann, one complaining that he "might have saved some of that concern he lavishes on the decline of the supernatural Christianity of the Middle Ages for the fate of a tradition that more nearly shared his own moral interest." To be fair, Lippmann had set himself against his Jewish upbringing a long time before. The writers for the liberal Catholic *Commonweal* witnessed in Lippmann's manifesto the "spiritual dissatisfaction of the modern Jew who has been severed from his religious community." They asserted that the Jew "who seeks to live as an individual in our at least nominally Christian world, who finds the way back into the temple obscured, inevitably surrenders that sense of 'being together with others' so essential in all Hebraic history." As confirmation of the *Commonweal*'s coverage of his homelessness, Lippmann offered one of his first positive evaluations of the "deeper fundamentalism" and "living authority" of Roman Catholicism in *A Preface to Morals*. His affiliation would deepen in subsequent years.[34]

Yet it was American Protestants who first saw an opportunity to bring Lippmann into the fold. Billy Sunday's evangelicals believed Lippmann was finally sad enough that they could convince him to accept Jesus as his personal lord and savior. Modernists, heavily influenced by James too, believed Lippmann's secular humanism to be compatible with their own quest for a scientific Christianity. Lippmann's work betrayed a generational gap within the Northeastern and Midwestern churches and seminaries where Modernists had been residing uneasily with Fundamentalists and moderates. One notable moderate, the globe-trotting evangelist John R. Mott, was so troubled by what he called the "powerful challenge of Humanism" that he began assembling a network of "Younger Theologians" to develop new defenses of Christian supernaturalism. Ironically, most Younger Theologians praised Lippmann's work. One called it an "indispensable preface to theology," providing the deconstructive context in which genuine faith could grow. Another, the socialist Christian pastor and Jamesian Reinhold Niebuhr, found Lippmann a kindred skeptic, calling his book "a relief and a joy." Lippmann returned the favor, telling Niebuhr "I have learned to look immediately for anything that you write."[35]

Niebuhr was just one of the Protestant leaders with whom Lippmann would maintain long-term relationships. Perhaps aware of Lippmann's connections to the World Alliance for International Friendship through the Churches, FCC leaders reached out to Lippmann in 1929 when they were drafting a new social creed for their churches. Lippmann was dismissive of such confessions, responding that "Christian ethics which would determine choices of decisions cannot be prescribed in easy, general phrases." His attitude toward the political impracticality of religions would not waiver over the course of his life, although he did express "great sympathy" with the FCC's revised statement of principles. Interestingly, Lippmann's denial of his Jewish heritage did not stop him from lending his name to the advisory council of the interfaith NCCJ. As early as 1924, Fosdick believed he and Lippmann had a lot in common—they both adhered to "reverent agnosticism"—and they continued corresponding even after Lippmann skewered Fosdick in print. Lippmann seemed so friendly to Christianity that future U.S. Senator H. Alexander Smith invited Lippmann to become an evangelist for the "Oxford Movement" project.[36]

*

Lippmann did undergo a conversion experience of sorts after 1929. According to Nevins, who had worked with Lippmann at the *World*, Lippmann had spent much of the decade reading religion, philosophy, and ethics. He would continue to do so in earnest as he began preparing a sequel to *A Preface to Morals*, including use of the *Catholic Encyclopedia*. Self-learning would reinforce Lippmann's desire (expressed to Helen) to belong to the Christian and not to the Jewish past. As Lippmann's affiliation with Christianity grew throughout world crises of depression and war, his political reporting and theorizing would change as well. His quest to leave "outmoded" Darwin behind in order to attain to "an objective understanding of what we really are"—a middle way between "nature" and "super-nature"— was a political as well as a religious crusade.[37]

As I have been arguing, Lippmann's transgression of binaries of the sacred and profane was a vocation, a forever mission. Nearly one-third of *A Preface to Morals* was about rebuilding government, economy, and family in reaction to modernity's acids. The ex-socialist Lippmann suggested that America's "disinterested" business class was now one of the most progressive forces around. Gone was any discussion of worker rights. Lippmann was at his most conservative—and disillusioned—when discussing sex and marriage. While he did say that more "experimenting" was needed in physical and social relations, he also condemned the "new hedonism" for its celebration of the destructive power of unchecked desire. Lippmann was indeed a Puritan in Babylon.[38]

In fact, *A Preface to Morals* faced its harshest criticism as an economic text. Frankfurter was vexed by Lippmann's seeming blindness to the way that disinterest could be coopted by corporate America. How could the editor of the *World* have become so indifferent to the ethical bankruptcy of the country's financial elite? Rubinstein wondered that as well. "All is not as it should be," she warned, "when we notice here that disinterestedness connotes a tremendous contraction of man's intellectual horizon, a pious faith that our finished piece of work will, somehow, fit in with other such pieces of work, and a practical justification in the increased efficiency such concentration will entail.... This is not a description of disinterestedness. It is not a description of anything but the resignation and surrender of utter weariness, a surrender colored by that resentment which any access of energy would kindle into futile rebellion." In other words, the liberation promised by pragmatism had settled into the prison of utilitarianism, and Lippmann did not seem to care. Lippmann would suffer harsher attacks after he joined a well-paying Republican newspaper during the Great Depression.[39]

Rendering Lippmann a "Tired Radical" (originally Weyl's term) has been commonplace but not really fair, as will be discussed in the next chapter on Lippmann as a political philosopher.[40] That is where most biographies of him typically start. They either ignore Lippmann the theologian or treat his extensive writings on religion as tangential. But there never was a "spiritual" or "secular" Lippmann: They were always one and the same person. His efforts to articulate, navigate, and ultimately manage what he saw as (but never termed) a post-Christian world intertwined the realms of politics and religions. The younger Lippmann's musings on statecraft must be understood as a form of public theology.

Notes

1. Walter Lippmann, to Helen Armstrong, Feb. 8, 1938, in WLP, Reel 111. See also Steel, *Walter Lippmann*, 265–7.
2. H. L. Mencken, to Walter Lippmann, Aug. 5, 1930, in WLP, Reel 17.
3. Walter Lippmann, *A Preface to Morals* (New York: Macmillan, 1929 [Reprint: Time Incorporated, 1964]), 19, 38–47, 133–4.
4. Lippmann, *Preface to Morals*, 56–9.
5. Lippmann, *Preface to Morals*, 106, 130, 178–80, 194.
6. Lippmann, *Preface to Morals*, 181–90, 204–5, 224–5, 305–7. On Santayana, Greek philosophy, and disinterestedness, see Annette T. Rubinstein, "Disinterestedness as Ideal and as Technique," *The Journal of Philosophy* 28 (Aug. 1931): 461–6.
7. Lippmann, *Preface to Morals*, 308–9; Steel, *Walter Lippmann*, 203. See Matthew S. Hedstrom, *The Rise of Liberal Religion: Book Culture and American Spirituality in the Twentieth Century* (New York: Oxford University Press, 2012).
8. Lippmann, *Preface to Morals*, 85–7, 234. I am indebted to Sarah Imhoff, "My Sons Have Defeated Me: Walter Lippmann, Felix Adler, and Secular Moral Authority," *Journal of Religion* 92 (Oct. 2012): 536–50, for highlighting Lippmann's connection of feminism and secularization.

9. James T. Shotwell, *The Religious Revolution of Today* (Boston; Houghton Mifflin, 1913), 9–10, 51, 151, 160–1; James T. Shotwell, *Intelligence and Politics* (New York: Century, 1921), 21, 31.
10. "Untitled essay on Billy Sunday" (circa 1917), in WLP, Reel 1.
11. Lippmann, to Albertson, Sept. 18, 1912.
12. Walter Lippmann, to Lucile Elsas, May 10, 1908, in Steel, *Walter Lippmann*, 24. Part of Lippmann's letter to Elsas was lost and only remains in Steel's biography. See Walter Lippmann, to Lucile Elsas, May 10, 1908, in *Public Philosopher*, ed. Blum, 4.
13. Walter Lippmann, "The Modern Spirit: Socialism as Attitude of Man," unpublished essay, n.d., in WLP, Box 19, Folder 80.
14. Lippmann, *Preface to Politics*, 138, 174, 225.
15. Lippmann, *Preface to Politics*, 150, 178, 229. "Beloved Community" was coined by James's rival Josiah Royce but was popularized Bourne. See McCarter, *Young Radicals*, 62, 122–6.
16. Lippmann, *Preface to Politics*, 40–4, 125.
17. Lippmann, *Drift and Mastery*, 155–7, 178, 196, 211, 276, 297, 302–3.
18. Walter Lippmann, to Van Wyck Brooks, Feb. 15, 1914, in *Public Philosopher*, ed. Blum, 17.
19. Walter Lippmann, "Unrest," *New Republic*, Nov. 12, 1919, in *Force and Ideas*, ed. Schlesinger, 279; Walter Lippmann, "The Patriotic Swindle," *World*, Apr. 7, 1927, 14. See also Philip Jenkins, *The Great and Holy War: How World War I Became a Religious Crusade* (New York: HarperOne, 2014). The best place to find Lippmann's *World* editorials cited in this and forthcoming chapters is RAC, Reels 4–7.
20. Walter Lippmann, to Oliver Wendell Holmes, Jr., Feb. 21, 1917, in *Public Philosopher*, ed. Blum, 62.
21. Walter Lippmann, *Liberty and the News* (New York: Harcourt, Brace, 1920), 47–8.
22. George Herbert Betts, *The Beliefs of 700 Ministers* New York: Abingdon, 1929), 60, 73–4; Joseph Wood Krutch, *The Modern Temper: A Study and a Confession* (New York: Harcourt, Brace, 1929), 18–19. See J. David Hoeveler, Jr., *The New Humanism: A Critique of Modern America, 1900–1940* (Charlottesville: University Press of Virginia, 1977). On the 1920s "spiritual depression," see Robert T. Handy, *A Christian America: Protestant Hopes and Historical Realities*, 2nd ed. (New York: Oxford University Press, 1984).
23. Walter Lippmann, "Living Truth and a Living Church," *World*, Jan. 23, 1922, 10. See Matthew Sutton, *American Apocalypse: A History of Modern Evangelicalism* (Cambridge: Harvard University Press, 2014).
24. Judith V. Grabiner and Peter D. Miller, "Effects of the Scopes Trial: Was It a Victory for Evolutionists?" *Science* (Sept. 6, 1974): 832–7.
25. John Dewey, "The American Intellectual Frontier," *New Republic*, May 10, 1922, 303–4; John Dewey, *Reconstruction in Philosophy* (New York: Henry Holt, 1920), 173.

26. On "Darwinism," see Walter Lippmann, *Men of Destiny* (New York: Macmillan, 1927), 29. On "great diversity" and "inquisitions," see Walter Lippmann, *American Inquisitors* (New York: Macmillan, 1928 [Reprint: Transaction, 1993]), 24, 34.

27. Lippmann, *American Inquisitors*, 84; Walter Lippmann, "Are We Degenerate?" *World*, Aug. 5, 1925, 10; Walter Lippmann, "What is Reason For?" *World*, July 18, 1925, 8. See also Clarence Darrow, to Walter Lippmann, Aug. 29, 1928, in WLP, Reel 7; and Felix Frankfurter, to Walter Lippmann, July 24, 1925, in WLP, Reel 10.

28. Lippmann, *American Inquisitors*, 75, 119–20.

29. Walter Lippmann, "The Foundations of Faith," *World*, July 17, 1925, 10; Walter Lippmann, "Political Churches," *World*, May 23, 1927, 12; Walter Lippmann, "A Free Church in a Free State," *World*, Oct. 3, 1928, 10. See also Walter Lippmann, "The Fundamentalist Churches in Politics," *World*, July 28, 1928, 12.

30. Lippmann, *American Inquisitors*, 120.

31. Walter Lippmann, "The South and the New Society," *Social Forces* (1927), in *The Essential Lippmann: A Political Philosophy for Liberal Democracy*, ed. Clinton Rossiter and James Lare (New York: Vintage, 1963), 43.

32. On "tear down," see Walter Lippmann, to Lynn Weldon, Mar. 23, 1931, in *Public Philosopher*, ed. Blum, 271. On "you are sympathetic," see Fremont Older, to Walter Lippmann, May 24, 1929, in WLP, Reel 25.

33. On Lippmann and the New Humanism, see Walter Lippmann, to Seward Collins, Mar. 25, 1930, in *Public Philosopher*, ed. Blum, 261–2. On "theocratic culture," see Lippmann, *Preface to Morals*, 206. On "doctrine of humanism," see Walter Lippmann, "Humanism as Dogma," *Saturday Review of Literature* 6 (1930): 817–19. On Lippmann and "Naturalistic Humanism," see Warren Allen Smith, "Authors and Humanism," *The Humanist* 11 (Oct. 1951): 199. On Lippmann as a "great humanist," see Allan Nevins, "Walter Lippmann and the *World*," in *Walter Lippmann and His Times*, ed. Childs and Reston, 66.

34. See Rubinstein, "Disinterestedness," for a critique of Lippmann's sources. See also Morrow, "Religion and the Good Life," 86–7; and "Faith on Easy Terms," *Commonweal*, Oct. 16, 1929, 604–5. See Lippmann, *Preface to Morals*, 32–3, on "deeper fundamentalism" and "living authority."

35. Letters encouraging Lippmann to convert to Christianity are scattered throughout his correspondence. On Mott and the Younger Theologians, see Mark Edwards *The Right of the Protestant Left: God's Totalitarianism* (New York: Palgrave Macmillan, 2012). For "preface to theology," see Walter Horton, *Theism and the Modern Mood* (New York: Harper and Brothers, 1930), 17, 90. For "relief and a joy," see Reinhold Niebuhr, "Review of *A Preface to Morals*," *World Tomorrow* 12 (July 1929): 313–14. See Walter Lippmann, to Reinhold Niebuhr, May 23, 1929, in WLP, Reel 24, for "I have learned."

36. On Lippmann and the World Alliance, see Fred B. Smith, to Walter Lippmann, Jan. 26, 1926; and Walter Lippmann, to Fred B. Smith, Mar. 1, 1926, both in WLP, Reel 33. On the FCC's social creed, see Edward Devine, to Walter Lippmann, Sept. 12, 1929; Walter Lippmann, to Edward Devine, Sept. 16, 1929; and Walter Lippmann, to Edward Devine, Oct. 29, 1929, all in WLP, Reel 7. On the NCCJ, see FCC, to Walter Lippmann, Apr. 25, 1927, in WLP, Reel 8; and Kevin M. Schultz, *Tri-Faith America: How Catholics and Jews Held America to Its Protestant Promise* (New York: Oxford University Press, 2011). See Harry Emerson Fosdick, to Walter Lippmann, Sept. 7, 1924, in WLP, Reel 9, on their relationship. On "reverent agnosticism," see Harry Emerson Fosdick, *As I See Religion* (New York: Harper and Brothers, 1932), 55. On the Oxford Movement, see H. Alexander Smith, to Walter Lippmann, Mar. 28, 1932, in WLP, Reel 92.

37. On Nevins's testimony, see David Elliott Weingast, *Walter Lippmann: A Study in Personal Journalism* (Westport, Conn.: Greenwood, 1949), 23. On writing a sequel to *A Preface to Morals*, see Walter Lippmann, to Graham Wallis, June 24, 1930, in WLP, Reel 32. See Lippmann, "Interview," 149–50, on Lippmann's use of the *Catholic Encyclopedia*. On Lippmann's affiliation with Christianity over Judaism, see Lippmann, to Armstrong, Feb. 12, 1938. For "objective understanding," see Walter Lippmann, to Newton D. Baker, May 15, 1929, in *Public Philosopher*, ed. Blum, 240–1.

38. Lippmann, *Preface to Morals*, 234–40, 257, 261–5, 282–7, 292.

39. Felix Frankfurter, to Walter Lippmann, Oct. 10, 1929, in WLP, Reel 10; Rubinstein, "Disinterestedness," 463.

40. Weyl had tried to publish an essay in the *New Republic* entitled "Tired Radicalism," but Lippmann refused to run it because it was aimed at him. See Forcey, *Crossroads of Liberalism*, 296.

3
The Priest, 1913–1930

If Nietzsche and Lippmann were right that all philosophy is autobiography—that "all philosophies are the language of particular men"—then what should we conclude about Lippmann's masterpiece of democratic theory, *Public Opinion* (1922)? Family problems informed his "high religion" of disinterestedness, so why not his politics? Lippmann had served his country well during World War I. He had then joined and eventually led the most powerful liberal publication in the country. Yet the daily grind of editorializing distracted him from the scholar's life he envied. His marriage to Faye was not going well. And try as he might to deny it, he was still a Jew in an anti-Semitic country. Lippmann felt the frustration of his "omnicompetent citizen," stuck in a world beyond his full comprehension and control.[1]

As with *A Preface to Morals*, the private discontentment around and within *Public Opinion* did not discredit Lippmann's revolutionary analysis, it crystallized it. "You cannot take more political wisdom out of human beings than there is in them," he summarized, "and no reform, however sensational, is truly radical, which does not consciously provide a way of overcoming the subjectivism of human opinion based on the limitation of human experience." For the postwar Lippmann, American democracy was in trouble because it was always in trouble. It was built upon the farce that persons were capable of greater intuition, integrity, and empathy than they actually were. According to Lippmann, "the world that we have to deal with politically is out of reach, out of sight, out of mind. Man is no Aristotelian god contemplating all existence at one glance. He is the creature of an evolution who can just about span a sufficient portion of reality to manage his survival, and snatch what on the scale of time are but a few moments of insight and happiness." This and other passages highlight how we need to reexamine the young Lippmann's political writings as indictments of civil religions.[2]

Walter Lippmann: American Skeptic, American Pastor. Mark Thomas Edwards, Oxford University Press.
© Mark Thomas Edwards 2023. DOI: 10.1093/oso/9780192895165.003.0004

Lippmann drew heavily upon James and Wallas in making his case for why American democracy needed a new cultural apparatus. Individuals rarely encounter reality directly and never fully, he argued. Rather, they are bound up in unsteady mental constructions that Lippmann called "pseudo-environments." Persons navigate their pseudo-environments by way of "stereotypes." Lippmann pioneered this concept and remains one of its most insightful theorists. Stereotypes are

> an ordered, more or less consistent picture of the world, to which our habits, our tastes, our capacities, our comforts and our hopes have adjusted themselves. They may not be a complete picture of the world, but they are a picture of a possible world to which we have adapted.... We feel at home there. We fit in. We are members. We know the way around. There we find the charm of the familiar, the normal, the dependable.... The stereotypes are, therefore, highly charged with the feelings that are attached to them. They are the fortress of our tradition, and behind its defenses we can continue to feel ourselves safe in the position we occupy.

Stereotypes, or the "pictures in our heads," are roadmaps of however much pseudo-environment we can handle. They are where will, perception, and reason meet. Stereotypes are also pathologies. They are the prisons we lock from the inside.[3]

For Lippmann, "we do not first see, and then define, we define first and then we see." This predicament of mediated existence was aggravated by the Great Society—Wallas's and Lippmann's name for large cities within industrial-capitalist nation-states. Earlier Progressives had called this new phase of human evolution "interdependence." In a Great Society, it was psychologically impossible for persons to achieve enough knowledge for political decision—to become "omnicompetent." Thus, public opinion was a delusion disguising the "manufacture of consent" by elites. Lippmann held up Wilson's "Fourteen Points" World War I peace program as an example of a manufactured symbol that had reorganized stereotypes in favor of global Americanism. Lippmann knew the program's failure as well as anyone: He had written most of it (more on that later).[4]

The takeaway for readers then and now? Free society is a sham, for most of us live in "subjection to symbols" that prey upon our wishes and whims. "By mass action nothing can be constructed, devised, negotiated, or administered," Lippmann recounted. Governments, schools, and churches labored in vain against "the more obvious failings of democracy, against violent prejudice, apathy, preference for the curious trivial as against the dull important, and the hunger for sideshows and three-legged calves." Lippmann no longer hid his disgust with Jeffersonian populism. Perhaps the "omnicompetent citizen" of yore had been able to master village and farm life, but Chicago and New York were no small towns. Nor should anyone look for solace in an "Oversoul" or spiritual collective. Lippmann decided Machiavelli had been right about human selfishness all along. Similar to but well before Reinhold Niebuhr, Lippmann was feeling his way toward a political doctrine of original sin. Both men would locate the incivility of civil societies in the cognitive quandary that James had called a "certain blindness" in humankind.[5]

Public Opinion has been passed over as a contribution to public theology (or, better, anti-theology). But there was a reason that liberal theologians were among the biggest champions of Lippmann's book. They appreciated his rejection of providential reasoning. As Lippmann observed,

> The tendency of the people who have voiced the ideas of democracy, even when they have not managed its action, the tendency of students, orators, editors, has been to look upon Public Opinion as men in other societies looked upon the uncanny forces to which they ascribed the last word in the direction of events. For in almost every political theory there is an inscrutable element which in the heyday of that theory goes unexamined. Behind the appearances there is a Fate, there are Guardian Spirits, or Mandates to a Chosen People, a Divine Monarchy, a Vice-Regent of Heaven, or a Class of the Better Born. The more obvious angels, demons, and kings are gone out of democratic thinking, but the need for believing that there are reserve powers of guidance persists. It persisted for those thinkers of the Eighteenth Century who designed the matrix of democracy. They had a pale god, but warm hearts, and in the doctrine of popular sovereignty they found their answer to the need of an infallible origin for the new social order.

Lippmann's investigation of public opinion was not an apology for elitist democracy, as it has often been remembered. The above passage suggests it was an effort to rob American nationalism of divine sanction. *Public Opinion* looked back to Lippmann's complaints about Rousseau in his Harvard essays. It anticipated his declaration in *A Preface to Morals* that "God"—or any benevolent supernatural provision—was dead. Now was the season for political theorists to stop looking to the stars and to start looking around them. It was time to put away childish things and to grow manly energies for moral reconstruction.[6]

Lippmann's prescription for post-Christian democracy was presented in secularist terms. He concluded that only experts had the resources to transcend their stereotypes and "pursue a more disinterested vision." Tailored democracy had already come to America, such as in the Census Bureau, but Lippmann believed it could become more stylish through the stitching together of networks of intelligence agencies. The new "special men," having secured their "freedom from clericalism," were able to play "Socrates" to elected officials. That said, Lippmann never completely endorsed Santayana's socialist aristocracy of secular saints. He feared self-interest would lead experts to form deep state bureaucracies. He thus recommended a "satisfactory decentralization" of policymaking. The goal should be "to separate as absolutely as it is possible to do so the staff which executes from the staff which investigates."[7]

A Preface to Morals might have been Lippmann's most revealing book, but *Public Opinion* was his most influential. Few read the former anymore. The latter still inspires scholars in media studies, political psychology, and related fields. But here is the point, and it must be insisted upon: We never would have gotten *Public Opinion* and its preparatory and succeeding material without the twenty-year religious and philosophical struggle that became *A Preface to Morals*. Leave it to an incurable eclectic to write his most famous treatise before he had figured out its foundations. However, reversing the publication order of the two books is necessary to understand how Lippmann's reflections on statecraft were shaped by the problem of ordering self and society in the absence of supernatural revelation. Lippmann was, from the start, a theologian and philosopher, a pastor and priest, under the masquerade of a political columnist.

It was Lippmann's refusal to submit to his own advice to compartmentalize faith and life which would make him one of the foremost post-Christian writers of his generation. He would hype Protestant and Catholic (rarely Jewish) ideals for achieving personal and public equilibrium. Again, that does not mean Lippmann ever adopted Christianity for himself. He recognized, like James and unlike Nietzsche, that God's expiration did not entail having to give up on divine companionship altogether. Fealty was optional—it could be superfluous for some and indispensable for others. Lippmann occupied both camps. In *Public Opinion*, he made the case that dispirited individuals needed effective organization and leadership. Just a few years later, he would be summoning the same "modern man" to become disinterested, to curate their souls more carefully in the face of modernity's acids.

In the long culture war between the RBNS and the SBNR, Lippmann refused to choose. Democracy depended upon developing robust mechanisms of government (the RBNS) while also nurturing superior personalities (SBNR). To save itself, a post-Christian America needed to magnify liberty and order simultaneously.

*

The younger Lippmann's trust that his country could do that had sprung from his socialism. He had approached it as a religious creed, we have seen. Lippmann found in socialism a fellowship that "homeless" Jews were denied at Harvard and around New York's leisure set. His conversion, though, was that of a privileged youth uplifting rather than joining the laboring masses like Reed and Eastman. Hence Lippmann's attraction to the bourgeois, non-statist socialism of the British Fabians. He was convinced that the socialist revolution could not develop from the top down but only through grassroots initiatives curated by the radical middle classes.[8]

That helps explain the nature and limits of Lippmann's feminism. While a student at Harvard, he had cited Wallas and James in defense of "militant" women's suffrage. In a long letter to Marie Hoffendahl Jenney Howe, the founder of the "Heterodoxy" women's club in Greenwich Village, Lippmann made his case for why feminists should become socialists. The present "emancipation of women" was the "dumb product of social conditions," Lippmann suggested. Feminism was not yet a self-directed movement, which was why women still found so many barriers to self-fulfillment in marriage and in the workforce. Lippmann believed they could achieve authenticity only as they committed themselves to building a socialist society. Conversely, Lippmann did not think socialism could triumph in America apart from a mass feminist movement. It was a bold and innovative argument—rooted in pragmatism yet anticipating leftist thought of the 1960s. It was also one that made feminism dependent upon the liberation of men and children from capitalism. Was there no place for an independent woman's vision of the good life?[9]

Lippmann struggled to reconcile personal autonomy and social solidarity in his early books. In *A Preface to Politics*, Lippmann marshalled James, Wallas, and Freud to lobby for synthesizing philosophy, psychology, and statecraft. As noted in the last chapter, the Nietzschean courage to recreate human existence, unencumbered by dead Christian mores, was paramount throughout the text. Iconoclasm was the spirit of the age, and who better to beckon it than feminists and trade unionists? Rather than disrupting such revolutions, Lippmann urged politicians to serve the needs of women, workers, and everyone else. He encouraged governments to surrender the role of "policeman" and to become the "producer" of a socialist commonwealth— meaning more efficient infrastructure, education, health care, and sanitation. Yet Lippmann's stress on civilizing irrational human impulses gave preference to the "Servile State" he feared except when he did not.[10]

James, through Wallas, helped Lippmann sublimate his Freudianism. Lippmann would return the favor by pushing a Wallas catchphrase for over fifty years. James had asked Wallas to write a follow-up to *Human Nature in Politics*, which he did called *The Great Society* (1914). Wallas had formulated the book in running conversation with Lippmann. He dedicated it to the twenty-five year old in hopes of steering him away from "certain forms of twentieth-century anti-intellectualism." It worked. Lippmann accompanied Wallas in searching for happiness within urban industrial capitalist society. But for what it was worth, Wallas did not think such contentment was possible. "If I try to make for myself a visual picture of the social system which I should desire for England and America," he concluded, "there comes before me a recollection of those Norwegian towns and villages where everyone, the shopkeepers and the artisans, the schoolmaster, the boy who drove the post-ponies, and the student daughter of the innkeeper who took round the potatoes, seemed to represent themselves, to be capable of Happiness as well as of pleasure and excitement, because they were near the Mean in the employment of all of their faculties." Lippmann, too, could appreciate a good Mean in the Aristotelian sense of avoiding excesses of pleasure, pain, but not privilege. He would later consider Wallas's manifesto "anti-socialist."[11]

That did not mean Lippmann was done with socialism, though. In *Drift and Mastery*, Lippmann still asked governments to join feminists, unionists, and "responsible businessmen"—that last one was a surprise—in working toward a more egalitarian social order. Lippmann was more dismissive of the political value of organized Christianity than he had been previously, and he was more insistent that agnosticism should be the starting point for any vital faith and politics. Yet, following Wallas, Lippmann was perturbed by the "complexity" of interdependence. He lamented that "our souls have become disorganized, for they have lost the ties that bound them."[12]

The demise of self-governance justified Lippmann in recommending more stringent social controls. Claiming (much like the old Lippmann) that "men will do almost anything but govern themselves," the younger Lippmann looked to science to save American democracy. Scientific criticism, the "inner sanctuary of civilized power," could provide planning and purpose where tradition and custom were flailing. Mastery remained a socialistic vision for Lippmann but also a snobbish one. "You can't build a modern nation out of Georgia crackers, poverty-stricken negroes, the homeless and helpless of the great cities," Lippmann insisted. "Before you can begin to have democracy you need a country in which everyone has some stake and some taste of its promise."[13]

At times, Lippmann's advocacy for scientific democracy demanded broader avenues of participation for women and the white working class. He maintained a certain blindness toward others, though, notably southerners. That is just another way to say that the radical Lippmann was making his peace with Progressivism, which generally ignored the plight of sharecroppers. The extent to which Lippmann remained a socialist after 1914 is a worthwhile question. Given his understanding of socialism as state-produced social capital, Lippmann never really gave it up. Yet it is more important to recognize here how Lippmann's skepticism informed his political performances. His first major works proved that Lippmann was a post-Christian thinker, longing after a tough-minded spirituality for what he thought was a tender-minded liberal democracy.

*

In the fight for Lippmann's ambition between Mabel Dodge's bohemians and the House of Truth's Progressives, *Drift and Mastery* signaled that the latter had won. Lippmann's book had been his admission to join the *New Republic* team. Croly told his friends the new journal was not socialist, while Lippmann confided that it was ("We shall be socialistic in direction, but not in method, or phrase or allegiance."). Croly's "Religion of Humanity" was not shared by Weyl and Lippmann. Yet one thing they could agree on: In the rap battle between America's founding fathers, Alexander Hamilton had more to say to an interdependent world than did Thomas Jefferson. "I regard Alexander Hamilton as the greatest constructive statesman that this country has ever produced," Lippmann charged. He and associates were hardly unaware of Hamilton's plutocratic devotions, nor were they unsympathetic to the pastoral virtues of Jefferson's Empire of Liberty. They wanted to combine "Hamiltonian means with Jeffersonian ends," in the words of one historian. Those ends, Croly said, were "essentially equalitarian and even socialistic." His editors talked frequently of "industrial democracy," but most broke from unionizing.[14]

The socializing of Hamiltonianism in Europe would be called "social democracy" or "democratic socialism." With the names "Democrat" and "Republican" already taken in America, *New Republic* editors adopted the label "liberalism" for their strong-state, anti-radical democratic nationalism. Thanks to Franklin Roosevelt, it stuck. Lippmann would continue to talk about the "marriage" of Jefferson and Hamilton well into World War II.[15]

But it was the other Roosevelt that *New Republic* men were smitten with. "He is the original and supreme Hamiltonian revivalist," Croly had confessed of Teddy in 1910. Croly launched the *New Republic* to help preserve Roosevelt's Progressive Party after its failed bid for the White House in 1912. Lippmann, too, had been enamored of Roosevelt from a young age and had cast the Rough Rider as a Nietzschean Superman in his first book. In 1935, Lippmann would describe himself as Roosevelt's "unqualified hero-worshipper" who had measured all succeeding presidents by him. Yet that fondness had not stopped Lippmann from once confiding to Frankfurter, "[Roosevelt] does not understand industrial preparedness; he does not know what he means by social justice." Lippmann admired assertive men so long as they conformed to whatever he felt was the good life and society at any particular moment—that was a pattern that would persist into his 1960s and 1970s. Still, Roosevelt's "New Nationalism" was an improvement upon "Congressional Government," which Lippmann held to be the chief defect of the U.S. Constitution ("There isn't a decent public servant in Washington who doesn't breathe a sigh of relief when Congress adjourns.").[16]

Roosevelt had read *A Preface to Politics* while on safari in Africa and had reveled in Lippmann's adulation. Upon returning stateside, he wrote a note of praise to the young man. In the spring of 1914, he invited Lippmann and Frankfurter to the Harvard Club to discuss the possibility of another presidential run in 1916. Later that November, Roosevelt welcomed the *New Republic*'s editors to his Oyster Bay home, where they talked politics well into the early morning. Afterwards, Lippmann told Dodge that he "loved him [Roosevelt] more than ever."[17]

In what was part surrogate campaign speech, part shout-out to James, the young Lippmann offered his vision of an "Integrated America." Lippmann praised Roosevelt for "aiming to draw Americans out of their local, group, class, and ethnic loyalties into a greater American citizenship." Such a period of nation-building had not been undertaken in North America since the days of Hamilton. Lippmann also faulted Roosevelt for trying to unify the country through universal military training. He pressed Roosevelt to learn from Hamilton's realism, particularly his scheme to form a United States through economic integration.[18]

Lippmann's moral equivalents to Roosevelt's warfare state were to nationalize the railroads and to develop federal insurance programs on unemployment, healthcare, old age, maternity, and accidents. "Only in some such great enterprise can Americans be expected to learn their most needed lessons: that a successful democracy must have a powerful government, that it must be a government which touches their lives if they are to cherish it, that it must be the custodian of interests so great that inefficiency and waste and the lack of public spirit are crimes against the state." Lippmann now sounded like his Harvard self who had wished for a religion of the State. There was always some continuity buried in his customary incongruity. In the long run, Lippmann's advice found acceptance in the New Deal and, appropriately enough, the Great Society. In the short run, his article did not matter. Roosevelt chafed under any criticism. He refused Lippmann's and friends' olive branches, calling them "the nice old ladies of the *New Republic*."[19]

Lippmann wasted no time in turning his democratic nationalist sights toward Wilson. The *New Republic*'s men imagined they could bring him over to their strong-state liberalism. In March 1917, Lippmann challenged Wilson to resist legislative government. "As compared with the other great states of the world," Lippmann assessed, "the United States to-day is in point of organization one of the most backward and intellectually one of the most timid." Western Europe had been busy building "the most drastic kind of collectivism." Wilson needed to follow in kind and lead America "towards a richer cooperative life, to intensify the war against poverty and ignorance and class rule, to integrate and democratize industry, [and] to make education national and modern." Wilson might have to act as a "benevolent despot," but Lippmann was convinced that there was no other way to save the American dream of upward mobility apart from "democratic collectivism."[20]

The *New Republic*'s liberalism was Lippmann's political answer to what he understood to be a spiritual problem. Secularization was making urgent how to build national community in the absence of a common core. As often as Lippmann criticized civil religions, he still believed healthy publics needed a replacement for religious orthodoxies. The older Lippmann would express a very different attitude toward his younger self's "collectivism" during the Great Depression. In typically ambivalent fashion, he would echo Progressives like Small and Croly in stressing the benefits of Christianity as enlightened social control. But, once again, I am running ahead of the story.

*

Lippmann spent World War I in and out of the *New Republic*. He was party to the journal's evolution from neutrality (1914) to "Aggressive Pacifism" (1915) and then to preparedness (1916). Croly and

Lippmann helped Wilson articulate his "Peace without Victory" early into his second term. Lippmann argued in favor of defending the "Atlantic community" as the first beacon of "civilization" itself (more on Lippmann's founding use of "Atlantic community" in Chapter 5).[21]

Lippmann had also been working out his own "America first" program—that was Wilson's phrase to describe neutrality—while reading Hamilton, celebrity naval theorist Captain Alfred T. Mahan, and Roosevelt's German counterpart, Chancellor Otto von Bismarck. The result was arguably Lippmann's most underappreciated work, *The Stakes of Diplomacy* (1915). The world war, he argued, emanated from imperialist adventures to exploit the planet's "weak" states, much as the Civil War had been fought between North and South for dominance of the West. The desire to subdue "anarchy" internationally—to "make civilization march" in the interests of market capitalist expansion—was inevitable. Nevertheless, imperialism produced "primitive" nationalisms, defensive reactions to the global other that invoked "God Almighty" to justify injustices. Imperialist Christian nationalisms crushed democratic aspirations, leaving the rubble of "homeless" denationalized multitudes.[22]

The only way to avoid planetary catastrophe was to organize what Lippmann termed "industrially backward" and "politically incompetent" peoples through international institutions. Lippmann's descriptions of the world's "weak" states often implied that they had brought their misfortunes upon themselves. Lippmann recalled missionary discourses that saw "heathen" nations as hereditarily disadvantaged. If such was the case, Western Christian imperialism might be accidental to the imperative of global economic integration. Yet Lippmann's distaste for empire was rooted in James's point that no one was perceptive or disinterested enough to speak for another. "Democracy is a meaningless word," Lippmann suggested, "unless it signifies that differences of opinion have been expressed, represented, and even satisfied in the decision."[23]

The foreign policy realism that Lippmann would call for in 1943, 1947, and 1965 was plain to see in *Stakes of Diplomacy*. Beneath idealist talk of building a "World State," readers could witness the older Lippmann's commitment to regionalism—to "local world governments" like the Atlantic community—as the proper location of international stability. Lippmann admitted that his mechanisms for modernization would still be intrusive and painful to "weak" peoples. Still, his analysis of why empires form and how to interrupt them was prescient.[24]

It was that acumen that also led Lippmann to fight a new kind of war. As a part of preparedness, Lippmann had recommended raising an army through conscription. When Wilson agreed, Lippmann reached out to Frankfurter to help him secure a post as an assistant to Secretary of War Newton Baker, where he thought he could be more useful than as a private. He was right. The newly wedded Lippmanns moved into the House of Truth full time, where Walter distinguished himself as Baker's whiz kid.[25]

A few months later, Lippmann was delighted to receive an invitation from Colonel Edward House to help lead a secret intelligence project. House was Wilson's most trusted advisor and had become close with the *New Republic* staff. The Lippmanns moved back to New York so that Walter could work in "The Inquiry." The Inquiry teams came from the new social sciences. Their mission was to formulate a "scientific peace." The Inquiry's leading lights, including Shotwell and the political geographer Isaiah Bowman, believed that organized religion was a relic hindering a verifiable knowledge of the world and human nature. Lippmann had not completed his masters before leaving Harvard, but he still felt he belonged among House's army of egghead secularists. Lippmann and other House of Truth Jews also hoped wartime service could curb anti-Semitism.[26]

The proudest moment of the younger Lippmann's life came while working with the Inquiry. Just two months into the mission, in December of 1917, House called upon him to draft a report that Wilson could use in response to the European secret treaties. Lippmann and a few others provided House their eight-point counteroffer three weeks later. Wilson added six of his own, the first five and the last. Wilson presented his "Fourteen Points" platform to Congress on January, 8, 1918. Wilson's additions are the only ones we remember—open diplomacy, freedom of the seas and international trade, self-determination for colonized peoples, and a League of Nations—but that did not stop Lippmann from exulting in his accomplishment. "This is the second time that I have put words into the mouth of the President," he told Bowman, not realizing how much

Bowman despised him. Lippmann then left the Inquiry to write open-minded propaganda as a captain in the London offices of the Military Intelligence Branch (MIB).[27]

In October, when Allied leaders meeting in Paris could not figure out the meaning of the Fourteen Points, House gave Lippmann one night to write a commentary. His explanatory notes suggest he shared Wilson's pledge to engage in the "peaceful conquest" of the postwar globe—Lippmann called it "peaceful penetration." That mission was evident on Point V regarding adjustments of colonial claims. Drawing upon *Stakes of Diplomacy*, Lippmann asserted that any colonizing power needed to act as a "trustee" of native populations and be subject to an international "code of colonial conduct." Military occupation should be forbidden, native culture respected, labor rights protected, and heavy investment be made in infrastructure and healthcare. Lippmann also counselled that "exploitation should be conducted on the principle of the open door," referring to the "Open Door Notes" that Secretary of State John Hay had written to the foreign governments occupying China in 1899. Open Door internationalism, or global free trade, would severely advantage the United States after the war, as the country had suffered minimal losses and made vast gains in manufacturing and financial supremacy. Lippmann was an anti-imperialist yet never subscribed to the anti-colonial ideal of self-determination (except for Russia, the subject of Point VI which he did write). The contradictions within Wilsonianism were Lippmann's, and they would follow the famed journalist into the geopolitical battles of the 1940s and after.[28]

What happened next is an often-told story: In order to secure British and French support for the League of Nations, Wilson bent to their demands for a harsh peace on Germany, which almost everyone knew would spark a second world war. "Peace without Victory" eluded the *New Republic* and the House of Truth. The "War to End War" was not to be. "I was the typical fool determined to hope to the bitter end," Lippmann said privately. He returned to the *New Republic*, where the editors sided with Senate Republicans in defeating the League's "collective security" measure, Article X, lest the United States give sanction to what liberals saw as an intolerable territorial settlement.[29]

Lippmann had experienced numerous personal slights by that time. Part of the reason he had taken the MIB post was to offer an alternative to the "tricky and sinister" state disinformation of the past, providing Wilson's own words as "something new and infinitely hopeful in the affairs of mankind." But Wilson had already soured on the young man after his criticism of Wilson's propaganda machine, the Committee on Public Information (CPI). When Lippmann convinced House to bring the Inquiry leadership to Paris to participate in the peace negotiations, the Inquiry pushed Lippmann to the sidelines. Before sailing home, his hopes of playing a role in the historic conference dashed, Lippmann learned that Bowman had been conspiring to drive him out of House's favor. The reasons were several, but anti-Semitism underlay it all. Lippmann should have been aware of this, for when Frankfurter had asked Lippmann to find a place for him in the Inquiry, House had told Lippmann to redirect him. "The Jews from every tribe have descended in force," House warned Wilson. "The objection to Lippmann is that he is a Jew, but unlike other Jews he is a silent one."[30]

*

Lippmann's liberals had believed they were entering a new democratic age of (Thomas) Paine. By 1920, they bore the pain of knowing they had supported a war that made democracy less safe everywhere. There was no Hamilton on their horizon, only Republican President Warren G. Harding, a very different breed of America firster. Lippmann had implored House to launch an Inquiry 2.0 to aid in the "scientific planning" of postwar industry and education, but that never happened. Instead, the New Era wedded isolationism with market imperialism over Western Europe, swinging metropolitanism with struggling agrarianism, and multiculturalism with violent Christian Americanism.[31]

Lippmann was no Tired Radical following the war, but he was tired of the *New Republic* and a bit sick of cities. "Living in the country redeems much," Lippmann wrote to Bernard Berenson, an art historian and one of Lippmann's closest confidants. "One gets so good a sense of the things that do not matter, and a decent relief from the feverish factionalisms of the city. But I'm afraid it's a long pull before any considerable number of us can cultivate our gardens. Sometimes I think we are a damned generation." Lippmann's reference to *Candide* (1759) by Voltaire—"let us cultivate our garden"—hinted that he wanted to be left alone for thought. But his passion to speak truth to and for powerful men was a fever he would never break.[32]

Lippmann determined that his wartime experience would not be in vain. If Washington was not going to safeguard America from disinformation campaigns—originating in the state or somewhere else—he would have to do it himself. Upon America's entry into the Great War, Lippmann had lobbied to put any domestic censorship under civilian authority, arguing that "it will be more important to control untruth than it will be to suppress truth." Wilson had chosen instead to unleash a "reign of terror," as Lippmann described it to Baker. The state-led Red Scare fueled anti-immigrant sentiments in general and anti-Semitism in particular, including a revival of the Ku Klux Klan (KKK). In 1920, Lippmann joined Faye and a friend in an analysis of *New York Times* coverage of the Russian Revolution. They concluded that the new priesthood of newspapermen was about as reliable as the old clergy had been.[33]

That same year, Lippmann published *Liberty and the News*, where he argued that "public opinion is blockaded" by the press's preference for "edification" over "veracity." The problem was compounded by the increasing complexity of urban life. "At the present time a nation easily acts like a crowd," Lippmann cautioned. As he told an associate, his first criticisms of mass American society had been occasioned by "the discovery that opinion can be manufactured." Lippmann thereafter assembled his masterwork about creating consent through the manipulation of stereotypes.[34]

That book, *Public Opinion*, should be read in light of Lippmann's reaction to the Red Scare. True, the "pictures in our heads" he made famous belonged mainly to his younger self. *Public Opinion* dramatized Lippmann's disenchantment with the notion that socialism could remain "non-coercive." His disgust with legislatures—"a group of blind men in a vast, unknown world"—had only ripened. But most importantly, Lippmann's recommendation for nonpartisan intelligence bureaus drew from his happier moments with the Inquiry and MIB. His wartime service had prefigured the CIA, Homeland Security, and other agents of elitist democracy. Nevertheless, *Public Opinion* was an attempt to ensure that Wilson's psychological warfare state could not happen again. As Lippmann argued elsewhere, the true liberal would be a "radical decentralizer and home-ruler" in both politics and economics.[35]

Lippmann's plea for "organized intelligence" reflected his Nietzschean urgency that moderns could not wait for a God to save them. Some readers foresaw that the book would become a classic in media studies. Older liberals appreciated Lippmann's work, but many younger ones did not. One reviewer resurrected the Tired Radical stereotype, anticipating charges Lippmann would face when he published *A Preface to Morals*.[36]

As mentioned earlier, Modernist pastors were among Lippmann's most sympathetic audiences. A seminary professor even wanted to apply *Public Opinion* to updating American churches. Christians, too, needed "some device for cooperative thinking through which some substitute basis for the formation of an intelligent public opinion can be brought about." Lippmann was mostly friendly to his liberal Protestant fans. A few years earlier he had told a Christian editor that churches should partner with him in the "purification of the news." No "single body of knowledge and ideals,"—as had typified the "ages of faith"—was possible in the "endless diversity" of Megalopolis, Lippmann ruminated in one editorial. His muse was the newly constructed St. John the Divine in upper Manhattan. Lippmann hoped the cathedral might still inspire moderns' thirst for discovery—and so advised that it give up its Episcopal identity in deference to New York's cosmopolitanism.[37]

Lippmann's counsel was a reminder that he was a post-Christian theorist of American democracy. *Public Opinion* was a public theology as well as a scorched-earth supplement to political philosophy. Consistent with the mission of other secularists, the younger Lippmann advocated for a dechristianized public square. Lippmann was convinced that modern men "make their wisdom" through strenuous effort. They do not kneel, pray, and wait to receive it.[38] But Lippmann's skepticism toward providence did not stop him from maintaining that everyone had a Jamesian right to take from religions what they wanted for self-preservation. Lippmann himself would borrow heavily from Christianity in the decades ahead to meet needs both personal and public.

*

One reason friends thought Lippmann was questioning his faith in democracy was because he was. The Red Scare had been terrifying enough. The Great Commoner, William Jennings Bryan, inciting Fundamentalists to attack public education was a Jeffersonian bridge too far. As we have seen, Lippmann opposed antievolutionism while maintaining the need for some type of civil religious minimum. Bryan's movement had been a national embarrassment for agnostics like Mencken, Lippmann, and Darrow. But that is not why Lippmann accused Bryan of "spiritual treason." That was because antievolutionists insisted they had an inalienable right to control thought. "The raising of a religious issue in American politics is more mischievous and wicked than anything any politician has stooped to in our time," Lippmann complained. Bryan sought to "unchain a sectarian fury" and "sectarian hatred" that would tear communities apart—and would cancel the scientific democracy Lippmann had sketched in *Public Opinion*. Lippmann called readers to defend the separation of church and state and resist the "state religion" of Fundamentalism.[39]

To combat Bryan's populism, it was not enough to mock it. One had to deconstruct the "mystical sense of equality" undergirding it. Even if it were true that all stand equal in heaven, that did not mean all were "equally good biologists before the ballot box in Tennessee." Lippmann continued, "there is nothing in the teachings of Jesus or St. Francis which justifies us in thinking that the opinions of fifty-one percent of the group are better than the opinions of forty-nine percent." In the final analysis, "the rule of the majority is the rule of force." Lippmann the proud "metropolitan" was more than a little disturbed by the resiliency of "village civilization." Building upon *Public Opinion*, he felt compelled to escalate the fight against the civil religion of Christian-Jeffersonian Americanism.[40]

"In our age the power of majorities tends to become arbitrary and absolute," Lippmann observed at the end of *American Inquisitors*. He was not ready to claim that majoritarian democracy was a road to totalitarianism, as he would in the 1950s. But Bryan's victory in Dayton had rattled him. "My own mind has been getting steadily antidemocratic," he confided. "The size of the electorate, the impossibility of educating it sufficiently, the fierce ignorance of these semiliterate priestridden and parsonridden people have got me to the point where I want to confine the actions of majorities." Lippmann's snobbery, sexism, and secularism intersected within his doubts regarding American's fitness for self-governance.[41]

Lippmann released his next book, *The Phantom Public* (1925), in the context of the Scopes trial. The book was part sequel, part how-to manual, part autobiography, but all revelry and despair. Lippmann rehashed the main points of *Public Opinion*: The modern urban world was too complex for anyone to achieve omnicompetence, and we should not look to "pantheistic powers" or a "voice of God" to bail us out. Lippmann no longer exempted experts from what he called "disenchantment." For Lippmann, disenchantment was religious as well as political—it was discouragement with the ennobling power of democracy and disillusionment with the supernatural force that was supposed to be on the side of the commoner. Public opinion might be useful in checking the "use of force" in a crisis, but otherwise it needed to live within its bounds. "The public must be put in its place...so that each of us may live free of the trampling and the roar of a bewildered herd." In the ongoing struggle between self and society for Lippmann's soul—between the RBNS and the SBNR—this time, self won. The disinterested, cosmically homeless "modern man" of *A Preface to Morals* would not be far behind.[42]

In *Phantom Public*, Lippmann sometimes recovered the Jamesian joy of his first book. He advised acceptance of the "deep pluralism" of experience, boasted that a universal moral code did not and could not exist, and asked citizens to keep "an open mind" about public affairs. But he also decided that democracies could not last. They must inevitably submit to a centralizing power because they could not manage their threats by popular means. Lippmann's personal displeasures, professional frustrations, and philosophical proclivities were leading him to conclude that freedom was the essential, impossible marker of the good life and society. He summarized his state of mind to the historian Charles Beard this way: "the answer, as far as I am concerned, to the question about the collective capacity of democracy to organize a state is emphatically 'no.'"[43]

*

Lippmann was working his way toward his argument in *A Preface to Morals* that citizens needed to have but could not have an external source of internal strength. But what if Lippmann's "no" was only to a kind of democracy? There were other ways of theorizing it, including the Chicago way.

Beginning in Jane Addams's Hull House, and then spreading out from John Dewey's work in philosophy and education, the experimentalists (Dewey's preferred term for pragmatism) demanded a new social order of everyday activism. The settlement house, according to Addams, would "socialize democracy." She believed urban-industrialism—Wallas's and Lippmann's Great Society—had made imperative the recovery of the "associated effort" of rural and small-town America. Chicago experimentalists prized openness to new experiences, critical engagement with tradition, and broad sharing in social life. They were aided by the philosopher and social worker Mary Parker Follett, who argued in *The New State* (1918) that "every man *is* the state at every moment." Addams, Dewey, Follett, and their many students were post-Christian. They repented of Calvinism yet appreciated theologies and churches that advanced real democracy. They updated older Progressives like Croly in erasing the distinction between the people and their governments. The experimentalists looked forward to what college students in the 1960s would call "participatory democracy."[44]

Scholars have used Lippmann to drive a wedge between James's elitism and Dewey's populism. Pragmatism, however, was a mutual appreciation society. Dewey had written frequently for the *New Republic* and had endorsed its stance that America could play a morally regenerative role in World War I. Dewey also took Lippmann's lessons about human limitation to heart. He called *Public Opinion* "perhaps the most effective indictment of democracy as currently conceived ever penned." To Dewey, Lippmann had smashed Jeffersonianism once and for all—that "particular Humpty Dumpty [that] can never be put back together again." Yet he also thought Lippmann's analysis pointed to another way of conjuring "organized intelligence" minus the bureaus of experts. In *The Public and Its Problems* (1927), Dewey cast out the demon of technocracy when arguing that Lippmann's Great Society had to become the "Great Community." The solution to the problem of democracy was more democracy of the Hull House type.[45]

Lippmann sympathized with participatory democrats' innovative nostalgia. At times, he even joined their Great Community. Lippmann did not have much if any contact with Addams, although he did eulogize her as a "saint" and a "witness to the ancient American faith that a democracy can be noble." Lippmann found Follett's work in "group psychology" valuable, although the two were more critical than constructive toward each other (he accused her of relying on "mosquito words" while she called him "a little daft" on state power). The *New Republic* had endorsed Follett's decentralism in 1916 when it prophesied that "great national organizations of teachers, social workers, business and professional men, farmers and trade-unionists" were fated to replace parties and legislatures as the "germinating centers of American opinion."[46]

Lippmann, Croly, and company had always been deferential toward Dewey. "There is but one kind of unity possible in a world as diverse as ours," Lippmann had written on democracy's shortcomings. "It is the unity of method, rather than aim; the unity of disciplined experiment. There is but one bond of peace that is both permanent and enriching: the increasing knowledge of the world in which experiment occurs. With a common intellectual method and a common area of valid fact, difference may become a form of cooperation and cease to be an irreconcilable antagonism." Lippmann had imbibed that Christianized language of associated effort from Dewey and Follett. Even *Public Opinion* looked to Dewey—"intelligence" was Dewey's word, after all, and Lippmann used it over forty times. That is not to say Lippmann and Dewey meant the same thing when they wrote about "organized intelligence." Nevertheless, the two remained cordial, sharing and commending each other's works.[47]

Dewey's and Lippmann's paths crossed indirectly within postwar participatory democratic circles. The 1920s and 1930s were experimentalism's brightest days, when the dream of growing democracy from the bottom up took root in adult and religious education, labor schools and colleges, social work, and public forums. Quoting Dewey to Theodore Roosevelt, Jr., Lippmann had argued that the best education for industrial workers was to unite for control of industry. That labor unions could serve as "hard schools of experience" for affecting industrial democracy was consistent with his idea that women would become feminists as they bonded to build a socialist society. Lippmann generally stayed away from experimentalist projects after the war, citing journalistic integrity, but he was glad others did not. Lippmann supported the Brookwood labor college run by Christian socialist pastor A. J. Muste, even though he refused to endorse the school or fundraise for it. Lippmann came closer to choosing sides when he advised liberal church organizations like the FCC and NCCJ. Aloofness aside, Lippmann appreciated the potential of advancing liberal democracy through "properly organized discussion," as he admitted to his friend Raymond Leslie Buell in 1939.[48]

By that time, Lippmann and Buell and been partnering for nearly twenty years to manufacture conversations on world affairs. A major part of Lippmann's work in the Inquiry had been to combat closed-door statecraft. After the war, he had demanded "a very open popular diplomacy." Lippmann supported Dewey, Addams, Buell, and others in starting the Foreign Policy Association (FPA) in 1921. The FPA was a revision of the League of Free Nations Association that the *New Republic* had helped launch three years earlier. It was also an extension of the vibrant adult education movement of the decade. Until the 1940s, the FPA produced literature on international developments for middlebrow consumption and hosted Saturday luncheons characterized by open discussion. Lippmann was never a leader in the FPA, but he did address FPA audiences on countless occasions and promoted their publications. In 1943, on the FPA's twenty-fifth anniversary, Lippmann praised the group's work "as a model of how free men look for truth and learn how to manage their affairs."[49]

When another group, the Council on Foreign Relations (CFR) made up of old Inquiry veterans, expanded their research and writing initiatives, they tapped Lippmann to help guide them. He would also contribute regularly to their journal, *Foreign Affairs*. Lippmann did not appear to have any connection to the CFR's local Foreign Relations Committees which had formed around the country in 1938, even though his comment to Buell hinted that he approved of their work.[50]

Certainly, Lippmann was never a devout participatory democrat. Entwining him and Dewey is just as misleading as imagining some ultimate combat as between them. There was too much Jefferson in Dewey for Lippmann's liking. Dewey and allies found Lippmann "a little daft" about Hamilton and Machiavelli. Later in life, Dewey would focus more on the role of the state in enabling democracy, while Lippmann would rediscover the importance of popular participation in politics. On one thing they could agree, though: "Nothing human is eternal." If God really was dead, then men must "make their wisdom." For Lippmann, he would increasingly affiliate with Western Christian theologies in defense of traditional American liberties. Dewey would ask churches to work with him in cultivating *A Common Faith* (1934). The secularism of both men was a post-Christian secularism.[51]

*

Lippmann and Dewey were implicated jointly in the failure of New England and (to a lesser extent) Chicago pragmatism to overcome a heritage of white Protestant male privilege. It did not have to be that way. For all the "normalcy" of the New Era, a revolution of rising expectations for women and minorities was afoot. The message of anthropologist Franz Boas that hierarchies of civilization did not exist circulated throughout American universities and high societies. His students Margaret Mead, Zora Neale Hurston, and others spread the good news of cultural relativism. They were aided by pop philosopher Horace Kallen, Lippmann's former Harvard classmate.[52]

These young cultural pluralists were preaching to the choir when it came to the pragmatists. Bourne's wartime essay "Trans-national America" (1916), where he had lifted the phrase "Beloved Community" from Josiah Royce, had dispensed with the melting pot in favor of celebrating difference. Before him, James and Dewey thought Darwinism demanded multiculturalism. "A progressive society counts individual variations as precious since it finds in them the means of its own growth," Dewey noted in 1916. Ten years later, he argued that the aim of government should be "securing a more equal liberation of the powers of all individual members of all groupings."[53]

The Coolidge administration could care less about what Dewey thought, but Lippmann did. In defining stereotypes as "the core of our personal tradition" and "the defenses of our position in society," Lippmann anticipated present-day discussions of positionality. Positionality means that all are situated in political and cultural contexts (i.e., the "position we occupy") that shape advantages and disadvantages in ways they may or may not recognize. Lippmann wrote *Public Opinion* in part to assist readers interrogate their prejudices and privileges. "What determines the quality of civilization is the use made of power," he asserted.[54]

Lippmann used his power of the press to challenge some stereotypes. By 1930, the New York *World*'s hundreds of thousands of subscribers had learned not to miss Lippmann's "op eds" (a concept the *World* had invented). Lippmann wrote mainly on politics and foreign affairs, but he also aided colleagues in advancing a "live and let live," social libertarian, Bobo lifestyle—Bourgeois-Bohemian. Before leaving the *New Republic*, Lippmann had argued that the peacetime extension of World War I's intelligence (I.Q.) tests was creating a new "caste" system discriminatory toward immigrants. He had then joined *World* columnists in their attack on the KKK, which Lippmann suggested was the American expression of the Italian Fascisti. As an anti-imperial voice, the *World* disarmed tensions between Mexico and the United States during the Cristero War (1927–29). Lippmann even traveled to Mexico to help broker a peace settlement between the Catholic Church and the government. Lippmann was still a secularist, albeit a post-Christian one, who believed limiting religions' public influence was essential to republican civility.[55]

The campaign of Catholic New York Governor Al Smith for the presidency in 1928 afforded Lippmann the opportunity to combat the most repressive elements of the New Era, namely prohibition and anti-Catholicism. Lippmann lauded Smith in the *World*, and Smith routinely sought or received Lippmann's counsel. As much as Lippmann feared the Great Society was overwhelming humankind's feeble rationality, Manhattan was still a marked improvement over the provincialism of Middletown, and Smith was its best representative. Smith lost to the small-town Protestant Herbert Hoover, one of Lippmann's former House of Truth associates.[56]

Still, Lippmann's pluralist commitments had been self-curtailed well before that election. As a Jamesian-Nietzschean with countercultural longings, the younger Lippmann could have kept an open mind regarding race, sex, and class. At times, he did. Lippmann sided with Black communities in 1915 when they began to organize a nationwide ban of the pro-Klan movie, *The Birth of a Nation* (1915). Lippmann was frustrated that the film had not been censured in New York and asked Native American rights activist John Collier to partner in turning public opinion against it. Lippmann had tried to get the scholar-activist W. E. B. Du Bois, a fellow Harvard man (Du Bois had graduated with his doctorate in 1895 when Lippmann was only six), admission into the Liberal Club in 1913. During World War I, DuBois had requested Lippmann's help in fighting racial discrimination in the armed forces. Du Bois had successfully sold Black Americans on participation in the war to assert their citizenship and demand for rights, but they were usually sent to manual labor battalions. It is unclear what help Lippmann provided Du Bois if any, and he never took up the issue in print. Following the war, Du Bois sent Lippmann reports on the first Pan-African Congress, about which Lippmann was "very much interested" but also never wrote about.[57]

Lippmann did pen the introduction to a study of racial violence during Chicago's "Red Terror." With the Great Migration of Southern Black Americans into Northern wartime cities, combined with the ravages of a global influenza pandemic, Chicago's South Side had blown up in 1919. Lippmann called out white supremacists, noting, "it is only the parvenue, the snob, the coward who is forever proclaiming his superiority." Lippmann argued that the uprisings were a "by-product of our planless, disordered, bedraggled, drifting democracy." A "dirty civilization" naturally led to race wars, while a "clean" one produced racial harmony.[58]

Lippmann's solution to the Red Scare, "race parallelism," was to satisfy pro-segregationists and Black nationalists simultaneously. Lippmann argued that racial apartheid was a recipe for the moral corruption of an entire society ("Those who degrade and terrorize are inevitably themselves degraded and terror stricken."). He identified another problem in what he had called earlier the "denationalization" of Black Americans. "So long as the status of the white man is in every way superior to that of the colored," he wrote, "the advancement of the colored man can mean nothing but an attempt to share the white man's privileges." Subjugation begets subjugation, in other words. But the solution was not "amalgamation" and "social mixture." It was opening "parallel" lines for Black self-development. "We shall have to work out with the Negro a relationship which gives him complete access to all the machinery of our common civilization, and yet allows him to live so that no Negro need dream of a white heaven and bleached angels." This was the "separate-but-equal" doctrine + the "pride of race" espoused at the time in (Marcus) "Garveyism" and, eventually, Black Power.[59]

Yet parallelism failed in theory by failing in practice. Recall Lippmann's observation from *Drift and Mastery* that you cannot build a nation out of "poverty-stricken negroes." That was a classic case of shaming the victims of racist policies. Lippmann lived segregated from persons of color (for instance, there is no evidence he interacted with the journalist and diplomat Lester Walton, who worked as an investigative reporter for the *World* during Lippmann's tenure). When Lippmann justified New York's "nullification" of prohibition by comparing it to the South's "nullification" of the Fifteenth Amendment—both safeguarded the "moral harmony" of their regions—he denied Black Americans the tool they needed to gain equal access to civilization's "machinery." When Lippmann supported conservative Southern Democrats like Virginia Governor Harry Flood Byrd, Sr., he chose to suppress Black civil rights. As Lippmann decided that "the disenfranchisement of the negro rests ultimately upon the superior force of the whites," he sanctioned might-makes-right ethics (i.e., "disenfranchisement would be impossible if the negro were stronger"). Lippmann feared Republicans would respond to the Great Migration by becoming a "white man's party" catering to white supremacists in the North and Midwest. That, in turn, would drive Black Americans to the "outer Left." Lippmann did not understand, or refused to admit, how his own inactions on race would make those fears a reality.[60]

Women did not fare much better in Lippmann's white-powered America. Jane Addams and many others had been busy socializing democracy before, during, and after Lippmann had asked them to do so. Beyond the familiar fields of education and nursing, women were pursuing careers in business and aviation, they were leaders in social work and the social sciences, and they were the energizers of liberal think tanks like the FCC and FPA. In *Drift and Mastery*, Lippmann had cheered women on in their efforts to bring scientific management to bear upon self, family, and society. Lippmann had also been an avid supporter of Sanger's Planned Parenthood (minus the eugenics) and of the global dissemination of birth control education by health care professionals. Yet during the 1928 presidential campaign, Lippmann advised Smith not to support the Equal Rights Amendment (ERA) for the same reasons that many women's groups did: They believed it would destroy their special protections.[61]

As historian Sarah Imhoff was first to notice, Lippmann quickly repented of the nineteenth amendment. On November 4, 1920, he hinted at his "profound discouragement with universal suffrage" for allowing Harding to win. "Ten years ago we should have said that democracies are educated," Lippmann warned in the runup to the 1924 elections. "Today with our experience of how the mind of the mass of men can be moved, with our enormously increased electorate and our greatly complicated life, we should be less certain that we wish to accentuate the struggle for power." Underlying and informing the anti-democratic turn of *Phantom Public*, and his concerns about the loss of authority in *A Preface to Morals*, were his doubts that the modern woman could "govern herself." Perhaps the flapper had been too much for Lippmann to bear. But he also feared a battle between the sexes for new positions in American society. That might be why he was reluctant to give credit to the women who assisted him with research, publications, and schedules, including Faye and, later, Helen.[62]

Lippmann's New Era too frequently looked back to the "White Man's Republic" of the nineteenth century. In resisting the Klan and I. Q. tests, Lippmann defended the rights of Southern and Eastern European immigrants to become American. Yet whenever he supported immigration restriction bills, and urged Smith to do the same, he extended the Red Scare's xenophobia. Lippmann even celebrated Smith for representing "the men and women drawn from all the white races of Europe." According to Lippmann, the "disappearance of free lands" and rise of cities over small farms meant the United States could no longer absorb millions of newcomers. Furthermore, the country's schools were not prepared to "assimilate successfully a great mass of children with very different social backgrounds from those of the mass of the American people" in the same way they could Northern Europeans, who were "much more nearly like the American." Still, Lippmann insisted this was not a matter of "superior" and "inferior" races, as eugenicists maintained. Lippmann's welding of antiracism and restrictionism must rank high among his most eclectic intellectual gymnastics.[63]

Lippmann's ambivalence toward the Sacco–Vinzetti case betrayed even further his deference to Klan politics while rejecting Klan civil religion. Frankfurter had labored to expose the unfairness of the trial of Nicola Sacco and Bartolomeo Vanzetti, two recent Italian immigrants and anarchists convicted of murder in 1921. Lippmann, too, argued for "mercy," by which he meant life imprisonment in place of execution. At times, he said he doubted the verdict and lobbied publicly for a retrial. In the end, however, Lippmann agreed with *World* conservatives that the decision was probably correct and praised investigators on both sides. Lippmann and fellow editors invited Sacco and Vanzetti's supporters to eschew "violent radicalism" while the two men awaited electrocution. Lippmann's response was a reminder of how harsh his assimilationism could be.[64]

Lippmann's Jewish friends at the House of Truth understood that better than most. Lippmann had loved seeing them promoted to top positions, including Brandeis to the Supreme Court and Frankfurter to a professorship at Harvard Law School. They had suffered together by being labelled "parlor Bolsheviks" during the Red Scare. Lippmann nonetheless refused to endorse his associates' Zionism. He was disturbed when Bourne grouped him in with Kallen, Frankfurter, and other Zionists in the *Menorah Journal*. Lippmann offered neither himself nor any other Jew a nationalist alternative—a "pride of race"—such as he had provided Black Americans. He was on his way toward erasing Judaism from history—his own as well as from the country's and the world's past.[65]

So maybe Lippmann was not the most open-minded person to write for the *American Hebrew* on how to foster better relations between Jews and non-Jews. His war on propaganda notwithstanding, Lippmann apologized for Henry Ford's funding of *The Protocols of the Elders of Zion*, which outlined a Jewish conspiracy to take over the world. Ford was a "rather kindly man," Lippmann claimed, who had been duped into thinking that Jewish bankers had started World War I. The whole matter was "nonsense" and certainly not the root cause of New Era intolerance. "I waste no time myself worrying about the injustices of anti-Semitism," he bragged. Who has the time for fretting about what clubs, hotels, or "college fraternities" one could or could not frequent? Only a people "cursed with a sense of inferiority" could be so "supersensitive to trivial prejudice in non-Jews and extraordinarily insensitive to the faults of the Jews." Of course, Lippmann had suffered injustices from anti-Semites at Harvard and in the Inquiry. Yet the only state he could commend to Jews was denial.[66]

If white Anglo-Saxon Protestants like Ford were not the source of anti-Semitism in America, who or what was? Lippmann's "Jewish anti-Semitism" fell heavily upon his Upsider community. He charged, "the rich and vulgar and pretentious Jews of our big American cities are perhaps the greatest misfortune that has ever befallen the Jewish people." Physical appearance and names already made Jews "conspicuous." Their use of wealth should not. The producer-capitalist, tough-minded Lippmann would never be comfortable with the rise of mass consumption, but he decided to see the vice of over-civilization as a particularly Jewish problem. When New York Jews "rush about in super-automobiles, bejeweled and furred and painted and over-barbered... they undermine the natural liberalism of the American people." If Jews wanted to feel welcome, Lippmann said that they needed to think twice as hard as others about how they were using the "opportunities" they already possessed. They had to "demonstrate the art of moderate, clean and generous living" such as Lippmann believed he had mastered.[67]

Yet Harvard's attempt to set a quota for Jewish admissions belied Lippmann's conviction that American Jews just needed to work hard and stay silent. Following other private schools, Harvard began considering a limit on Jewish enrollment after the war. Lippmann, in the *World*, lamented his alma mater's "change of soul" from the era of Emerson and James. He charged it with adopting the "prejudices of a summer hotel" and "standards of a country club." Behind the scenes, he had been expressing support for Harvard's fears about "too great a concentration" of Jews. Yes, the country had a responsibility to educate its "vast alien population," but perhaps the state could establish a new public university under Jewish leadership "to persuade Jewish boys to scatter."[68]

The scattering was key. In a (probably) unsent letter to another member of the committee on Jewish admissions, Lippmann argued against any kind of race-based quota system. He recommended that the school raise its entrance examination scores which would weed out the "less able" Jews and achieve an informal quota of around fifteen percent. "A concentration of Jews in excess of fifteen percent will produce a segregation of cultures rather than a fusion." That, in turn, would perpetuate the "tribal mysticism" and "tribal inbreeding" so injurious to Jewish Americanism. Lippmann believed that the secularization ("breakdown") of "Jewish theological exclusiveness" needed to run its course, not be repackaged into Zionism. Zionism, Lippmann expressed, was a "romantic lost cause" fueled by those not courageous enough to accept the "moral anarchy" of the present interregnum. As for Lippmann, "my sympathies are with the non-Jew" whose "personal manners and physical habits" were "distinctly superior" to that of American Jews. It was time for the Jews to "scatter" by intermarrying with the superior race. Reducing Harvard's Jewish population would be in their best interest in the long run, even if in the short term it meant denying them the opportunities Lippmann had been talking about.[69]

The best evidence for Lippmann's argument that colonized peoples take on the customs of their oppressors was Lippmann himself. Everyone agreed he was one of the Progressive stalwarts of the postwar era. His remedies were intended to save, not curse, the "omnicompetent citizens" who found themselves lost in Great Societies. Yet Lippmann was also making his conservative mission to tame disorderly desire explicit. Throughout the 1920s and after, he positioned himself as a post-Christian priest of democratic survival through the sacrifice of substantive democratic rights for large sections of the American population.

*

Sometimes it was hard to believe that Lippmann was one of the country's chief advocates for disinterestedness. He offered a nightmarish vision in *A Preface to Morals* of a damned generation—of men without chests and girls gone wild. Yet he also blessed the New Era's "religion of success," as he had negatively termed it in *Public Opinion*. European socialists had been wrong to think that "collectivism" was the destiny of modern man. "The more or less unconscious and unplanned activities of businessmen are for once more novel, more daring, and in a sense more revolutionary, than the theories of the progressives," Lippmann told *Vanity Fair*. "The economic position is as easy as it's ever been in this generation," he reported to a British friend. America's economy had finally wedded material abundance to an "amazing distribution of wealth." Labor was happy and farmers were holding their own. "Lord knows I don't know what we've done as a nation to deserve these things," he concluded. When the *World* finally closed its doors in 1931, Lippmann recalled the ten years he had been at the paper with pride. *Time* magazine's cover story on Lippmann that year declared him liberalism's "Moses."[70]

Lippmann's friends worried about their once-young prophet, now forty-two years old. But they were wrong to consider him a Tired Radical. Lippmann had never been a radical to become tired of. Like James, Dewey, Santayana, and Wallas, Lippmann's socialism had been of a middle-class paternalist variety. Lippmann's understanding of democracy, at both a national and international level, had long been tempered by a realism about the limits of human perception and good will. Ever since Lippmann had argued for immigrant restriction at Sachs, he had been deferential to white Northern European Protestant males, especially when their last name was Roosevelt. But above all, Lippmann had been skeptical of universals from a young age, in religion as well as in politics. That skepticism was a main source of his many paradoxes—or, in his words, eclecticism.

Lippmann's real transformation came about after 1930. He would decide that the Great Society could not be humanized, let alone stabilized, apart from Christian traditions he knew he could never make his home. If having an "unwritten book" (*A Preface to Morals*) had once fed feelings of "tyranny" and "compulsion psychosis," then the older Lippmann would remain prisoner and potentate, patient and punisher, long after his first blockbuster. Still, Lippmann would find spiritual satisfaction in art and nature, especially during those weeks each year that he and Faye could get away to Europe. Upon exiting the *World*, when colleagues like Walton were thrown into personal financial crisis, the Lippmanns headed to Greece and Florence, "the loveliest joint product of providence and man that I know of" he told Baker. Soul care was something that could only happen beyond the "bewildering herds" of an unrighteous, impoverished republic.[71]

Notes

1. "Omnicompetent citizen" is a repeated reference throughout Lippmann's book, *Public Opinion*. On "all philosophies" and Nietzsche, see Lippmann, *Preface to Politics*, 5, 177.
2. Lippmann, *Public Opinion*, 19, 190.
3. Lippmann, *Public Opinion*, 13, 51. See Walter Lippmann, to Malcolm M. Willey, Jan. 13, 1925, in *Public Philosopher*, ed. Blum, 173–4, where

Lippmann explains, "by 'stereotypes,' I mean certain fixed habits of the cognition. I use the word to describe part of the process by which the pseudo environment is pieced together in our heads. It is a pathological term for the kind of cognition which classifies and abstracts falsely and generally violates the scientific canons for dealing with fact."

4. Lippmann, *Public Opinion*, 44, 103, 123.
5. Lippmann, *Public Opinion*, 114, 117, 129–35, 176.
6. Lippmann, *Public Opinion*, 125. On the application of Lippmann's book to churches, see William Adams Brown, to Walter Lippmann, Mar. 9, 1922, in WLP, Reel 4.
7. Lippmann, *Public Opinion*, 21, 50–1, 176–81, 184, 195.
8. McCarter, *Young Radicals*; and Riccio, *Walter Lippmann*, 1–27.
9. Walter Lippmann, "In Defense of the Suffragettes," *The Harvard Monthly* (1909), in *Essential Lippmann*, ed. Rossiter and Lare, 441–2; Walter Lippmann, to Marie Hoffendahl Jenney Howe, Feb. 16, 1915, in WLP, Reel 14.
10. Lippmann, *Preface to Politics*, 47, 152–3, 203.
11. Graham Wallas, *The Great Society* (New York: Macmillan, 1914), v.; Lippmann, "Interview," 40.
12. Lippmann, *Drift and Mastery*, xxi, 64, 171.
13. Lippmann, *Drift and Mastery*, 189, 255, 269, 273–4.
14. See Forcey, *Crossroads of Liberalism*, for a general overview of the *New Republic* and Lippmann's place in it. The phrase "Hamiltonian means with Jeffersonian ends" is often attributed to Croly's *The Promise of American Life*. Although that is a good summation of Croly's views expressed in the text, he never used that exact phrase. Forcey offered a variation (29). Yet the originator was George Mowry, *Theodore Roosevelt and the Progressive Movement* (Madison: University of Wisconsin Press, 1946), 145. On the "socialistic" Hamilton, see Croly, *Promise of American Life*, 43. See Lippmann, to Brooks, on the "socialistic" direction of their journal. For Lippmann's comments on Hamilton, see Walter Lippmann, to the editor, *Democratic Chronicle*, Apr. 26, 1919, in *Public Philosopher*, ed. Blum, 113.
15. Lippmann, "Living Past," 15. See Ronald D. Rotunda, "The 'Liberal' Label: Roosevelt's Capture of a Symbol," *Public Policy* 17 (1968): 377–408.
16. Forcey, *Crossroads of Liberalism*, 129. For Lippmann's views on Roosevelt, see Lippmann, "Interview," 55; Walter Lippmann, "A Tribute to Theodore Roosevelt," essay for The Women's Roosevelt Memorial Association, Oct. 27, 1935, in *Essential Lippmann*, ed. Rossiter and Lare, 487; and Walter Lippmann, to Felix Frankfurter, June 30, 1916, in *Public Philosopher*, ed. Blum, 52. On Lippmann's views on Congress, see Walter Lippmann, "And Congress," *New Republic*, Mar. 10, 1917, in *Force and Ideas*, ed. Schlesinger, 152.
17. Steel, *Walter Lippmann*, 64–5; Walter Lippmann, quoted in Dodge, *Movers and Shakers*, 164.

18. Walter Lippmann, "Integrated America," *New Republic*, Feb. 19, 1916, 62–5.
19. Lippmann, "Integrated America," 65–7. On the *New Republic*'s fallout with Roosevelt, see Forcey, *Crossroads of Liberalism*, 244–5.
20. Walter Lippmann, "In the Next Four Years," *New Republic*, Mar. 10, 1917, in *Force and Ideas*, ed. Schlesinger, 147–50.
21. Forcey, *Crossroads of Liberalism*, 246, 249, 266–8. See also Walter Lippmann, "The Defense of the Atlantic World," *New Republic*, Feb. 17, 1917, in *Force and Ideas*, ed. Schlesinger, 73.
22. Lippmann, *Stakes of Diplomacy*, 66, 87–9, 98, 152–3, 170–2. On Lippmann's reading list, see Walter Lippmann, to Graham Wallas, Aug. 15, 1915, in *Public Philosopher*, ed. Blum, 29. The "America first" reference was common among both political parties throughout this era. For Lippmann's use, see Lippmann, "Integrated America," 64.
23. Lippmann, *Stakes of Diplomacy*, 47–8, 87–110.
24. Lippmann, *Stakes of Diplomacy*, 129, 144–9, 203–4.
25. The best general overview of Lippmann's war service is Steel, *Walter Lippmann*, although see also McCarter, *Young Radicals*; and Snyder, *House of Truth*.
26. Lawrence E. Gelfand, *The Inquiry: American Preparations for Peace, 1917–1919* (New Haven: Yale University Press, 1963).
27. The Lippmann comment comes from Bowman's diary entry of Oct. 5, 1939. See Snyder, *House of Truth*, 646n3.
28. Walter Lippmann, Memorandum, to Edward House, Oct. 28, 1918, in WLP, Reel 35, reprinted in *Public Philosopher*, ed. Blum, 97–105. See Cara Lea Burnidge, *A Peaceful Conquest: Woodrow Wilson, Religion, and the New World Order* (Chicago: University of Chicago Press, 2016).
29. Walter Lippmann, to Bernard Berenson, July, 16, 1919, in WLP, Reel 4.
30. On House's comment to Wilson, see Steel, *Walter Lippmann*, 129–30. On Lippmann's troubles with Wilson and in Paris, see Steel, *Walter Lippmann*, 145–54; and McCarter, *Young Radicals*, 254–6.
31. Walter Lippmann, to Edward House, May 11, 1918, in *Public Philosopher*, ed. Blum, 89–92.
32. Lippmann, to Berenson, July 16, 1919.
33. Walter Lippmann, to Woodrow Wilson, Feb. 6, 1917, in *Public Philosopher*, ed. Blum, 61; Walter Lippmann, to Edward House, Apr. 12, 1917, in *Public Philosopher*, ed. Blum, 65–6; Walter Lippmann, to Newton Baker, Jan. 17, 1920, in *Public Philosopher*, ed. Blum, 133–4. On the *Times* survey, see Steel, *Walter Lippmann*, 172–3.
34. Walter Lippmann, *Liberty and the News* (New York: Harcourt, Brace and Howe, 1920), 9–11, 37–8, 56; Walter Lippmann, to Ellery Sedgwick, Apr. 7, 1919, in *Public Philosopher*, ed. Blum, 112.
35. Lippmann, *Public Opinion*, 27–8, 57, 141; Walter Lippmann, "Liberalism To-Day," *World*, July 31, 1924, 6.
36. Ernest Gruening, "Public Opinion and Democracy," *Nation*, July 26, 1922, 98.

37. Walter Lippmann, "The Building of a Great Cathedral," *World*, Dec. 23, 1924, 12; Walter Lippmann, "Bishop Manning Should Reconsider," *World*, Feb. 13, 1925, 10. On "device," see Brown, to Lippmann, Mar. 9, 1922. On "purification," see Walter Lippmann, to Albert G. Dieffenbach, July 12, 1920, in *Public Philosopher*, ed. Blum, 136.
38. Walter Lippmann, "Second-Hand Statesmen," *Yale Review* 11 (1922): 681. For "make their wisdom," see Lippmann, *Public Opinion*, 190.
39. Walter Lippmann, "The Spiritual Treason of Bryan," *World*, July 15, 1925, 10; Walter Lippmann, "The Rise of Sectarian Politics," *World*, July 10, 1925, 10; Walter Lippmann, "Keep Religion Out of Politics," *World*, July 8, 1925, 12; Walter Lippmann, "The Separation of Church and State," *World*, July 1, 1925, 10.
40. Walter Lippmann, "Why Should the Majority Rule?" *Harpers* 152 (1926), 399, reprinted in *Essential Lippmann*, ed. Rossiter and Lare, 11. On "metropolitan" versus "village civilization," see Lippmann, *Men of Destiny*, 28, 85.
41. Lippmann, *American Inquisitors*, 111; Walter Lippmann, to Learned Hand, June 8, 1925, in *Public Philosopher*, ed. Blum, 176.
42. Walter Lippmann, *The Phantom Public* (New York: Macmillan, 1925 [Reprint: Transaction, 2004]), 10–11, 56–9, 145, 187–8.
43. Lippmann, *Phantom Public*, 25, 87, 132, 179–80; Walter Lippmann, to Charles Beard, Sept. 5, 1925, in WLP, Reel 3.
44. Jane Addams, *Twenty Years at Hull House* (New York: Macmillan, 1910), 453; Jane Addams, *Democracy and Social Ethics* (New York: Macmillan, 1907), 2–3, 93, 138, 269–77; Mary Parker Follett, *The New State: Group Organization the Solution of Popular Government* (New York: Longmans, Green, 1918), 12, 34, 43, 161.
45. John Dewey, "Public Opinion," *New Republic*, May 3, 1922, 286–8; John Dewey, *The Public and Its Problems* (New York: Henry Holt, 1927), 116, 213, 215–17. For the long history of juxtaposing Lippmann and Dewey, and the dangers of doing so, see Tom Arnold-Forster, "Democracy and Expertise in the Lippmann-Terman Controversy," *Modern Intellectual History* 16 (Aug. 2019): 561–92.
46. For Lippmann's thoughts on Addams, see Walter Lippmann, *Interpretations, 1933–1935*, ed. Allan Nevins (New York: Macmillan, 1936), 381–2. On Follett, see Walter Lippmann, to Mary Parker Follett, Sept. 9, 1919; Mary Parker Follett, to Walter Lippmann, Dec. 23, 1919, both in WLP, Reel 9; and "Editorial Notes," *New Republic*, July 15, 1916, 264.
47. Walter Lippmann, "The Basic Problem of Democracy," *Atlantic Monthly* 62 (Nov. 1919): 616–27 (626); Lippmann, *Public Opinion*, 43–4, 171–200; John Dewey, to Walter Lippmann, May 4, 1922; Walter Lippmann, to John Dewey, Jan. 14, 1930, both in WLP, Reel 7.
48. Walter Lippmann, to Theodore Roosevelt, Jr., Feb. 18, 1915, in *Public Philosopher*, ed. Blum, 23–5. On Brookwood, see A. J. Muste, to Walter Lippmann, Sept. 30, 1926, in WLP, Reel 20. On "discussion," see Walter Lippmann, to Raymond Leslie Buell, May 17, 1939, in WLP, Reel 49.

49. Lippmann, *Men of Destiny*, 151. On the FPA, see David John Allen, "Every Citizen a Statesman: Building a Democracy for Foreign Policy in the American Century" (PhD diss, Columbia University, 2019).
50. On the CFR, see Robert D. Schulzinger, *The Wise Men of Foreign Affairs: The History of the Council on Foreign Relations* (New York: Columbia University Press, 1984).
51. Walter Lippmann, *Interpretations, 1931–32*, ed. Allan Nevins (New York: Macmillan, 1932), 27.
52. Charles King, *Gods of the Upper Air: How a Circle of Renegade Anthropologists Reinvented Race, Sex, and Gender in the Twentieth Century* (New York: Doubleday, 2019).
53. Randolph Bourne, "Trans-national America," *Atlantic Monthly* 118 (July 1916): 86–97; John Dewey, *Democracy and Education* (New York: Macmillan, 1916), 357; Dewey, *Public and Its Problems*, 192.
54. Lippmann, *Public Opinion*, 50–1, 152.
55. Walter Lippmann, "Live and Let Live," *World*, Jan. 1, 1925, 10; Walter Lippmann, "Fascisti and the Ku Klux Klan," *World*, July 26, 1922, 8. On Lippmann and I. Q. tests, see Arnold-Forster, "Democracy and Expertise in the Lippmann-Terman Controversy," 561–92.
56. Lippmann, *Men of Destiny*, 2–9, 28.
57. Walter Lippmann, to John Collier, Mar. 22, 1915, in *Public Philosopher*, ed. Blum, 26. On Lippmann's efforts to get Du Bois admitted to the Liberal Club, see Steel, *Walter Lippmann*, 39. For DuBois's letter seeking help for a Black soldier denied promotion, see W. E. B. DuBois, to Walter Lippmann, June 29, 1917, at https://credo.library.umass.edu/view/full/mums312-b010-i161 (last accessed 8/1/20). On Lippmann's interest in the Pan-African Congress, see David Levering Lewis, *W. E. B. Du Bois: A Biography, 1868–1963* (New York: Henry Holt, 2009), 379.
58. Walter Lippmann, "Introductory Note," in Carl Sandburg, *The Chicago Race Riots, July 1919* (New York: Harcourt, Brace, and Howe, 1919), iii–iv.
59. Lippmann, "Introductory Note," iv. On the Black Nationalism of Marcus Garvey in Chicago, see Erik S. McDuffie, "Chicago, Garveyism, and the History of the Diasporic Midwest," *African and Black Diaspora* 8 (Apr. 2015): 129–45.
60. On the Fifteenth Amendment, see Walter Lippmann, to William Borah, Aug. 3, 1926, in WLP, Reel 4. On Lippmann's ties to Byrd, see their correspondence in WLP, Reel 50. For "superior force," see Walter Lippmann, to W. W. Ball, Jan. 14, 1926, in WLP, Reel 3. See Walter Lippmann, to C. P. Scott, Aug. 6, 1919, in *Public Philosopher*, ed. Blum, 125–6, for Lippmann's prediction about the Republican party.
61. Walter Lippmann, to Alfred E. Smith, Sept. 17, 1928, in *Public Philosopher*, ed. Blum, 230. On Lippmann's support for Sanger and birth control, see Margaret Sanger, *Margaret Sanger: An Autobiography* (New York: W. W. Norton, 1938), 199.

62. Imhoff, "My Sons Have Defeated Me," 536–50. See Walter Lippmann, to Graham Wallas, Nov. 4, 1920, in *Public Philosopher*, ed. Blum, 137, for "discouragement." On "ten years ago," see Walter Lippmann, "The Setting for John W. Davis," *Atlantic Monthly* 133 (October 1924): 534–5. See Lippmann, *Drift and Mastery*, 218–19, on "govern herself."

63. Walter Lippmann, "Rather Vague Ancestors," *World*, Apr. 9, 1924, 12. See Walter Lippmann, "Gov. Smith on Immigration," *World*, Aug. 27, 1928, 10, for Lippmann's counsel to leave immigration reform out of the election. On "white races," see Walter Lippmann, "History in the Making," *World*, Nov. 2, 1928, 12.

64. Walter Lippmann, "Mercy," *World*, Aug. 10, 1927, 12; Walter Lippmann, "An Appeal to Governor Fuller," *World*, Aug. 6, 1927, 10; Walter Lippmann, "Threats and Irritation," *World*, Aug. 18, 1927, 8; Walter Lippmann, "Doubt That Will Not Down," *World*, Aug. 19, 1927, 12. See Walter Lippmann, "The Lowell Committee Report," *World*, Aug. 8, 1927, 10; and Walter Lippmann, "Patriotic Service," *World*, Aug. 24, 1927, 12, on Lippmann's agreement with the trial verdict. See Walter Lippmann, "Calmness and Fairness Needed," *World*, Apr. 18, 1927, 10, on "violent radicalism."

65. See Lippmann, to Berenson, July 16, 1919, for "parlor Bolsheviks." See Walter Lippmann, to William Allen White, Jan. 4, 1926, in WLP, Reel 33, on his anti-Zionism.

66. Walter Lippmann, "Public Opinion and the American Jew," *American Hebrew* 110 (Apr. 14, 1922): 575.

67. Lippmann, "Public Opinion," 575.

68. Walter Lippmann, "Harvard Loses Its Bearings," *World*, Jan. 12, 1923, 12; Walter Lippmann, to Arthur N. Holcombe, June 14, 1922, in *Public Philosopher*, ed. Blum, 148.

69. Walter Lippmann, to Lawrence J. Henderson, Oct. 27, 1922, in *Public Philosopher*, ed. Blum, 148–54. Steel was unable to determine if Lippmann ever sent the letter. See Steel, *Walter Lippmann*, 613, chapter 15, note 13.

70. Lippmann, *Public Opinion*, 57. On "businessmen," see Lippmann, *Men of Destiny*, 26. For "economic position," see Walter Lippmann, to S. K. Ratcliffe, Oct. 9, 1925, in *Public Philosopher*, ed. Blum, 178. See Steel, *Walter Lippmann*, 276–8, for the context of the *Time* story.

71. Walter Lippmann, to Learned Hand, Sept. 11, 1927, in WLP, Reel 12; Walter Lippmann, to Newton Baker, Feb. 26, 1931, in *Public Philosopher*, ed. Blum, 270.

PART II

The Older Lippmann

Part II covers the years 1930 through Lippmann's death in 1974. Chapter 4 examines Lippmann's response to the Great Depression and the New Deal. It concludes with a look at Lippmann's misunderstood manifesto, *The Good Society* (1937), and the start of his "Catholic phase." Chapter 5 considers Lippmann's critical take on American foreign policy during World War II and the Cold War. He moved further into and away from Washington politics simultaneously. Chapter 6 shows how Lippmann's worries about the country's diplomacy led him to argue for a stronger executive, a more enlightened republic, and a greater welfare state. A close reading of Lippmann's last major work, *The Public Philosophy* (1955), is central, although his celebrity status will also be profiled and interrogated. Lippmann's break with Cold War liberals over the civil rights movement and Vietnam War is the focus of Chapter 7. Lippmann's deepened affiliation with and distance from Christian traditions, as well as his embrace and rejection of civil religions, is emphasized throughout.

4
The Evangelist, 1930–1939

"I am a conservative; I think I always have been. But that doesn't mean that I'm a conservative who agrees with William Buckley. I never joined Barry Goldwater or anyone like that. I don't consider myself that kind. I hope and trust I am a conservative in the line of Edmund Burke. I believe in certain fundamental things in philosophy and constitutional law which are conservative as against the Jacobins." That was Lippmann's confession to biographer Steel and their *Washington Post* and *New Republic* readers in 1973, a year before Lippmann's death. The lifelong devotee of the Roosevelts had just voted for Richard Nixon in the presidential election (he had in 1968 as well). By "Jacobins," Lippmann meant those devotees of the French Revolution who boasted that human beings could achieve their full potential if freed from society's restraints. He named Nixon's opponent, the South Dakota Senator and liberal stalwart George McGovern. "Man is not naturally good," Lippmann countered, "nor is his nature perfectible by economic means."[1]

Lippmann had first started praising Burke during the 1930s. While endorsing Burke's view of legislatures as deliberative bodies unbeholden to public opinion, Lippmann declared that the British statesman had been "one of the wisest men of his century and among the profoundest political thinkers of the tradition which we inherit." But which tradition was Lippmann talking about, Jefferson's Declaration of Independence or Burke's *Reflections on the Revolution in France* (1790)? More to the point: What intellectual wilderness had liberalism's Moses wandered into? If Lippmann had been a conservative all along, why had he not made common cause with Buckley and Goldwater, the spokespersons of post-World War II conservatism?[2]

The older Lippmann would prove the even older adage that the more things change, the more they stay the same. Lippmann only

Walter Lippmann: American Skeptic, American Pastor. Mark Thomas Edwards, Oxford University Press.
© Mark Thomas Edwards 2023. DOI: 10.1093/oso/9780192895165.003.0005

seemed to make himself over during the Great Depression. One biographer explained it this way: "His counsel was no longer 'express yourself' of the halcyon days before World War I, but rather, 'control yourself.'" That was a smart observation but a bit overstated. Mastery of self and society had been on Lippmann's mind from the start. Shut out of white Northern European Protestant circles at Harvard, the younger Lippmann had drifted into socialism and bohemianism without much resolve. *Public Opinion* had made his frustrations with the disorders of Jeffersonian democracy plain. *A Preface to Morals* had then divulged the post-Christian skepticism that had been hiding in plain sight in Lippmann's political writings. That book had been less successful in charting a way forward for swinging individuals and society, however, who remained disinterested in Lippmann's drab secular humanism. He had immediately set out to write a sequel.[3]

The sequel would take eight years to publish—really twenty-six years—and even then Lippmann never finished it. In persevering through the morass of modernity, the older Lippmann realized something that the younger had not: He needed a MORE as well. Lippmann the None discovered that a pragmatic affiliation with the "classical and Christian heritage," as he named it, could fix several problems at once. Lippmann recommended a new public role for religions during the depression and war years that would have shocked his former SBNR self. Yet he never accepted Christianity as true in a metaphysical sense, only in a utilitarian one. Lippmann remained a faithful critic of Christian American nationalism even when indulging anew Roman Catholicism.

Much of the older Lippmann's work from the 1930s through the 1960s would center around the conduct of states and state actors. He would endorse novel spiritual foundations for strong-state liberalism and articulate a realist Wilsonian foreign policy that he would term "neo-isolationism." He would defend heterosexual white male positionality through his silence regarding civil rights and liberties. Still, Lippmann never forgot that the relationship between personal and social life was dialectical if not paradoxical. A Great Society that could no longer count upon the moral training of a sickening Christian culture had to find alternative ways to cultivate and then interrelate hearty personalities and healthy institutions of democratic governance. As much as they might hate each other, the SBNR and the RBNS had to stick together for the sake of the Great Community.

*

Lippmann's mission to rescue American democracy from itself became more urgent in a time of civilizational collapse. The Great Depression of the 1930s encompassed more than mass unemployment and ecological and agricultural devastation. It was an era of despair in which it appeared that the "American Way of Life" was over. With producer capitalism speciously dead, many wondered if state socialism of the European fascist or communist varieties should happen here. Franklin Roosevelt's New Deal was seen as vital to combatting the psychological as well as the financial effects of the depression. At the same time, the United States indulged in xenophobic "us vs. them" sentiment toward Europe and Asia. Lippmann, for his part, would stoke fears of subversion from within while casting himself as an evangelist bringing good news of serenity in this world. Lippmann did not manufacture the social crisis, but he sure took advantage of it.[4]

Lippmann would occupy one of the largest platforms on the planet to market a mere Christian humanism for what ailed the upside-down West. When the *World* shuttered in 1931, friends thought Lippmann might settle for an academic post—Harvard offered him a chair in its government department, while the University of North Carolina at Chapel Hill invited him to be its president. Lippmann surprised everyone when he joined the prominent Republican newspaper, the *New York Herald Tribune*, and began writing "Today and Tomorrow." The thrice-weekly op-ed would become syndicated in over two hundred newspapers and reach an audience of ten-to-twelve million. By 1940, Lippmann would be the fourth most popular columnist in America, surpassed only by Walter Winchell, Dorothy Thompson, and Boake Carter. Among "prosperous" publics, Lippmann ranked second behind Thompson (who joined the "*Trib*" in 1936). Lower-income readers turned to Winchell first and Lippmann last. Still, Lippmann took comfort in the knowledge that he was probably the highest-paid journalist around. Republican friends like Thomas Lamont, the head of J. P. Morgan bank, found good reason to go on European vacations with the Lippmanns and to get Walter admitted to New York's (ethnically) exclusive clubs.[5]

Given that Lippmann's most avid subscribers were categorized as "potential Republicans," is it finally permissible to lament his deradicalization? The answer is still no—and an emphatic no to Amos Pinchot, the Progressive-era holdout and Lippmann's harshest critic. In four articles for *The Nation* in 1933, Pinchot dubbed Lippmann the "Obfuscator de Luxe" and "salesman of plutocracy" who was "once a votary in the house of Marx" but "now worships in the house of Morgan." Lippmann had never been a Marxist, and he also never stopped advocating for piecemeal measures of socialism. Lippmann was as troubled by the unequal distribution of wealth in America as his closest friends and proposed using the inheritance tax to "level down" prosperity. That said, Lippmann's exodus from labor unions made his ties to New York's Old Left and the "Red Decade" tenuous at best.[6]

Lippmann's *Trib* work clearly narrowed his focus. Of the nearly 1500 "Today and Tomorrow" columns he penned between 1931 and 1946, two-thirds were about economics. The younger Lippmann had taken a few classes on the subject while at Harvard, but he still must have laughed at his older self's reputation as a "public economist." Lippmann's passion for the dismal science entangled with his evolving religious and philosophical interests. Recognizing "no copyright on ideas," Lippmann plagiarized liberally from many fields of inquiry, especially from theology. "When things seem particularly sick in Washington," one critic complained of Lippmann's style, he "deplores the confusion and then goes cosmic, becomes so pontifical and profound that no one can follow him." Lippmann remained an articulator of other people's ideas. It was what he was best at.[7]

Lippmann stayed torn between "the contemplative and the active life" as expressed in his commencement address at Columbia, "The Scholar in a Troubled World" (1932). Lest his undergraduate audience think he was offering "a mere elegy to a fugitive and cloistered virtue," Lippmann concluded that only "the men who have stood apart" from daily grinds and generational crises could recover the "general principles" and "intellectual clarity" necessary to revive democracy. Lippmann invoked the nation's founders as an ideal type of stand-apart men. He had long admired Hamilton, but during these years he rediscovered James Madison. Lippmann envied *The Federalist Papers* and hoped to write something like them that would survive the test of time. But that magnum opus would have to be achieved in the stolen moments between morning newspapers and drafts, afternoon meetings with research assistants, tennis and the gym, planning excursions to Maine and Europe, and evening cocktail parties and dinners with friends with money. Lippmann was too enamored of being the talk of the town to be seduced absolutely by the life of the mind.[8]

*

The Great Depression did not affect Lippmann in the material way that it did millions of Americans, but the confusion it produced made him go cosmic. He was not alone: Many public intellectuals and reformers welcomed economic devastation as an opportunity to moralize about the sins of the New Era. They would turn to varieties of Christianity to resist the encroachments of fascism and communism—the imagined diseases of an invented Western heritage.

These were boom years for the "Puritan" Lippmann, who scolded the Gatsbys for their "soft living" (even though he was one with them in metropolitan spirit). In column after column, Lippmann condemned the "greed" that he claimed was the real source of his country's upset. In "The False Gods" (1932), Lippmann blasted political and economic elites for teaching people "to be acquisitive, to seek feverishly to become richer and richer, to prostrate themselves before the Golden Calf." Now, the masses must pay the penalty for their leaders' idolatry. As Lippmann explained,

> A demoralized people is one in which the individual has become isolated and is the prey of his own suspicions. He trusts nobody and nothing, not even himself. He believes nothing, except the worst of everybody and everything. He sees only confusion in himself and conspiracies in other men. That is panic. That is disintegration. That is what comes when in some sudden emergency of their lives men must find themselves unsupported by clear convictions that transcend their immediate and personal desires.

To Lippmann, cultural, spiritual, and economic catastrophe proceeded together. Elsewhere, he claimed that a "new generation" of Americans was rising that were "tired of the fawning and the flattery, of the evasiveness and the straddling, of the soft and the fat and the timorous, of the shoddy optimists, the ignobly self-indulgent, the greedy and the parvenu who battened upon the distortion of values which the inflation produced."[9]

But from where was this reboot of Roosevelt's strenuous life to come from? What the younger Lippmann had termed James's "Right to Believe" took on fresh relevance in the Great Depression. The New Era had convinced Lippmann that man "does not domesticate perfectly. There is a strain of wildness and of excess in him which cannot be regimented or caged, and this wildness, which may drive him to the savage or the sublime, he cannot satisfy with mediocre distractions." Lippmann unloaded on this vice of over-civilization ("mediocre distractions") in the *Women's Home Companion*. Yet had not the flappers proven that women, too, were hard-wired toward wildness? Or was Lippmann chiding the ladies for refining Rough Rider masculinity out of existence? At any rate, Lippmann repurposed himself as partisan of the depression-era drive to revive self-reliant American manhood. But to do that, his once-emancipated, now emaciated modern man would have to bow to Jesus or maybe Buddha: "There is no substitute by the mere arrangement of outward activities for that radical arrangement of inward activity which in its many manifestations men have called religion." Lippmann continued to expound freedom from and freedom for religious affiliation.[10]

Lippmann himself began to fraternize with those who presumed a more affirmative role for religions in society. Out were Freud and Nietzsche. In were persons like the Harvard metaphysician Alfred North Whitehead, Niebuhr the Christian realist, and the British historian and political advisor Arnold Toynbee. Lippmann had been elated that Whitehead had found a spot at Harvard to continue the legacy of James and Santayana. Lippmann recovered the doctrine of original sin ("the satanic will") alongside Niebuhr, but with a broader audience.[11]

Lippmann copied Toynbee the most. In response to worldwide war and depression, Toynbee had taken up the questions of what civilizations are and how they rise and fall. His twenty-nine world civilizations assumed a working relationship between religions and cultures, although he had not decided which one was primary. Lippmann devoured the first three volumes of Toynbee's *A Study of History* (1934) with great interest. He took Toynbee concepts as his own, including the terms "external proletarians" and "internal proletarians" (those alienated from the material security of the ruling classes). The fantasy that Toynbee would term "post-Christian" in 1940 was, for Lippmann, already morphing from a welcome aspiration into a grave concern.[12]

Lippmann's reading of Toynbee reinforced the former's "civilization" versus "barbarism" discourse. Lippmann had always used "civilization" and "civilized" to refer to Europe and the United States. In the 1930s, however, secularist trans-Atlantic public intellectuals like Lippmann joined Christian and Jewish thinkers in redeploying the civilization-barbarism framework. Most did so to defend Western cultural exceptionalism. Warning college students of the "loud-mouthed barbarians," Lippmann recounted, "we had no idea how men behave when their customary way of life is disrupted and their familiar habits are disordered. We had no idea of how fragile are the bonds of a civilized existence." His assertion that Great Societies were poised to "stampede back into barbarism" was a professional middle-class jab at the labor movement he was estranged from. Still, humble self-awareness of the enemy within could at times slip into Lippmann's elitist speech. "In some degree the disposition to crime is present in us all," Lippmann concluded about a triple homicide. "The best of us is only a recently and partially civilized barbarian."[13]

The recently and partially civilized Lippmann was now a nonpracticing Jewish celebrity columnist who congratulated Christian cultures for their contributions to social order. That was vintage RBNS: Respect for conventional religious nationalist expressions irrespective of personal devotions. It was quite the sea change from *A Preface to Morals*, the instant SBNR classic that had pitted the moral man against the immoral society. Lippmann might have lost some of his *World* fans over his new cosmic tone, but anti-fascist Catholics were loving it. In the past, Lippman had appealed to Modernist Protestants while holding Roman Catholics at a distance and worrying about a Vatican alliance with Mussolini. In the wake of his work on the Smith campaign and fight against the Klan, though, Lippmann had encouraged the *Commonweal*'s liberal Catholics to resist fascist "*totalitaria*" (this was apparently the first use of the word "totalitarianism" in the American press). Lippmann believed

Catholics would make the best anti-totalitarians, as they had pioneered the core democratic idea of the separation of powers during the Middle Ages. He bid them return to (St. Thomas) Aquinas and natural law defenses of limited government. *A Preface to Morals* had also commended Catholicism's ability to conserve and promote humanistic values. In the years ahead, Lippmann aided Catholic confidants in finding enemies to fault for the spread of totalitarian barbarism throughout Western civilization.[14]

The civilization-barbarism continuum could paper over other transgressions as well. Lippmann would never warm up to Mussolini, even after interviewing him in 1929, but he would find some nice things to say about Adolf Hitler. Most of the time, Lippmann was outspoken in calling the Nazi party a group of "barbarized" thugs carrying out "planned, organized and centrally directed terrorism" against Jewish populations. Still, Lippmann agreed with Hitler that Germans were right to feel "intrinsically outcast" by the World War I peace settlement. In one column, Lippmann applauded the Nazi leader's "very statesmanlike address" and considered him "the authentic voice of a genuinely civilized people." As Lippmann explained, "to deny today that Germany can speak as a civilized power, because uncivilized things are being said and done in Germany, is in itself a deep form of intolerance. Like all intolerance, it betrays a lack of moral wisdom, in this case the moral wisdom of religious insight into the dual nature of man." Unless Americans wanted to be judged by their worst representatives, in other words, they should not consider Nazi Germany beyond redemption. Lippmann called for open-mindedness even when friends and readers wished he would not.[15]

One such person was Frankfurter. It was bad enough watching his friend praising Hitler. When, in the same editorial, Lippmann charged that some Jews were "parvenus," it seemed Lippmann was (again) saying that Jews had brought persecution upon themselves. Frankfurter immediately cut off all communication. Lippmann could not care less, as he had grown weary of the self-described "threesome" that he, Felix, and Faye had enjoyed. By the time of their breakup, Frankfurter was writing two or three long letters for every one of Lippmann's. Having Felix as a pen pal had grown "frightening to me," he later confessed.[16]

*

The Evangelist, 1930–1939

Lippmann had more interesting men to be nervous about, at least as he defined interest. Strong-state liberals like himself had languished throughout the 1920s. The Great Depression presented the perfect moment for them to flex their Hamiltonian muscle of executive over legislative authority. But Franklin was not the Roosevelt Lippmann had been looking for. Lippmann had hoped his old benefactor Newton Baker would run for the Democratic nomination in 1932. Lippmann thought Baker the model of the disinterested statesman, while Roosevelt was a "weaseling mind" and a "kind of amiable boy scout." No doubt a Baker presidency would have served Lippmann's ambition to be an influencer behind the throne. Lippmann did not endorse Roosevelt until shortly before the election, after which time he lunched with the President-elect and alerted him that he would have to assume "dictatorial powers." For his part, Roosevelt found Lippmann generally more helpful than not. He invited him to the White House to problem solve on more than a few occasions.[17]

Lippman recognized the New Deal as a return to the Progressivism-liberalism he had championed as cofounder of the *New Republic*. Roosevelt's administration, like Lippmann's earlier journal, became another center for Jewish lawyers and professors left homeless in an anti-Semitic age. House of Truth graduates Brandeis and Frankfurter, along with their disciples, advised on and administered federal operations to an unprecedented degree (even if only one person of Jewish descent, Henry Morgenthau, Jr., served in Roosevelt's cabinet). Along with them, Lippmann argued that strong federal leadership was imperative to keep the country from falling into the clutches of reactionaries and revolutionaries. Recall his Harvard writings in which he had suggested that the State become a religion to lead America. Like Small's "American Religion" and Croly's "Religion of Humanity," Lippmann's strong-state liberalism was conservative—Lippmann would say Burkean—originating in the first Roosevelt's expansion of government to hold the United States together against disintegrative forces. Yet Lippmann credited the innovative conservatism of the New Deal to Hoover (another House of Truth fellow), whom he argued was its true architect despite being its main opponent.[18]

Lippmann found much to criticize in Roosevelt's reforms. The one agenda item that both men loyally supported was keeping America white, Northern European, and mostly Protestant. Franklin appeared to be a kinder and gentler nation builder than Teddy. Yet the New Deal era was a lot like the New Era in perpetuating a racist Christian Americanism. "You know this is a Protestant country, and the Catholics and Jews are here under sufferance," Roosevelt once told a Jewish advisor. "It is up to you [and other Jews] to go along with anything I want." Roosevelt found support from Lippmann's Harvard classmate, the ex-secular humanist poet T. S. Eliot, who asserted in 1934 that the West needed to rebuild Christian societies in which "any large number of free-thinking Jews" like Lippmann would be "undesirable."[19]

Baker encouraged his friend and protégé to stand against such bigotry when he invited Lippmann to attend an NCCJ conference with him (Baker was a chairman of the organization). Lippmann was overseas when the offer arrived but would have declined anyways. It was hardly uncommon for Lippmann to turn down offers to join pressure groups, citing journalistic integrity—which, he admitted privately, was "an excellent excuse for not doing things I don't want to do." In this instance, the true excuse was a lack of "enthusiasm" for interreligious work. This was just one indication that Lippmann would never share the "Judeo-Christian" enthusiasm of mid-century America.[20]

Lippmann instead used his media platform to uphold Red Scare bans on immigration. He was familiar with the "science of settlements" of his old Inquiry detractor Bowman. He offered that as a basis for his contention that the United States should not reopen its borders to Jews and others fleeing oppression in Europe. During the 1920s, Lippmann had complained that America had turned its back on political refugees. Now, without evidence or explanation, Lippmann claimed that it was "entirely impossible" to allow mass migration to "settled communities" or to move "overcrowded people" to an "overcrowded" city. Instead, Jews and other persecuted peoples should be relocated to "backward and empty regions" like Africa. Here was the "moral justification for empire," Lippmann maintained: to remake beleaguered city folk into "pioneers" and agents of modernization. "It is a task as inspiring as it is great," said Lippmann of settlement science, "one to enlist the genius of the imperial nations, and to revive in the world that feeling of hope in the expansion of human energies which it has lost."[21]

Lippmann still fled the peril of being a successful Jewish American through deflection. In this instance, he turned refugees away from

American shores to preserve the Protestant white male Rooseveltan republic—and his revered status within it. The younger Lippmann had urged fighting the KKK during the 1920s, but the older one normalized Klan ideology even as that movement fractured. Under pressure from Dorothy Thompson, Lippmann's *Trib* colleague, Roosevelt softened on immigration. Lippmann never did. As one later observer put it, Lippmann "thought he could choose not to be a Jew."[22]

*

Isolationism—political, economic, military, and religio-racial—was foundational to Roosevelt's early New Deal, and Lippmann's contrarian spirit vetted it. The Stoic individualism of Lippmann's SBNR sensibility, always opposed to religious institutions and systems, now had to share space with his RBNS feeling that the dechristianized masses needed moral regimentation. Privately, Lippmann bemoaned that the economies of Great Societies had to be managed by centralized authorities. Publicly, he was one of the country's foremost proponents of federal responsibility to maintain the "popular standard of life." Yes, the New Deal was "strong medicine" for a democratic people, but the American invalid would not survive without emergency action.[23]

Lippmann believed the country was ready for another shot of tough-minded leadership. Weak opposition to Hoover's and Roosevelt's recovery efforts signaled that "laissez-faire is dead and that the collectivist principle is now generally accepted. The great issues of the contemporary world, as between conservatives and progressives, fascists, communists, and social democrats have to do with the kind of collectivism, how it is to be established, in whose interests, by who it is to be controlled, and for what ends." Americans need not fear that Roosevelt was leading the country into fascism or communism because those were the "alien stereotypes" of the "ancient despotism of the East." Both were external to "Western civilization" and the "Western way of life." The New Deal, in contrast, was descended from the transcendent wisdom of the founding fathers as updated through Roosevelt, Wilson, Hoover, and Roosevelt again. At times, Lippmann was liberalism's most earnest champion—its Moses.[24]

Yet Lippmann's "yes" to the Rooseveltan state was tempered by a resounding "no." That would not have been surprising to followers who knew of the younger Lippmann's oscillations between advocacy for State religion and fears of the "Servile State." For many public intellectuals, they welcomed parts of the New Deal but feared the whole of it. It was the reverse with Lippmann. He argued repeatedly for "concentration of authority" in the executive branch while condemning most of Roosevelt's signature policies. Between 1933 and 1938, ninety percent of Lippmann's references to the New Deal would be judged later to have been negative or neutral. He was especially relentless in his assault on the National Recovery Administration (NRA), the initial centerpiece of the New Deal. Lippmann condemned the NRA as "moral coercion" through its civil religion of the Blue Eagle. Not only were its practices of wage and price fixing hindering recovery, they were also leading to "excessive centralization" and a "dictatorial spirit" that was "producing a revulsion of feeling against bureaucratic control of American economic life."[25]

Lippmann had other problems with the New Deal. He was ambivalent about the Social Security program, while 94% of his mentions of minimum wage legislation would be deemed negative. He privileged local over federal relief efforts and counseled against direct assistance programs that would "demoralize others by destroying their incentive to work and to fend for themselves." Federal welfare programs had the potential to create a new "caste" instead of a "fellowship of morally equal men." Lippmann's erratic response to Roosevelt's reforms was typical of a generation that was struggling to balance competing political values of freedom and security.[26]

If Lippmann's attacks anticipated those of later libertarian conservatives, he never shared their fear that the New Deal was "creeping socialism." As the old Red Scare became the long Red Scare, Lippmann stood against it as part of his general suspicion of civil religions. He kept faith that the expanding republic, the Great Society that Madison and the founders had inaugurated, remained immune from outside agitators. Instead, a true conservative knew that civilizations rot from within. The "internal proletarians" were always more dangerous than the "external" ones. As Lippmann explained it, "I am no believer in the literal inspiration of the Constitution or in its rigid interpretation. But those who do not see that liberty and progress in America both depend upon limiting the power of all government, upon preserving its federal nature, upon protecting local authority, are, I believe, tragically blind to the plainest lesson of the world they live in. For once a people let all power become concentrated at one point, it is like an army trapped in a salient." That statement squared with Lippmann's claims about enhanced executive power, which he hoped would be a temporary emergency expedient.[27]

One thing seems clear: Lippmann's anti-democratic turn never really happened. He parroted Burkean talking points about the unruly masses, but he also found new responsibilities for organized publics to safeguard the nation's freedoms. Lippmann insisted that this was a spiritual-philosophical problem first and a political-economic one second. A post-Christian people must figure out how to keep faith in themselves even as they safeguarded freedom from outmoded faith.[28]

*

And who better to assist in conserving American values than a Brit? Besides James and Wallas, Lippmann would count his friendship with the world's most famous public economist, Lord John Maynard Keynes, as the "most happy" of his life. The two had first met during the World War I peace talks. They remained friends and collaborators into the Great Depression years, including an all-night damage control session at the American embassy in London after Roosevelt had blown up international currency discussions. Lippmann complained to Keynes about the failings of the NRA, while Keynes explained his theory of how governments could mitigate boom-and-bust cycles through fiscal policy. Lippmann found Keynes's magnum opus, *The General Theory of Employment, Interest, and Money* (1936), "unreadable." Nonetheless, Lippmann described himself as an "ardent, amateur Keynesian" into the 1960s.[29]

Lippmann was one of Keynes's most avid translators for a popular audience. He would laugh at today's caricatures of Keynesianism as a slippery slope toward totalitarianism. Rather, Keynes was pointing the world toward a "Compensated Economy," or "free enterprise compensated by government action." Lippmann was encouraged that Roosevelt bought into Keynesianism in the form of federally funded public works programs like the Civilian Conservation Corps (CCC) and the Works Progress Administration (WPA). Adventures in government deficit spending (economic stimulus) would make up for market failures while maintaining values of dignified work and self-reliance. To Lippmann, Keynesianism promoted an Aristotelian "middle condition" for America as opposed to plutocratic privilege and proletarian insecurity. Building upon Keynes, Lippmann imagined future WPAs and CCCs rolled out in response to market collapses. As he told the historian Henry Steel Commager in 1947, he had objected to the technique, not the substance, of the New Deal. Lippmann believed the promises of both liberalism and socialism could be realized through the right method of intermingling free enterprise and compensatory government action—a "Free Collectivism" as a moral equivalent for "Absolute Collectivism."[30]

As the master of meliorism, Keynes was the William James of political economy. He was also something else. Keynes was the Burke that post-Christian, ex-socialist liberals like Lippman cried out for. Keynes offered a third way between what Lippmann believed to be the discredited utopian extremes of libertarianism and socialism. Even Keynes was convinced that Burke would have chosen that path as well. "It is not wise to look too far ahead," Keynes had summarized Burke in 1906. "Our powers of prediction are slight, our command over results infinitesimal." In Lippmann's estimation, Keynes was disinterested in the best sense of the word, humble in the face of human limitation yet still determined to live MORE for self and others. Lippmann was more than pleased to play evangelist to his friend's divine intuitions.[31]

In case Lippmann's conflation of Keynes, James, and Burke is too much for you to bear, remember that this is the same man who had helped the *New Republic* convert Alexander Hamilton into a socialist. The key to all those intersections was Lippmann's skepticism. James's hatred of absolutes remained at the core of Lippmann's being, but he still allowed others to move in and out of his intellectual orbit as the times—or column deadlines—demanded it. Lippmann's fellow travelers, living and dead, helped him craft an American liberalism characterized by a balance between personal liberty and group security. Like he explained to Baker, "I really believe that these free countries have evolved by trial and error a method of social control which no one conceived a priori."[32]

Lippmann preferred Keynes's Burkean pragmatism to what he saw as the overreaction of government-mandated unionism. Underlying Lippmann's one-man war on the NRA had been his Jamesian sense that it was impossible to manage a free market. Yet he had worried as well that the agency was being used to strengthen the power of corporations. His call to bring back trustbusting reflected his (classical as well as strong-state) liberal faith in equalizing opportunity and increasing competition. That context must be kept in mind if we are to understand Lippmann's disgust with the National Labor Relations Act of 1935 (NLRA), also known as the Wagner Act. What would become the most important piece of labor legislation in American history looked like "forcing" workers to join unions. Lippmann asserted that the Wagner Act made the federal government the "promoter of a particular kind of unionism" to serve Roosevelt's lust for building a "radical farm-labor party." Lippmann demanded that the entire law be thrown out.[33]

With his new Madisonian logic (from *Federalist* No. 10) on full display, Lippmann argued that unions like corporations must fight it out in the private sector. The federal government should stay a disinterested referee, not a partisan picker of winners and losers. Lippmann's missives against Wagner and Roosevelt fell pleasantly upon the *Trib*'s prosperous Republican ears. Like his critics, they could pretend that Lippmann was a partisan for corporate domination. But the point was rarely as it seemed with Lippmann. His older self no longer backed a participatory form of industrial democracy, but he still believed unionization would and should advance.[34]

*

Lippmann's conservativism was, like most of his intellectual life, of a heterodox variety. In many ways, it was another name for his contrarian style. It also signaled a self-confidence that had eluded him for much of his life. The sources of that blessed assurance were multiple. For one, Lippmann had found his soulmate, and it was not Faye. It was Helen Byrne Armstrong, the wife of one of Lippmann's closest friends and biggest fans, Hamilton Fish Armstrong, the editor of *Foreign Affairs*. Walter and Helen's romance began in the spring of 1937, conducted mainly through love letters. It was quickly found out by one of Hamilton's secretaries. They asked their partners for a divorce, and the two married in early 1938. Lippmann told Helen that his marriage had been "a failure from the very start" and that Faye was a "coward about life." In her deposition, which was quoted by the Associated Press, Faye described Walter as "a facile veteran in the use of invective and development of criticism, a phase of his equipment that he constantly uses in administering verbal punishment upon complainant." There is no reason to doubt her assessment.[35]

"Fish" dropped Lippmann from his roster of contributors, not allowing him even to be mentioned in *Foreign Affairs* for thirty years. Lippmann gave up his seat at the CFR roundtable to not add insult to his friend's injury. He also gave Faye everything she wanted in the divorce, including most of their friends. The entire episode was an unusually brash move for Lippmann, as it promised to draw unwanted scrutiny and to threaten his precarious status as a Jewish public intellectual. But Lippmann did not care since Helen's love and admiration made him happier than he had ever been. It restored what he called his "juice for life." Thanks to her, "I have something to say not merely to the minds but to the hearts of a few in this generation and perhaps to more in another."[36]

Lippmann also had to thank God, or at least his theological studies, for his ego boost. Ironically, Lippmann married the ex-Catholic Helen at a time when his affiliation with Christianity and especially Catholicism was peaking. His interest in Niebuhr notwithstanding, Lippmann remained cordially indifferent to the FCC's "fluffy" social gospel. He had started reading more into religions and philosophy in preparation for *A Preface to Morals*. His compulsion to write a sequel had bent him even further toward the "classical and Christian heritage" and further way from Judaism, as he told Helen. Lippmann's latest muses included the *Catholic Encyclopedia* but also *L'esprit de la philosophie médiévale* (1932) by Neo-Thomist philosopher Etienne Gilson. Gilson's innovative nostalgia for the Middle Ages was exactly what Lippmann sensed was needed to counter the wasting away of Western values. Still, Lippmann preferred to see older-times religions through the lens of spiritual cosmopolitans like Madison and Hamilton. The incurable eclectic was discovering the personal and professional benefits of thinking within a tradition, even if he refused to swear allegiance to one.[37]

Lippmann's first attempt to devise a "central" Western tradition as a solution to *A Preface to Morals* was entitled "The Image of Man." It was a cosmic version of the younger Lippmann's belief that liberal democracies were disintegrating because they had banked on a false conception of human nature. Here, Lippmann endorsed "classical" anthropologies over "secular" ones like Dewey's experimentalism and Croly's "Religion of Humanity." He testified, "I do not believe there is more than one ideal of civilization." Gilson and others had taught him that free persons and societies depended upon submission to a "superhuman" or "ultimate principle of order" such as had been found among the Greeks, Romans, and Christians. Lippmann once again ignored Jewish influences.

Lippmann's affiliation with Christianity proceeded as he decided (while touring Europe) that "a civilization must have a religion." Sounding more like Royce and Santayana than James, Lippmann proclaimed, "it is in God that mankind is bound together." He claimed that America's founders had understood the need for a humanism bigger than humanity, which is why they invested no "absolute sovereignty" in simple majorities. Lippmann wanted readers to follow the founders' example in conducting their private and public lives in conformity to "natural law" and the "universal moral order." Those words, like all the words in "The Image of Man," fell like bricks upon the Nietzschean Lippmann. As it turned out, his manuscript would never have any readers—he would only publish it in scattered parts—but it was essential to his older self's pragmatic conservativism. It was also a reminder of how theology and politics were forever intertwined in Lippmann.[38]

*

Amid the ruins of economic depression and the specter of another world war, Lippmann felt freer than he ever had—free to love and to be loved, free to believe and to be believed, and free to appear to renounce his Progressivism-House of Truth-*New Republic* liberal lineage. Lippmann had encouraged Roosevelt's dictatorial powers so long as he thought they would be temporary. When the Supreme Court struck down the NRA, Lippmann thought he had been wise to suspect governmental overreach. Through frequent trips and letters to the White House, Lippmann was sure he had impressed upon Roosevelt the need to listen to Republican concerns and freeze the national experiment. However, the NLRA and "court-packing" plan convinced Lippmann that the president was "recklessly reckless." Lippmann broke with the administration and began advising

Roosevelt's conservative Democratic (Byrd) and Republican (Alf Landon) opposition.[39]

Lippmann drafted a counter-New Deal "Declaration of Principles" to rally disillusioned Democrats. Lippmann's mistrust of bureaucracy had originated on the left before swinging to the right. It had first evidenced itself in Lippmann's bohemian fear of the "Servile State" and his Fabian socialism. He had also waged war on Prohibition for spreading of "the bureaucratic control of people's private affairs" as well as for the "degradation in the respect for law which always and everywhere throughout history has followed bureaucracy and meddlesomeness." Now, Lippmann argued that the political ideal of "monopolistic or quasi-monopolistic control"—instituted by New Era Republicans and extended by New Deal Democrats—could lead "only to the progressive impoverishment of the people and the destruction of their liberties." Concentrations of power in industry, agriculture, and labor inevitably produced an "excessively powerful government." To combat the "evils of bureaucracy" resulting from the "evils of private privilege," Lippmann called for legislative over executive authority, a graduated income tax, and "genuinely free bargains in the open market" through the removal of corporate "immunities and privileges."[40]

Lippmann's Principles were a pox on both parties. They were his stumbling further toward a Jamesian–Keynesian–Burkean third way of political economy. Lippmann hoped against hope that Roosevelt might become the next trustbuster. But he was not willing to wait to find out. In the throes of an affair and theological awakening, Lippmann expanded upon his Principles to explain how a listless Great Society might approximate *The Good Society* (1937). The book was not another "Preface," but it was an "Inquiry." What else could it be when claiming inspiration from Wallas, Keynes, and the soon-to-be leaders of libertarianism Ludwig von Mises and Friedrich von Hayek, author of the anti-statist manifesto, *The Road to Serfdom* (1944)? Perhaps that heterogeneity explains the confession which opened the work:

> For more than twenty years I found myself writing about critical events with no better guide to their meaning than the hastily improvised generalizations of a rather bewildered man. Many a time I have wanted to stop talking and find out what I really believed. For I should have

> liked to achieve again the untroubled certainty and the assured consistency which are vouchsafed to those who can whole-heartedly commit themselves to some one of the many schools of doctrine. But I was not able to find in any of the schools a working philosophy in which I could confidently come to rest.

Lippmann still desired to be a stand-apart Scholar for a world in jeopardy. *The Good Society* wedded Lippmann's post-Christian affirmations from "The Image of Man" with Helen's devotion, which he privately acknowledged "unfroze his spirit" and empowered him to write more boldly.[41]

Lippmann the public economist was reborn as an evangelist ready to go forth with a gospel of ordered liberty. Eight years earlier, he had doubted that eighteenth-century liberals had anything to say to an Einsteinian world. Now he admitted that Adam Smith had been right all along. *The Good Society* was an attack on parts of the New Deal yet also an autopsy of where and how liberalism had gone wrong. The problem, Lippmann decided, was not that liberalism had been tried and found wanting. It was instead that "liberals failed to develop the promise of liberalism." Westerners and especially Americans had to "find again the conviction of their forefathers that progress comes through emancipation from—not the restoration of—privilege, power, coercion, and authority."[42]

Lippmann decimated the notion that a free enterprise system of a free people could be "planned." His nuanced distinction between "Absolute" and "Free Collectivism" was gone. He instead sided with Mises and Hayek in condemnation of Soviet, Nazi, and Rooseveltian statism ("collectivism"). He also revisited James and Wallas, who reminded him that the ability to control reality diminishes the more complex our environments become. The one exception in which economies could be directed was in times of war, but that just betrayed the real problem. Collectivist states, even democratic ones, merged economic and military might, making civil and world wars more likely. It was smart analysis that anticipated later theorists like C. Wright Mills, the author of *The Power Elite* (1956). But for Lippmann the problem was spiritual: "Men find themselves in a troubled world where they no longer look confidently to God for the regulation of human affairs, where custom has ceased to guide and tradition to sanctify the accepted ways."[43]

Lippmann pleaded with the disenchanted masses to turn away from worship of the "Providential State" and join him in a "renascence of liberalism." This was not his father's liberalism, however. For all the talk of Adam Smith, Lippmann's recreation was closer to his work at the *New Republic* than it was to any laissez faire revival. Lippmann chastised "humane collectivists" like Lewis Mumford at the same time that he complained about corporations becoming "departments of the government."[44]

Lippmann's new liberalism called for economic decentralization and submission to a "common law" (he had been reading the British jurist Sir William Blackstone, too). By common law, Lippmann had something like an economic Bill of Rights in mind, but one that was elastic enough to provide for the "applying and perfecting [of] reciprocal relations" through adjudication. It was vague but not without precedent: The younger Lippmann had proposed a judicial process for affecting industrial democracy after World War I. To practice what he preached, Lippmann advised Roosevelt to prefer "more uniform legislation" to regulate industry in place of blessing the special interests of corporations and unions.[45]

The Good Society was a strange, unexpected book, but that did not excuse how badly critics stereotyped it. Older, wealthier friends like John W. and Norman P. Davis found it a necessary corrective to the New Deal. General readers described it as "defeatist" and a "liberal swansong." One reviewer dubbed Lippmann the "Pundit in a Penthouse." Another accused him of advocating a "liberalism of the right." Lippmann "preaches the futility of any attempt to deal with modern problems in their own terms and thereby rationalizes and blesses the status quo," charged still another. Pinchot lumped Lippmann in with Hamilton as perpetrators of "plutocratic fascism." The journalist John Flynn complained, "when that the poor banker and broker hath cried, Lippmann hath wept." Flynn and Pinchot became involved in the America First committee against U.S. intervention into World War II, a movement inclusive of anti-Semites and Nazi sympathizers. Flynn went on to become an apologist for the second Red Scare, siding against Lippmann.[46]

Lippmann's dalliance with Hayek lent credence to portrayals of Lippmann as a right-wing agent. Lippmann reached out to Hayek after drafting his manuscript, and the two quickly bonded over opposition to the "planned economy." Fearing that economic and intellectual suppression went hand in hand, the two began collaborating on an international think tank of anti-collectivist "genuine liberals." Their efforts became the Mont Pelerin Society, one of the makers of Milton Friedman and twentieth-century libertarianism. Their first meeting in August of 1938 in Paris, where the term "neoliberalism" was coined, was entitled the "Walter Lippmann Colloquium."[47]

The word "neoliberal" today has become shorthand for libertarian efforts to dismantle regulatory welfare states at home and abroad. Yet the only thing more diverse than neoliberalism at mid-century was Lippmann's own conservatism or liberalism or humanism or republicanism or socialism. Lippmann's invectives against "collectivism" and "planning" remained bounded by Keynesianism. Lippmann argued that public investments in education and poor relief, paid for by taxes on unearned income, were the "cultural equipment" necessary for a middling free society. More radically, Lippmann suggested that the "good life" depended upon the localized "deep associations" of a less mobile labor force. He also endorsed the massive federal infrastructure project, the Tennessee Valley Authority (TVA), as a "prototype" for government-controlled resource management. He never turned against all federal economic planning.[48]

In a "Today and Tomorrow" companion to his book, Lippmann presented a nightmare scenario of a Toynbee proletariat, bereft of savings and property, being "absorbed into a mass" and becoming "a frightened crowd ready for a master." He countered, "a resolute democracy should favor the dispersion of industry rather than its concentration, and it should favor the rise in as many communities as possible of different kinds of enterprise rather than a high degree of specialization on some one product." Better to value fraternity over Fordism, even if that meant having to use government to break up Great Societies. Lippmann never became active in Mont Pelerin, and he never forgave Hayek for not talking more about how big business could be just as destructive to individual liberty as big government. The author of *Public Opinion* was advocating for enlightened populism. "The only conceivable source of authority is the power of the people," Lippmann concluded, "and the only hope of good government is the progressive refinement of the popular will."[49]

*

On a theological level, it looked as if America's star skeptic had become one of its prominent pastors. Lippmann's most attentive interest group were American and European Catholics. Their affection for him had grown in direct proportion to Lippmann's budding romance with Christian heritages. Church leaders, too, believed that "refinement" of soul and society could only come through what Lippmann, in *The Good Society*, called "the higher law." Incorporating text from "The Image of Man," Lippmann described the higher law as a "prayer" handed down from the Stoics and Aristotle, to Aquinas and Roman Catholics, and on to America's founders. The higher law was "the denial that men may be arbitrary in human transactions." Stated positively, it was the insistence that all human beings are "inviolable persons" with an "immortal soul" and "inalienable essence." Lippmann had espoused makeshift humanism for years, but his tone was more plainly Christian now. National and world unrest had humbled him: "We are not so full of wisdom, and so comfortably masters of our fate, that we can afford summarily to reject the underlying conception upon which so many sages and saints and heroic leaders have based their hopes of a happily ordered existence."[50]

In his recent book, *Why Liberalism Failed* (2018), Catholic political scientist Patrick Deneen referenced Lippmann only once. But Deneen's argument—that liberalism had both derived from and destroyed the "classical and Christian" understanding of human nature to its detriment—belonged to the self-described "classical and Christian" Lippmann.

Lippmann had been loath to accept that humankind needed organized religions before and during *A Preface to Morals*, but no longer. He instead subsumed the Catholic argument that secularism and totalitarianism were inextricably linked. As he explained at the end of *The Good Society*,

> Collectivist regimes are always profoundly irreligious.... By the religious experience the humblest communicant is led into the presence of a power so much greater than his master's that the distinctions of this world are of little importance. So it is not an accident that the only open challenge to the totalitarian state has come from men of deep religious faith. For in their faith they are vindicated as immortal souls, and from this enchantment of their dignity they find the reason why they must offer a perpetual challenge to the dominion of men over men.

Lippmann never experienced any "power" apart from rapturous moments in art and nature. Nevertheless, in books and columns he offered a Christian-inflected anti-totalitarianism to the delight of church folk.[51]

The years 1938 to 1948 might be described as Lippmann's "Catholic phase," when his affiliation-minus-allegiance was at its strongest. The RBNS that had always inhabited him now wanted to overtake his SBNR persona. Bishop Fulton Sheen commended Lippmann for his "genuinely solid and spiritual outlook." Other Catholics, including the *Commonweal*, claimed Lippmann as one of their own. Rumors even circulated that Lippmann had converted. In support of such claims, Lippmann eulogized Pope Pius XI as the world's greatest defender of "the basic and universal faith of Western men" against the barbarians at the gates. Of course, Lippmann never did join the church—or any church, for that matter. Yet the Lippmann–Roman Catholic alliance helped each to verify their Americanisms. In adopting Christian diagnoses of civilizational decline, Lippmann positioned himself as a part of that tradition (rather than as a Jewish subordinate in Roosevelt's Protestant America).[52]

Lippmann's warnings about "spiritual proletarians"—his rebranding of Toynbee's "internal proletarians"—was a conservative exercise in creating an ingroup by casting an outgroup. The spiritual proletarians were the "masses without roots" and "crowds without convictions." They were city folk who were cut off from the "elemental experiences of life." Their "disbelief in the existence of a central tradition of human wisdom" meant that the spiritual proletarians were "the chaos in which the new Caesars are born."[53]

Perhaps milking cows and manuring fields was not next to godliness. Still, Lippmann was in good left-liberal company when he blamed "the privileges of the few" for the impoverished conditions that proletarians found themselves in. Lippmann and Catholic friends believed Christianity could be a source of more holistic thinking about the human condition. Waxing cosmic after a tour of the 1939 World's Fair, Lippmann concluded, "the variety of man's interests and talents, the endless ingenuity and courage of his enterprises, will surely distract and destroy mankind if men cannot find once again that sense of the universal in the particular, the allegiance to that which is catholic in that which is diverse, of which for more than two thousand years Rome has been the center and the symbol."[54]

Since 1776, however, Rome had resided in Washington D.C., not Italy. Lippmann found that the best way to Americanize Catholicism, and himself, was to Catholicize Americanism. That revisionist history was manifest in Lippmann's new celebration of the Bill of Rights as an expression of natural law, something "self-evident, inalienable, eternal, and universal." The renovation of the founders into divine doctors was not uncommon in American Catholic writings, but it was unusual for a Hamiltonian political realist like Lippmann to rely so much on Jeffersonian rhetoric. Lippmann blamed the "sophists," nineteenth-century philosophers and twentieth-century historians, for obscuring the founders' belief that "the rights of man were not Caesar's but the things of God."[55]

Lippmann was unclear on where Washington and company had learned that lesson, though. He bragged that faith in liberty as humankind's natural condition had come about "by means of a progressive revelation which began in the Mediterranean world. On this revelation of man our civilization was founded. This revelation was the central belief of the enduring religion; it is the argument of the perennial philosophy; it is the beginning and the end of the developing science; it is the subject matter of the expressive arts; and it is the major premise of the laws and institutions of the civilized world." Lippmann did not mean by "revelation" and "religion" what his Catholic and Protestant subscribers did. No amount of inspirational words uttered in public could compensate for his private skepticism toward systematized spirituality. At the same time, his RBNS side asserted itself in ways that spotlighted Catholic perspectives on national and world order.[56]

Protestants never lost interest in Lippmann, though, nor he in them. The two reconnected in 1939 after the publication of Lippmann's column, "The Reconstruction of the Democratic Philosophy." Appearing to forget all his editorializing against Fundamentalist political religion during the 1920s, Lippmann endorsed a Roosevelt speech claiming that Christianity was foundational to democratic government. "Freedom, nationalism and religion are so inseparable in our civilization that when they are separated, each in itself becomes destructive and reactionary," Lippmann wrote. Totalitarianism was a spiritual threat against societies that had once been rooted in the conviction that persons were "made in the image of God." The older

Lippmann had came to believe that secularists were more dangerous than communists and fascists in juxtaposing church and state. Instead, a lost liberal generation should follow the president in rediscovery of "religion as the source of democracy."[57]

Given his several diatribes about civil religions and other forms of ideology, it is easy to imagine the younger Lippmann standing aghast at his new Christian American self. Or, better, post-Christian American self. Lippmann's desire for a MORE from life—to resolve issues of personal identity, professional advancement, and public harmony—did not stem from any kind of theological certitude or commitment. Lippmann never ceased to doubt, even when he embraced civil religion half-wholeheartedly during the 1950s. His ecumenical Protestant fans did not care, for appearances could be as useful as the real thing. One FCC founder, Charles Stelzle, encouraged Lippmann to keep pushing the social value of religion and offered to have the FCC reprint his column. Lippmann was aiding in the "spiritual rehabilitation" of the nation, another pastor responded, which would lead to "economic stability."[58]

*

Finding stability was always paramount for Lippmann. Somehow, he had followed his heart in reckless abandon, and had groused about the tyranny of his own strong-state liberalism, all the while preserving a regimented daily schedule, attended to by multiple women and filled with meetings with powerful men. The Lippmanns' removal from New York to Washington, D.C., following their divorces cut them off from the Lamonts. Yet their fall from grace brought them among the Dulles and Kennedy dynasties. The couple would enjoy an influence and renown unprecedented for an editorialist, especially a Jewish one. Walter would cultivate attachments to white male state actors as never before. Meanwhile, he continued to ignore professional women, even those in his immediate spheres of influence. Lippmann's research associate, Frances van Schaik, read and organized books and articles for him. She also conducted interviews and attended press briefings on his behalf. Only rarely did Lippmann admit that his success was a team effort rooted in the exploitation of female office spaces.[59]

Beset by threats to his republic at home, at work, on the streets, and abroad, the older Lippmann fixated on the need for "order" in the face of mounting "disorder." The real "New Order" on earth did not belong to "unregenerate" Nazis, he announced. It had appeared two thousand years ago in the recognition of "the higher law" of "man's dignity." It had been advanced by and through what Lippmann called "Christendom." Christendom would remain an ill-defined abstraction in Lippmann's writings throughout World War II—but the slipperier, the better, for the chameleon Lippmann. The United States, composed of "the same rules of public law and the same system of public morals" as the earlier Christendom, was now the world's greatest representative of that transhistorical order. There was no reason to fear alien subversion. "Did Christendom become Mohammedan after it had fought the Moslems right up to the gates of Vienna," Lippmann asked? Instead, the true enemies of a civilization were "decay, demoralization, and disbelief." In do-it-yourself Christianity, Lippmann found a cultural politics that matched his personal and social life.[60]

But what made Lippmann a conservative after Burke and Toynbee and not Buckley and Goldwater was his insistence that humankind's "disposition to evil" and "slumbering barbarism"—its original sin—was innate and not external to any people. Human beings had a nature, and it was not all good. As the crisis of national depression became the calamity of world war, Lippmann remembered the personal and domestic sources of international anarchy. The will to power had to be balanced by a will to self-control, and that necessitated a revival of Christian humanism. Lippmann began to sound like a highbrow Christian nationalist while, in truth, he was one of their harshest critics.[61]

Notes

1. "Walter Lippmann at 83," C4. See also Ronald Steel, "Walter Lippmann: An Interview with Ronald Steel," *New Republic*, Apr. 14, 1973, 16–17.
2. Lippmann, *Interpretations, 1931–1932*, 329. On Lippmann as a pragmatic Burkean conservative, see Robert J. Lacey, *Pragmatic Conservativism: Edmund Burke and His American Heirs* (New York: Palgrave Macmillan, 2016).
3. Wellborn, *Twentieth Century Pilgrimage*, 56. See Walter Lippmann, to Graham Wallas, June 24, 1930, on the sequel to *A Preface to Morals*.
4. See Ira Katznelson, *Fear Itself: The New Deal and the Origins of Our Time* (New York: Liverlight, 2014).

The Evangelist, 1930–1939

5. See Steel, *Walter Lippmann*, 269–82, on Lippmann's transition to the *Herald Tribune*. On his salary and rankings, see Weingast, *Walter Lippmann*, 32.
6. Walter Lippmann, to Felix Frankfurter, Apr. 5, 1932, in WLP, Reel 61. On Pinchot's critiques, see John Mason Brown, *Through These Men: Some Aspects of Our Passing History* (New York: Harper and Brothers, 1952), 218.
7. Craufurd D. Goodwin, *Walter Lippmann: Public Economist* (Cambridge: Harvard University Press, 2014). On Lippmann's plagiarism and defense, see Weingast, *Walter Lippmann*, 26; and Forcey, *Crossroads of Liberalism*, 55. For "goes cosmic," see Frank Kent, quoted in Weingast, *Walter Lippmann*, 29.
8. Walter Lippmann, "The Scholar in a Troubled World," *Atlantic Monthly* 150 (1932), in *Essential Lippmann*, ed. Rossiter and Lare, 509–16.
9. Walter Lippmann, "Today and Tomorrow: The False Gods," *New York Herald Tribune*, May 20, 1932, in *Essential Lippmann*, ed. Rossiter and Lare, 466–8. On "soft living," see Walter Lippmann, "Today and Tomorrow: Reflections on the Public Nerves," *New York Herald Tribune*, Jan. 1, 1932, in *Essential Lippmann*, ed. Rossiter and Lare, 124. On "greed" and "demoralization," see Lippmann, *Interpretations, 1931–1932*, 14, 26–7, 241–2, 247–8, 327. On "tired," see Walter Lippmann, "Today and Tomorrow: The New Congress," *New York Herald Tribune*, Dec. 8, 1931, in *Essential Lippmann*, ed. Rossiter and Lare, 122.
10. Walter Lippmann, "Free Time and Extra Money," *Women's Home Companion* 57 (April 1930), in *Essential Lippmann*, ed. Rossiter and Lare, 440.
11. Walter Lippmann, to Felix Frankfurter, Mar. 4, 1927, in *Public Philosopher*, ed. Blum, 200; Walter Lippmann, "Today and Tomorrow: Ice-Cold Evil," *Washington Post*, Oct. 30, 1941, 13.
12. Walter Lippmann, to Bernard Berenson, Mar. 23, 1935, in *Public Philosopher*, ed. Blum, 326.
13. Walter Lippmann, "Loud-Mouthed Barbarians: The Passionate Unreasonableness of Mankind," *Vital Speeches of the Day* 3 (July 1937): 587–9. On "craving," see Walter Lippmann, "Today and Tomorrow: Crazy as a Bedbug," *New York Herald Tribune*, July 3, 1937, 13.
14. Walter Lippmann, "Autocracy versus Catholicism," *Commonweal*, Apr. 13, 1927, 627. On Lippmann's article and the origins of "totalitarianism," see K. Healan Gaston, *Imagining Judeo-Christian America: Religion, Secularism and the Redefinition of Democracy* (Chicago: University of Chicago Press, 2019), 79.
15. Walter Lippmann, "Today and Tomorrow: Hitler's Speech," *New York Herald Tribune*, May 19, 1933, 19. For a more typical Lippmann essay on Hitler, including the "terrorism" charge, see Walter Lippmann, "Today and Tomorrow: Ghosts of the Past," *New York Herald Tribune*, May 31, 1933, 15. For "barbarized," see Lippmann, *Interpretations, 1933–1935*, 326.
16. Walter Lippmann, "Interview," 166–7. Lippmann had once written to Frankfurter, "Faye knows all about you, what friends we are, and we'll make it a threesome." See Walter Lippmann, to Felix Frankfurter, Apr. 23, 1917, in WLP.

17. On Baker as president, see Walter Lippmann, to James Angell, Dec. 23, 1937, in WLP, Reel 42. See Walter Lippmann, to Newton Baker, July 29, 1932, in WLP, Reel 44, for "weaseling mind." On "boy scout," see Walter Lippmann, to Newton Baker, Nov. 24, 1931, in *Public Philosopher*, ed. Blum, 280–1. Lippmann's meeting with Roosevelt was described in a private letter from Lippmann to Steel. See Steel, *Walter Lippmann*, 300, 618.

18. See Lippmann, *Interpretations, 1933–1935*, for a collection of his "Today and Tomorrow" columns regarding federal authority (2–10) and about Roosevelt (249–95). On Hoover, see Walter Lippmann, *The Method of Freedom* New York: Macmillan, 1934), 32; Walter Lippmann, *The New Imperative* (New York: Macmillan), 13–27; and especially Walter Lippmann, "Today and Tomorrow: The Dream of Troubled Spirits," Jan. 20, 1949, in *Essential Lippmann*, ed. Rossiter and Lare, 341–3. See also Leonard Dinnerstein, "Jews and the New Deal," *American Jewish History* 72 (June 1983): 461–76.

19. Franklin Roosevelt, quoted in Gerstle, *American Crucible*, 185. T. S. Eliot, *After Strange Gods: A Primer of Modern Heresy* (London: Faber and Faber, 1934), Preface.

20. Newton Baker, to Walter Lippmann, Sept. 17, 1931; Walter Lippmann, to Newton Baker, Sept. 21, 1931, both in WLP, Reel 44. See Walter Lippmann, to Hans Morgenthau, Apr. 24, 1955, in WLP, Reel 81, on "excuse."

21. 'Walter Lippmann, "The Moral Isolation of America," *World*, July 29, 1926, 12; Walter Lippmann, "Today and Tomorrow: The Problem of the Refugees," *New York Herald Tribune*, Nov. 17, 1938, 21; Walter Lippmann, "Today and Tomorrow: On Opening up a New World," Nov. 24, 1938, 25.

22. Joseph Kraft, "Lippmann: Yesterday, Today, Tomorrow," *Washington Post*, Sept. 11, 1980, A19.

23. See Walter Lippmann, to John P. Davis, July 1, 1933, in WLP, Reel 56, for his misgivings about government management of the economy. On "popular standard," see Lippmann, *New Imperative*, 1–3, 8–37; Lippmann, *Method of Freedom*, 1–36. For "strong medicine," see Lippmann, *Interpretations, 1933–1935*, 6.

24. On "laissez-faire is dead," see Lippmann, *Method of Freedom*, 37–8. On "alien stereotypes" and "ancient despotism," see Lippmann, *New Imperative*, 4–7; and Walter Lippmann, "Today and Tomorrow: Watchman, What of the Night?" *New York Herald Tribune*, Jan. 1, 1935, 23.

25. For the statistics on Lippmann's New Deal columns, see Weingast, *Walter Lippmann*, 61, 73, 76. On the NRA, see Lippmann, *Interpretations, 1933–1935*, 98–9 (89–125 more generally).

26. For local over federal relief, see Lippmann, *Interpretations, 1931–1932*, 140–3. See Lippmann, *Interpretations, 1933–1935*, 248; and Lippmann, *Method of Freedom*, 106, on Lippmann's problem with direct assistance.

27. Walter Lippmann, "Today and Tomorrow: On This Rock," *New York Herald Tribune*, December 10, 1935, in *Essential Lippmann*, ed. Rossiter and Lare, 220–2.
28. On the Great Depression as a spiritual problem, see, for one example, Lippmann, *New Imperative*, 38–42.
29. See Lippmann, "Interview," 152–5, on "friendship." For "ardent Keynesian," see Walter Lippmann, to John Kenneth Galbraith, Dec. 23, 1965, in WLP, Reel 63. On the NRA, see Walter Lippmann, to John Maynard Keynes, Apr. 17, 1934, in WLP, Reel 71. See Steel, *Walter Lippmann*, 306–7, on the American Embassy meeting.
30. Walter Lippmann, to Henry Steel Commager, May 31, 1947, in WLP, Reel 53. On "Compensated Economy" and "Free Collectivism," see Lippmann, *Method of Freedom*, 38. See Lippmann, *Interpretations, 1933–1935*, 269–70, for the "free enterprise" quotation. On Roosevelt following Keynes, see Walter Lippmann, to John Maynard Keynes, Jan. 9, 1936, in WLP, Reel 71. For Lippmann's thoughts on public works, see Lippmann, *Method of Freedom*, 106–10; Lippmann, *Interpretations, 1931–1932*, 79–82; and Lippmann, *Interpretations, 1933–1935*, 228–48. On "middle condition," see Lippmann, *Method of Freedom*, 91–112.
31. John Maynard Keynes, "Burke's Timidity on Embarking on War," unpublished ms., 1906, quoted in "Keynes on Burke," https://www.theatlantic.com/daily-dish/archive/2007/02/keynes-on-burke/231119/ (last accessed 10/28/20).
32. Walter Lippmann, to Newton Baker, June 13, 1934, in WLP, Reel 44.
33. For a sample of Lippmann's editorials on the Wagner Act, see Walter Lippmann, "Today and Tomorrow: Sailing under False Colors," *New York Herald Tribune*, May 5, 1938, 21A; and Lippmann, *Interpretations, 1933–1935*, 126–54. On "farm-labor," see Walter Lippmann, "The Reaction against the C. I. O.," *New York Herald Tribune*, July 1, 1937, 23.
34. See Lippmann, *Method of Freedom*, 91–2, for an example of his Madisonianism.
35. On Lippmann's affair and marriage to Helen, see Steel, *Walter Lippmann*, 342–66 (quotations taken from 265–66 and 359). Steel's narrative draws upon personal conversations with Helen.
36. Lippmann, quoted in Steel, *Walter Lippmann*, 357.
37. On "fluffy," see Walter Lippmann, to Hamilton Fish Armstrong, Apr. 4, 1935, in WLP, Reel 42. On Gilson's influence on Lippmann, see Walter Lippmann, "The Image of Man," Unpublished Manuscript, n.d. (circa 1930s), 34, 117–25, in WLP, Box 221, Folder 317.
38. Lippmann, "Image of Man," 18–20, 43, 90–2, 112–13, 123, Part III 3; Lippmann, "Men and Ideas."
39. Lippmann, "Interview," 167–8.
40. Walter Lippmann, "Mrs. Asquith on Prohibition," *World*, Mar. 7, 1922, 10; Walter Lippmann, to Lewis Douglas, Apr. 16, 1936, in *Public Philosopher*, ed. Blum, 348–50.

41. Walter Lippmann, *An Inquiry into the Principles of the Good Society* (Boston: Little, Brown, 1937), vii–xi. Lippmann's book was called *The Good Society* for short. On Helen's impact on Lippmann's writing, see Walter Lippmann, quoted in Steel, *Walter Lippmann*, 35.
42. Lippmann, *Good Society*, xi-xiii, 201–2.
43. Lippmann, *Good Society*, 23, 35, 90–130, 176, 198.
44. Lippmann, *Good Society*, 6, 52, 207, 217, 260–6, 289.
45. Lippmann, *Good Society*, 260–6, 289; Walter Lippmann, "Can the Strike Be Abandoned," *New Republic*, Jan. 21, 1920, in *Force and Ideas*, ed. Schlesinger, 224–32. See Lippmann, "Image of Man," 34, for his reading of Blackstone. For "uniform legislation," see Walter Lippmann, to Franklin Roosevelt, Jan. 6, 1937, in WLP, Reel 88.
46. Walter Lippmann, to John P. Davis, Oct. 22, 1937, in WLP, Reel 56; Norman P. Davis, to Walter Lippmann, Aug. 10, 1937, in WLP, Reel 56. On "defeatist," see Charles Elcock, to Walter Lippmann, Nov. 3, 1938, in WLP, Reel 127. On "swansong," see Ed Dokin, to Walter Lippmann, Nov. 3, 1938, in WLP, Reel 127. On the published criticism of Lippmann and his book, see Weingast, *Walter Lippmann*, 112–16.
47. Walter Lippmann, to Friedrich von Hayek, Mar. 12, 1937; Friedrich von Hayek, to Walter Lippmann, Apr. 6, 1937; Walter Lippmann, to Friedrich von Hayek, Apr. 9, 1937; Friedrich von Hayek, to Walter Lippmann, Nov. 12, 1937; all in WLP, Reel 66. On the Lippmann Colloquium and Mont Pelerin Society, see Angus Bergin, *The Great Persuasion: Reinventing Free Markets since the Depression* (Cambridge: Harvard University Press, 2015).
48. Lippmann, *Good Society*, 214, 223–30, 236. On Lippmann's criticism of Hayek, see Walter Lippmann, to Friedrich von Hayek, Dec. 5, 1960, in WLP, Reel 66. On TVA, see Walter Lippmann, "Today and Tomorrow: The Trouble in the T.V.A.," *New York Herald Tribune*, Mar. 8, 1938, 19A.
49. Walter Lippmann, Today and Tomorrow: How Liberty is Lost," July 16, 1938, in *Essential Lippmann*, ed. Rossiter and Lare, 43–5; Lippmann, *Good Society*, 260.
50. Lippmann, *Good Society*, 334–51, 337, 372–8.
51. Lippmann, *Good Society*, 382. See also Gaston, *Inventing Judeo-Christian America*.
52. Walter Lippmann, "Today and Tomorrow: Pius Xi," *New York Herald Tribune*, Feb. 11, 1939, 15. On Catholic support for Lippmann, see Fulton Sheen, to Walter Lippmann June 10, 1939, in WLP, Reel 91; F. A. Mulesky, to Walter Lippmann, Dec. 7, 1938, in WLP, Reel 127; and Louis J. A. Mercier, "Walter Lippmann's Evolution," *Commonweal*, Aug. 4, 1939, 348–50. On rumors about Lippmann's conversion, see Wellborn, *Twentieth Century Pilgrimage*, 134.
53. Walter Lippmann, "Today and Tomorrow: The Modern Malady," *New York Herald Tribune*, Nov. 3, 1938, 21.

54. Walter Lippmann, "Today and Tomorrow: A Day at the World's Fair," *New York Herald Tribune*, June 6, 1939, 25A.
55. Walter Lippmann, "Today and Tomorrow: The Bill of Rights," *New York Herald Tribune*, Dec. 14, 1939, 25.
56. Lippmann, "Bill of Rights," 25.
57. Walter Lippmann, "Today and Tomorrow: The Reconstruction of the Democratic Philosophy," *New York Herald Tribune*, Jan. 7, 1939, 13.
58. Charles Stelzle, to Walter Lippmann, Jan. 10, 1939; and M. Wright Conant, to Walter Lippmann, Jan. 10, 1939, both in WLP, Reel 127.
59. On Schaik, see Steel, *Walter Lippmann*, 499–500, which was probably based on interviews with Walter and Helen (Steel does not offer sources for this information).
60. Walter Lippmann, "Today and Tomorrow: On a New Order in the World," *New York Herald Tribune*, Oct. 10, 1940, 23; Walter Lippmann, "Today and Tomorrow: Our Order and Their Disorder," *New York Herald Tribune*, Nov. 26, 1940, 21; Walter Lippmann, "Today and Tomorrow: The Quick Predictors," *Washington Post*, Dec. 23, 1939, 11.
61. Walter Lippmann, "Today and Tomorrow: The Pair of Winged Horses and the Charioteer," *New York Herald Tribune*, Nov. 15, 1938, 25A.

5
The Prophet, 1939–1949

Reading Lippmann's "Today and Tomorrow" columns in the 1940s, it was sometimes easy to forget that the world was not quite ending. Liberalism's Moses had been to the mountaintop and was returning with a message of fear before hope: Western society was in decline, and Lippmann (quoting Toynbee) said it was "not murder but suicide." Americans and Europeans had turned their backs on the "great tradition" derived from "Roman law and Christian order." To save themselves, they had to reject the fascist doctrine that human beings were hapless victims of impersonal forces. Thirty years earlier, Lippmann had boasted that the "Christian dream" was dead. Now, he insisted that "the inviolability of the human soul, or in the ancient language of faith, the fatherhood of God" was real. There was an "indestructible essence" in man "by which he can by repentance and reparation redeem himself."[1]

Lippmann's post-Christianity flourished amid global destruction. His growing affiliation with Christianity served his entangled aims of assimilation into an anti-Semitic society, protection of white male positionality, and promotion of republican civility within a mass democracy. Speaking before the American Catholic Philosophical Association, Lippmann charted the downward spiral from "modern man" to "secular man" and onward to "unhappy man." The "dangerous man" of totalitarianism would not be far behind. Lippmann's speech was an act of contrition for having valorized the detached "mature man" ten years earlier. Again citing Toynbee, Lippmann reiterated the threat posed by the "horde of beings without autonomy, of individuals uprooted and so isolated and disordered that they surrender their judgment and their freedom to the master of the horde." Only the "classical and traditional conception of human nature," espoused by Plato and Aquinas, could mollify the muddled soul and enable genuine fraternity. "As perfected in the religious tradition of the West," Lippmann reported, "the good life is an imitation of God—that is to say, the cultivation of the reason, which is an imitation of His omniscience, and of the only true freedom—the freedom to follow the dictates of reason—which is an imitation of His omniscience." No wonder that so many of Lippmann's readers believed (wrongly) that he had built a new home in an old faith.[2]

Lippmann had trafficked heavily in the Christian revivalist discourses of trans-Atlantic public intellectuals after detailing *The Good Society*. This era saw the publication of T. S. Eliot's *The Idea of a Christian Society* (1939) and the French Catholic Jacques Maritain's *Integral Humanism* (1936) which called for the establishment of a "new Christendom." The cultured social gospel of an Eliot, Maritain, and their ecumenical communities diverged significantly from the well-oiled, richly funded Christian libertarianism led by Billy Graham. The latter were littering the country with projects to restore "One Nation Under God," not the New Deal. Still, most liberal and conservative Christians coincided in promotion of "Judeo-Christian" nationalism. In realization of Albion Small's American Religion, Catholics, Protestants, and Jews were asked to come together to defend the "American Way of Life" against any number of outgroups.[3]

Lippmann's religious tongues aside, he never became a Christian nationalist. He did not use the term "Judeo-Christian" and only rarely said anything nice about Judaism—although many of his readers no doubt felt reassured in their tri-faith civil religiosity. Lippmann complained, in more general terms, that the interwar years had been "the most un-American period in the history of our nation." At his thirty-year Harvard reunion, he claimed that "Western civilization" was dissolving because its peoples had chosen the "easy way" of existence. Lippmann continued to roast the "fat" abundance of the "jitterbug age." The "organized mechanized evil loose in the world," he charged, was the result of "the lazy, self-indulgent materialism, the amiable, lackadaisical, footless, confused complacency of the free nations of the world." His solution recalled his rough-riding hero Roosevelt: "We shall turn from the soft vices in which a civilization decays, we shall return to the stern virtues by which a civilization is made, we shall do this because, at long last, we know that we must, because finally we begin to see that the hard way is the only enduring way." The younger Nietzschean Lippmann would have found much to agree with in that statement. The older Burkean Lippmann's message that a "free society" required "ancient faith" in a "greater community" of honor would have been more disturbing.[4]

Lippmann believed that educational reform was vital to the moral renewal of American democracy. He repented of "progressive education," confiding to Roosevelt, Jr., that pragmatism was a "dangerous disease" that had produced the "unrestrained materialism" of the 1920s and the "grandmotherliness" of the New Deal. As Lippmann explained to a group of scientists, "a society can be progressive only if it conserves its traditions."[5]

In attacking "modern education" for destroying Western civility, Lippmann suppressed his earlier commitments to scientific democracy. He emphasized instead the manufacture of consent:

> There is an enormous vacuum where until a few years ago there was the substance of education. And with what is that vacuum filled: it is filled with the elective, eclectic, the specialized, the accidental and incidental improvisations and spontaneous curiosities of teachers and students. There is no common faith, no common body of principle, no common body of knowledge, no common moral and intellectual discipline.... When one realizes that [students] have no common culture, is it astounding that they have no common purpose? That they worship false gods? That only in war do they unite? That in the fierce struggle for existence they are tearing Western society to pieces?

Lippmann called for a return to classical liberal arts education inclusive of Graeco-Roman and Christian subject matter. He commended a Catholic form of the "Great Books" program for reinstating loyalty to a "great central tradition." By recovering the "great inheritance" or "revelation" of truth, goodness, justice, and sacrifice—the "virtuous habits" of the early American republic—modern man could subdue "the jungle around him and the barbarian within him." For his part, Lippmann kept trying to tame his "Image of Man" manuscript. That would pay off in the 1950s when Lippmann, a veteran opponent of civil religions, published his own public philosophy.[6]

Lippmann's complicated relationship with Jewish and Christian traditions should be obvious by now. His younger self had indulged in freedom from religions, especially the political ones. Yet he had long held that skepticism—his own and his generation's—was destructive of social order. Modern man had to be, but could not afford to be, a None, as he had outlined in *A Preface to Morals*. From the mid-1930s throughout the Cold War, Lippmann followed a road well-traveled by other ex-secularist celebrity thinkers toward the re-enchantment of the West. Yet Lippmann remained a post-Christian thinker of both the SBNR and RBNS types, never committing privately to the theologies he endorsed publicly. Lippmann relocated convictions about large, interdependent nation-states ("Great Societies") needing a common culture or "religion" to the forefront of his media persona. He clung to an innovative Jamesian skepticism all the same.

Unsurprisingly, Lippmann's books, essays, and editorials were devoted to war and peace after 1942. He was well situated to address the topic, as he and Helen had moved to Georgetown in 1938 to escape their marital scandal and to enjoy leisurely walks with their first loves, their prize-winning poodles. The newlyweds frequented the company of Washington's power elite. Walter's social, symbolic, and literal capital skyrocketed. The Lippmanns also traveled through England and France in the summer of 1939 conducting interviews about the coming conflagration. Walter did not take on a formal wartime position as he had during World War I, but he still played an important supervisory role around the beltway. Helen would be at his side the entire time—assisting him, promoting him, protecting him.

We must continue to read Lippmann's writings on foreign affairs as public theologies, however. Like his earlier work on politics and economics, his brinkmanship was informed by the prophetic and pastoral columns discussed at the outset of this chapter. Though Lippmann seemed to trade in his earlier Wilsonianism for tough-minded realism, it was truer to say that Lippmann modeled the Christian Wilsonian as realist and the realist as Christian Wilsonian. Lippmann's eclecticism made it easier for friends and foes to dismiss his several sacred texts as passing fancies rather than to see them for what they were: More "prefaces" in one pilgrim's progress toward the satisfaction of the good self and society.

*

Lippmann had been reflecting on world affairs since 1914, often in line with East Coast white male elite opinion (the so-called "American

Establishment"). At the end of *The Stakes of Diplomacy*, Lippmann had juxtaposed the "true internationalist" with the "unreasoning patriot." The former "preserves his country in trust for that greater state which will embrace civilization. He regards his allegiance as a stewardship." Educated in the realism of Roosevelt and Mahan, with its emphasis on balances of power between great states, Lippmann in 1919 had not been ready for the United States to ensure collective security through the League of Nations. At the same time, Lippmann had been a Wilsonian committed to the "peaceful penetration" of foreign markets.[7]

During the 1920s, Lippmann had invited "unconscious" Americans to own up to their imperial status. Given his early advocacy of a good neighbor policy toward Mexico and South America, the pro-empire contours of Lippmann's thought were often overlooked. Dominance of the Caribbean alone meant that the United States was no longer a "virginal republic in a wicked world" but instead an unprecedented "world power." Empire denial left the administration of American expansion to businessmen and inept politicians. Better for the country to accept its share of responsibility in the "civilizing work" of "backward" peoples. That had been the unofficial policy of the CFR, where Lippmann had aided its research initiatives and drafted its *The United States in World Affairs* books (1932, 1933). Lippmann had only reluctantly endorsed the Washington disarmament conferences and the "Outlawry of War" movement. Truer to form, he had decried America's "kid-glove diplomacy," encouraging stronger executive leadership dedicated to the resolution of European disorders. The United States could do empire better than any nation before it—it was "one of the possible destinies of Western civilization." Lippmann associated the "America First" movement with the KKK and lamented all the "bedazzled suckers" who followed them.[8]

Lippmann had acquiesced to America's isolationist turn during the 1930s more than actively supporting it. As he had told Armstrong in 1935 (when they were still friends), the only way to achieve peace through collective security was the Wilsonian way of stimulating global economic interdependence. Yet by that time he had also despaired of the Democratic party's will-to-internationalism. Public opinion was against sane measures like ending American neutrality and canceling Europe's war debts, Lippmann had told Norman Davis, soon to be the CFR's president. Thus Lippmann had announced publicly—and privately to Roosevelt's Secretary of State Cordell Hull—that a "direct intervention in Europe is impossible, would be ineffective and would be undesirable." He maintained that position even as Hitler's ambitions became manifest.[9]

The imperative for the United States was "disentanglement," Lippmann said. Disentanglement was an isolationist mantra recalling Jefferson's and Washington's "no entangling alliances" counsel. Lippmann would return to it repeatedly in the years ahead. Still, he hoped that the American Great Society, once resettled securely upon a Keynesian hill, might "exercise some moral authority" regarding human rights and international law. He looked forward to a "European Union" or "United States of Europe" founded upon a Hamiltonian ideal of economic over racial-cultural integration.[10]

Lippmann's trust in the resilience of the West had also come with a warning of a global race-class war. Clearly the world's protectionist response to the Great Depression proved that there would be no "steady and predestined advance toward a universal civilization" such as nineteenth-century intellectuals, missionaries, and politicians had dreamed of. Instead, those Western Christian imperialists had "awakened" the "masses" of the Near and Far East, along with the American and European working classes, out of their "docility" and "ancient lethargy." The rising Majority World were not the "grateful receivers of blessings provided." They were "active, clamorous, contentious men insisting upon their own notions of their own just deserts." The older Lippmann expressed little sympathy for peoples who were desiring a greater piece of the Fordist pie. He had started "othering" in earnest—finding "barbarians" hiding everywhere—during the Great Depression. He continued to do so for the purposes of lowering his readers' expectations for world peace. Americans needed to rid themselves of the "illusion that the great masses of men could enter into civilization quietly, without first going through the immense, the catastrophic, agitation of their own awakening, that a world-wide civilization could come into being without the labor pains of so great a birth."[11]

World War II fulfilled Lippmann's prophecy. He saw the moment as pregnant with possibilities for a new national and world order. By 1938, Lippmann was already telling friends that the United States needed to confront the fascist threat with "overwhelming superior force." He was advising Washington to "prepare totally for war" against totalitarian states. It should therefore be no surprise that Lippmann joined CFR associates in 1939 in advancing the interventionist cause against America First isolationists. Lippmann was an early advocate for repealing the country's neutrality laws, arguing that aid to England and France would "keep Americans 3,000 miles from the war and keep the war 3,000 miles from Americans." He also met behind the scenes with New York's finest in the Century Club, a standing dinner party of white men in support of U.S. intervention. Lippmann's greatest contribution to the Club was his convincing of legendary General John Pershing to give a speech on behalf of the defense of Great Britain. Pershing's speech (which Lippmann helped write) swayed public opinion in favor of Roosevelt's "destroyers for bases" deal with Prime Minister Winston Churchill and then the "lend-lease" program which ended neutrality. Lippmann still criticized Roosevelt's weakness on foreign affairs and preferred his Republican rival Wendell Willkie until the Japanese attack on Pearl Harbor.[12]

Lippmann's most significant publication during the intervention debate was written before Hitler's invasion of Poland. Assuming the role of national therapist in Henry Luce's *Life* magazine, Lippmann diagnosed that his countrymen were suffering from a serious case of denial. Americans were pretending like they were not the "controlling power" of "Western civilization." They were reactionary, fearful, and defensive when they should have been bold, decisive, and enterprising. American Destiny, Lippmann explained, was the same that Rome had assumed in the ancient world and Great Britain in the modern one: To be the center, model, and enforcer of a planetary civilization. This was the older Roosevelt's strenuous life ideal yet updated to a global scale. Lippmann believed that the American people were ready to exchange their "indecision" for "confidence"—although he had no clue that it would take a fifty-year war to bring it about. Luce stole much of Lippmann's article and renamed it "The American Century." Lippmann, however, was always closer to Vice-President Henry Wallace's "The Century of the Common Man" (1942), in which the fellow agnostic argued that it was America's Christian responsibility to modernize the Majority World in a post-colonial way.[13]

Lippmann's destiny as a tough-minded prophet came to fruition as a spokesperson for national mission. He had been telling friends and readers for decades that they could not wait on divine intervention to solve their problems, that they had to rely upon themselves and each other. His voluntarist outlook—in the same vein as Nietzsche, James, Wallas, and Keynes—had been the controlling principle of his strong-state liberalism. Now it was foundational to his foreign policy outlook. More than ever, a planet in chaos needed Lippmann's secularist-turned-hybrid Christian humanist message of disinterested self-reliance.

*

Lippmann applied his constructive post-Christian skepticism to global reorganization during World War II and the Cold War. The initial result was his best-selling book, *U.S. Foreign Policy: Shield of the Republic* (1943). Though forgotten outside of international relations circles—where scholars still talk of the "Lippmann gap"—the book sold more copies than *A Preface to Morals*.[14]

The chief problem of American foreign policy, Lippmann argued, was that there was none. Any grand strategy had to assume that "the nation must maintain its objectives and its power in equilibrium, its purposes within its means and its means equal to its purposes, its commitments related to its resources and its resources adequate to its commitments." In other words, do not overreach yourself, either rhetorically or in actuality. Americans had been tolerating a breach between its "commitments" and its "power" since the Monroe Doctrine of 1823 if not earlier. Nevertheless, the gap was mainly a twentieth-century failing. Lippmann condemned the "bankruptcy" of American foreign policy between the Spanish-American War and World War II, including the country's "emasculation" during the 1930s. He repented in shame of his own "innocence" that American economic and cultural expansion could be accomplished absent political and military strength. Lippmann found America an abortive world power, and he blamed tender-minded manhood for it.[15]

Lippmann protested too much about his younger self's ignorance. Before and during World War I, he had been ambivalent about the League of Nations, preferring regional alliances like the "Atlantic community." (Some scholars today remember Lippmann as the progenitor of "Atlantic community" studies.) Lippmann returned to that multi-power arrangement along with Atlanticists in America and England, including Toynbee, but now with a "C." As Lippmann explained, America's "military isolation" due to its island status demanded that it entangle itself with Europe. Lippmann offered martial reasons for an alliance with the British, though he talked elsewhere about their shared language, culture, and religions. Lippmann wanted it to be clear to readers that the Atlantic Community was a "community of interest" and "system of security," not a "scheme for empire" or a "plan for the combined domination of the world." He did not obligate the United States to become "the Good Samaritan of the entire world" like Luce's American Century had.[16]

Indeed, Lippmann wrote his book to prevent that from happening. His greatest fear was that his countrymen would overcommit themselves and neglect the "order of power," by which he meant the ranking of world states most vital to American interests. Lippmann was confident that Russia would be preoccupied by its own "internal development" after the war and would not seek communist expansion. Central and Eastern Europe were "beyond the reach of American power" and so their "neutralization" in any contest between East and West was paramount. Meanwhile, Lippmann thought the Pacific would remain unstable for years to come.[17]

In short, Lippmann wanted Americans to accept that their opportunities for worldmaking were limited. Their priorities should be as well. Still, Lippmann believed the North Atlantic states must lead in building a "nuclear [intimate or close] alliance" with the planet's other great regional powers, namely the Soviet Union and China. The big four in concert would form the basis of a broader organic coalition of states dedicated to enlightened hegemony. Lippmann's concluding vision of a "world-wide system of liberty under law" anticipated the United Nations (UN) that was then under construction.[18]

U.S. Foreign Policy was ignored as a religious text, although that dimension of Lippmann's work was unmistakable for those with the eyes to see. He was drafting the book during his Catholic phase when he was chiding citizens for having abandoned their "ancient faith" and "great inheritance." This point about the loss of a common core intersected with Lippmann's worry about the absence of a clear American mission. "A free people cannot and should not be asked to fight and bleed, to work and sweat, for ends which they do not hold to be so compelling that they are self-evident," he admonished.[19]

Yet Lippmann only appeared to be calling for a new national consensus consistent with his minimalist Christian humanism. Following World War I, Lippmann had condemned foreign policymakers' indenture to "illusions." He now spent over one quarter of his bestseller deconstructing the "illusions" and "mirages"—the stereotypes—that he believed had trapped America's leaders for so long. For Lippmann, there was no "Holy Writ of American tradition," and he thought that attempts to conjure up one did more harm than good. The dream of "international collaboration," minus the will to power to see it through, represented an invasion of "cosmic transcendentalism" into statecraft, as he lectured one Republican senator. Eschewing "grandiose and global plans," Lippmann said there was no "single carpet by which mankind can overlap the jungles and the mountains and land plump and breathless in the promised land." Once again, he both rejected and demanded a civil religion to bind together interdependent peoples. Such was the ongoing dilemma of the post-Christian intellectual, caught between the feeling for truth and the fact of relativity.[20]

*

Per usual, Lippmann's inner conflict between freedom and authority—between Jefferson and Hamilton; between the SBNR and the RBNS—played out on a big stage. *U.S. Foreign Policy* generated substantial praise and criticism. One unexpected detractor was Lippmann's Catholic correspondent Maritain. Lippmann had welcomed Maritain's interventionist writings and had hoped that America and France would collaborate in defense of "Western civilization." In response, Maritain had faulted Lippmann for failing to advance an "ultimate ideal" that could inspire readers to sacrifice. Lippmann countered that "security against great aggression" was a more responsible ideal than was Maritain's "promotion of civilization." The problem, as Lippmann saw it, was to keep church and state separate. "The policeman must not be regarded as a potential priest, teacher, and constructer of the good life," he thought. Rather, disciplinary power "should be confined to the limited task of preserving an order within which the priest and teacher and constructer can proceed." The older

Lippmann believed that the SBNR could only thrive in an order set by the RBNS.[21]

For Lippmann, "if the ultimate ends of human society were entrusted to the foreign offices in London, Moscow, Chungking, and Washington," such an "insidious temptation to imperialism" would lead to a "new version of Kipling and the white man's burden." He continued to channel James's anti-imperialism. Granted, Lippmann's ambivalence toward marrying religions and foreign affairs was hard to square with his concurrent claims about Christianity and democracy. It is even more puzzling when we consider that, during these very years, Lippmann lauded the Republican lawyer John Foster Dulles's work for a "Just and Durable Peace" on behalf of the FCC and the rest of the world Protestant ecumenical community. Hopefully, it is evident by now that Lippmann never was a "prisoner of consistency" (his words). His pragmatic paradoxy—to hold conflicting positions in equal measure—frustrated more than a few friends and enemies.[22]

U.S. Foreign Policy was better received by Washington's insiders despite its iconoclasm. They, too, were tired of utopian schemes for "One World" (Willkie) or an "Atlantic Charter" (Roosevelt). They, too, wanted to focus more on "national security," a phrase that Lippmann had popularized in his book. In truth, Lippmann preferred the leadership of General Charles de Gaulle to any American politician. "Men like that have always fascinated me," he would later tell Nevins about the French resistance leader. Lippmann would talk fondly of de Gaulle well into the 1960s, having opportunities to interview him and relay messages to Washington on his behalf.[23]

Nevertheless, before and during the war Lippmann strengthened his ties across the American Establishment. He counted among his confidants Ambassador Joseph P. Kennedy, whom he had coaxed away from appeasement and toward interventionism. Before the release of *U.S. Foreign Policy*, Lippmann had tutored, or had been sought out to tutor, the U.S. State and War Departments, including various military commanders. He had sent a lengthy memorandum to Hull and Assistant Secretary of War John McCloy about how General Eisenhower could restore French control over North Africa. General Mark Clark, commander of the United States Fifth Army, wrote Lippmann in appreciation of his book, which afforded Lippmann the opportunity to lecture Clark on why the United States should be more supportive of the Gaullists. The Secretary of the Navy, James Forrestal, looked to Lippmann for advice on the German postwar settlement. Emboldened by Helen's partnership and his deepened affiliation with the "classical and Christian heritage," Lippmann was delighted to serve as a "One-Man State Department." The public theologian, public opinionator, and public economist had become a public diplomat advocating for a less-than-grand geopolitics.[24]

*

Yet Lippmann always defied easy categorization. Steel's claim that Lippmann quit Wilsonianism to become the "apostle of a hardheaded realpolitick" during World War II is misleading. Until the Vietnam War, Lippmann's realism was conducted within a messianic Wilsonian context. Wilsonianism—the belief that the United States should exert itself as a great world power—did not die following World War I. It dissipated and proliferated. Lippmann had stood with other of the CFR's realistic Wilsonians in pressuring countrymen to assume diplomatic and military responsibilities commensurate with their economic supremacy. Where Lippmann broke with the CFR (John Foster Dulles being the exception) was in adopting an affirmative attitude toward world Christian moral influence that he also negated.[25]

Wilson had resided in the global social gospel camp, while Lippmann found organized religions to be obstacles as well as aids to American destiny. That was revealed in Lippmann's daily columns and in his addendum to *U.S. Foreign Policy*, entitled *U.S. War Aims* (1944). Lippmann spent much of the new book lambasting the "Wilsonian gospel" and the "Error of 1919" even more harshly than he had in its predecessor. Lippmann believed Wilson and his team, which had included himself, had been willfully innocent about their impulse toward dominion. They had hidden behind illusions like "collective security" and "self-determination" rather than facing the anarchy of the real world. Their goal of global community had been good, but their fluffy means had made foreign affairs so much worse.[26]

According to Lippmann, "we cannot build a universal society from the top downwards." He reinstated his point from a year earlier—but originally from 1915—that world order had to grow organically from the "regional grouping" of states. Peoples occupying the "same strategical neighborhood" should combine for their common defense and prosperity. Hence, Lippmann's continued stress on the promotion of the Atlantic Community. The United States must work with the British in building up preponderant hard and soft power across the pond. But they had to respect that the Russians and Chinese had some degree of right to do so in their orbits. If Germany and Japan could be pacified following the war, and the great states could learn to practice the good neighbor principle, Lippmann believed a chastened worldwide Americanism or at least a long peace was in reach.[27]

U.S. War Aims spent a few weeks on the bestseller list but was eclipsed by the onslaught of texts calling for one world government. Lippmann was particularly upset with the attention garnered by former under Secretary of State Sumner Welles's *Time for Decision* (1944), which called for the UN to serve as a planetary peacekeeping force. To be sure, Lippmann recognized the need for international organization. He endorsed the UN's economic foundation, the Bretton Woods system (1944), which was intended to jumpstart postwar reconstruction and America's peaceful penetration into foreign markets. Lippmann was less enamored of the later Dumbarton Oaks proposals, which he thought followed Welles's prescriptions rather than his own. It was foolish to believe that "everything is everyone's business," Lippmann chided. "We must not write into the constitution of the world society a license to universal intervention."[28]

The older Lippmann remained a Jamesian prophet of limitation in foreign as well as in domestic policymaking. He protested to one Dumbarton supporter that the UN was a mirage since world order could not be conjured via ink. Yes, the thirteen colonies had sort of accomplished it with their U.S. Constitution, but that was only because they had a shared history, culture, and interest. To Lippmann, the Dumbarton attendees were putting the cart of globalism before the horse of regionalism. Only as the United States, Britain, Russia, and China policed their own neighborhoods could something like a world union of states become real. For Lippmann, forming a UN was a question of method and of vision. He questioned the former but heartily endorsed the latter. As a "truly universal society" and planetary "concert of power," Lippmann told readers that the UN was the early fulfillment of "an ancient dream of the saints and sages."[29]

Lippmann's sacralizing of the UN was a Wilsonian tribute, however unintentional. It was also typical of how Lippmann reframed America as a Christian-informed superpower after 1941. Following World War I, he recounted, the United States had acted irresponsibly, breaking up the Atlantic Community and acting like a debtor nation instead of the financial juggernaut it had become. "The boy had become a man. But the man behaved like a boy," was how Lippmann put it. Now, he believed it imperative that the country take stock of its limits but also its responsibilities.

> We are the latest great power developed by and committed to the tradition of the West. We are among the bearers of this tradition, and we are numbered now among its proudest defenders. That is the polestar by which we must set our course. At the center of that tradition resides the conviction that man's dignity rises from his ability to reason and thus to choose freely the good in preference to evil. We may claim without offense that this inner principle of the Western tradition is not local, tribal, or national, but universal, and in so far as we are its faithful servants, we shall, in learning how to use our power, win the consent of mankind.

Lippmann did not care to notice that his counsel to build consent for universal ideals required Americans to leave their neighborhood on an ideological crusade. His statement on "American purpose" in *U.S. War Aims* contained a similar mixed message: The country's "highest interest" was to "live in a world environment which contains no dangerous and alien powers." That was the language of Luce's American Century which, in turn, had been derived from Lippmann's original.[30]

The conclusion of *U.S. War Aims* was even more remarkable for its Christianization of American involvement in the world. It, too, was entitled "The American Destiny," but it bore no resemblance to Lippmann's prewar article. The United States, Lippmann boasted, was the "center" of Western civilization and the guarantor of the "eternal promise" of the "ancient faith" derived from the "Mediterranean world of the ancient Greeks, Hebrews, and Romans" (this was a rare occurrence where Lippmann included Jews within the Western tradition). America must prevent Europe from becoming a "decaying and disorganized fringe" around the Soviet Union and Asia. It is "historic and providential," Lippmann continued, "that the formation of the first universal order since classical times should begin with the binding together of the dismembered parts of Western Christendom. From this beginning a great prospect offers itself: that the schism between East and West, which opened up in the Dark Ages from the fifth to the eleventh centuries of our era, may at last be healed." This was the Christianized language of Lippmann's "Today and Tomorrow" op eds detailed at the outset of this chapter.[31]

Lippmann's self-described "prophecy" of redeemer Americanism had been preceded by his rejection of self-determination. That was a reminder that Lippmann's Wilsonianism was a realistic one. As the policy of both the Southern confederacy and Adolf Hitler—of secession and of national aggrandizement—self-determination was "deeply un-American and uncivilizing." The older Lippmann's critique of self-determination originated in his lifelong instinct to minimize disorder and maximize order. "There is no end to this atomization of human society," he threatened. "Within the minorities who have seceded there will tend to appear other minorities who in their turn will wish to secede." Lippmann furthermore contended that self-determination was a rejection of the West's "great tradition" of the "ideal of a state within which diverse peoples find justice and liberty under equal laws and become a commonwealth." Like his updated "American Destiny," Lippmann stressed the need for public obedience to a trans-historical if not transcendent standard of living. He remained an anti-imperialist but a confused one.[32]

Lippmann did not become more coherent when attending to the working-class prerequisites for American Destiny. His censures about alliance-building outside of one's neighborhood was typical of conservative and even isolationist thought—recall that Lippmann would tell Nevins that he had always been a conservative. Nevertheless, Lippmann's catching of the "full employment" fever during the war years placed him in the center of New Dealism. A country committed to full mass production and abetted by Keynesian strategies, he argued, might finally eliminate the chronic diseases of unemployment, poverty, and private over public-mindedness. Not only would full employment mitigate industrial warfare dating back to the Wagner Act, Lippmann believed the demand for U.S. goods would provoke industrial capitalist prosperity at home and abroad, thus obviating the need for sustained foreign aid. "There is no basic conflict between the national interests of the American people and their international interests and responsibilities," he reassured. It was a provocative argument—and a self-serving one for an anti-radical liberal.[33]

Lippmann wanted to see his United States become a world manufacturing, trading giant with a tamed labor movement. He also believed the country had to lead in modernizing the majority world. Lippmann remained steeped in the racialized language emanating from the ages of European imperialism. Yet he was closer to Wallace than to Luce in advocating for the self-development of post-colonial peoples. Africa was still "too primitive" for independence, Lippmann wrote, yet he hoped that the UN might be able to "relieve and transmute the problems of empire" by fostering the "exchange of scientific knowledge, inventions, technology, and of cultural achievements." America's "Great Adventure" was to take charge of the "great development" of the "primitive places" in the world. Stimulating urban-industrial growth abroad would make full employment at home all the easier, and vice versa. Economic interdependence would also be a great boon to world peace. Lippmann was no fan of the Atlantic Charter's idealism, yet he foretold that "freedom from want" would result in "freedom from fear."[34]

I am not certain I can reconcile Lippmann's thoughts about foreign affairs between 1938 and 1945, nor that I should try. Lippmann was among the most articulate and influential foreign policy realists of his time. Like Niebuhr, Lippmann offered theological caution to citizens to respect the bounds of their habitation. But he remained a Wilsonian in the sense of believing in transcendent values that a particular nation must embody and spread—in effect, a universal nationalism. As Lippmann had deepened his affiliation with Christianity during the 1930s to address issues of personal identity and social unrest, so in the 1940s and 1950s Christian relics proved useful to Lippmann's imagining a more glorious, circumscribed position for America in the world. He remained ensconced in the white world order of the imperial West, but he also suggested ways to move beyond it. Lippmann's realistic Wilsonianism was always an unstable compound of patriotic congratulation and critique.

*

Lippmann had been more in than out of Washington during World War II. One issue over which Lippmann broke with the American

Establishment was Russia. Lippmann's Point VI of the Fourteen Points had affirmed Russian self-determination, and Lippmann had insisted on it to Baker. The consolidation of Stalinism had not deterred him. Per his theory of regionalism, the Soviet Union was entitled to exercise power within its neighborhood. Nearing the end of World War II, Lippmann was uncharacteristically optimistic that Stalin would not stand in the way of America's Great Adventure. He supposed Russia too devastated by war to resume the mantle of international communism's powerhouse. Yet he also hoped that the Yalta Conference (on the postwar planning of Germany and Europe) had set the Soviets on a pathway to democratization, at least regarding Eastern and Central Europe. "There are no direct conflicts of vital interest as between the Soviet Union and the United States," Lippmann reported to one former military intelligence commander. A Russian-American war was "a virtual impossibility," Lippmann told readers, although he thought they might be brought to blows indirectly.[35]

The contrarian Lippmann reasserted himself after 1945. He warned against fanatical faith in atomic supremacy, insisting that "American power is limited." There were no "absolute weapons," and the belief that there were kept the United States from developing a measured military policy. Lippmann preferred the dollar diplomacy of his friend James Byrnes, Truman's Secretary of State, who was working to convince the Soviets to accept American aid.[36]

Privately, Walter and Helen became more critical of U.S. policy after Winston Churchill's unveiling of the "Iron Curtain" imagery in his Fulton, Missouri, speech in March of 1946. The Lippmanns were first drawn into debate at a dinner party at Undersecretary of State Dean Acheson's house along with Russian expert Charles Bohlen and Wallace (now Secretary of Commerce). Acheson and Bohlen took Churchill's side, while the Lippmanns preferred Wallace who stressed the need for cordial relations with the Russians. They had a more heated confrontation with Bohlen at a later gathering. At one point, Helen announced, "well, Chip, all I can say is that in your war I won't be a nurse's aide!" (Helen had served as a nurse's aide in World War I and had directed the program during World War II.) The Lippmanns would not support Wallace's Progressive Party in 1948, but nor would they have a good relationship with Truman.[37]

Lippmann disarmed Red Dawn scenarios just as he had before the war. He also channeled his inner Lincoln when warning that "the world order cannot be half democratic and half totalitarian." Lippmann joined ecumenical church leaders in advising Acheson on the need for a "declaration of human rights" (which the UN released in 1948). At some point, Lippmann said, the Soviets would have to adopt the "same ultimate standards of value" as the West regarding the "inviolability of the human spirit." "Without an ultimate standard of morals," he preached, "a universal society does not exist." Yet, in the very same book, Lippmann rebuked readers for not recognizing the "spiritual error" of Wilsonianism:

> It is the error of forgetting that we are men and of thinking that we are gods. We are not gods. We do not have the omniscience to discover a new moral law and the omnipotence to impose it on mankind. When we draw up lists of general principles which we say are universal, to which we mean to hold everyone, we are indulging in a fantasy. We are imagining ourselves as beings who are above and outside mankind, detached from the concrete realities of life itself, and able to govern the world by fiat. We are mere mortals with limited power and little universal wisdom.

Lippmann continued to sound the Nietzschean–Jamesian alarm against absolutism that he had voiced in *Public Opinion* and *A Preface to Morals*. Elsewhere, he lectured a Republican senator on the need for inconvenient compromise for the sake of superpower cooperation: "We ought to remember that the men who wrote the Bill of Rights into our Constitution were willing to pay the price of accepting slavery and the slave trade and the Fugitive Slave Laws in order to have a constitution at all, and I think there is a moral in that for us in our dealings with Russia."[38]

Lippmann's love–hate relationship with "ultimate standards of value" was the backdrop against which he laid his Cold War countermeasures. Recall his take on the Truman Doctrine. It was a "strategic monstrosity" hell bent on an "ideological crusade." What was required instead was a reasoned estimate of American interests and the commensurate power to see them through. Elsewhere, Lippmann mocked the containment policy as "a combination of Moses, Julius Caesar, Santa Claus, and Mr. Fixit to all mankind." He blamed postwar Britain's poor domestic planning and declining colonial leadership for causing a "transfusion of American power, based on our fear of Soviet Russia, our quest for oil, and an unconsidered, half-baked form of American imperialism." Lippmann did not coin the term "globalism" that was just surfacing in the English language, but he did as much as any writer to ensure that it would be a pejorative.[39]

Lippmann's anti-globalism is more welcome in our day than it was in his own. In that time, the State Department began strategy sessions with a discussion of why and how Lippmann was wrong. One official sick of reading Lippmann's warnings was Acheson. At another dinner party, he accused Lippmann of "sabotaging" American national security. The ensuing hot war of words was just one moment that left Lippmann feeling "rather lonely" in Washington. All the same, Lippmann was becoming friends with the head of the State Department's policy planning staff, George Kennan, the foil of his *Cold War* series. Lippmann would eventually win Kennan over to his side.[40]

*

But the reverse was more immediately true. As biographer Steel noticed, "whenever containment was put to the test as a policy choice rather than as an abstract doctrine, [Lippmann] went along with it." It was ironic as well that Lippmann the agnostic turned to religions to make sense of international disorders more frequently than did Kennan the supposed Christian crusader. Lippmann asserted in his *Cold War* essays that the Atlantic Community was founded upon the "common traditions of Western Christendom." He also resumed his argument from the 1930s that Russia was "alien" to that heritage. It was a part of the authoritarian, slavery-ridden Asia that knew nothing of the chivalry of Rome and Geneva. Thus, for Lippmann, the world order problem was not communism. It was the eternal struggle between East and West—between civilization and barbarism. Lippmann was optimistic that free market capitalist expansion might be able to open all Iron Curtains in the future. But until that time, the Atlantic Community would have to "live and let live" with Russia. Lippmann highlighted rapprochements between Protestants and Catholics as evidence that East–West coexistence was possible.[41]

At the tactical level, however, Lippmann was a Cold Warrior offering only nuanced opposition to Truman's signature policies. He held steadfast that U.S. and Soviet "zones of power" were the best that could be hoped for until the former forced, bought, or begged the latter off the continent. He scolded Washington for building a global anti-Soviet coalition instead of prioritizing the creation of an "all-European Union" under British and French leadership. Yet Lippmann also endorsed Truman's request for aid to Greece and Turkey and an expanded naval presence in the Mediterranean. The most important matter in postwar American foreign policy, Lippmann told one confidant, was building up enough military might to scare the Soviets into going home without provoking them to start World War III. Soviet newspapers had already decided by 1946 that Lippmann was a "representative of imperialist ideology."[42]

As a Cold Warrior, Lippmann backed a broader European Recovery (Marshall) Plan—including the Soviet Union—and a more limited North American Treaty Organization (NATO)—excluding Germany. Despite their falling out, Acheson would deliver a speech on behalf of European recovery that was derived from a Lippmann article. Lippmann supported both anchor policies because he believed they were rejections of Truman's globalism. Like the administration, Lippmann did not talk about how the Marshall Plan helped preserve white world order by propping up European imperialism in Africa and elsewhere. For him, the Marshall Plan's Keynesian strategies could steer Europeans away from the "swelling bureaucracy" of socialism and restore a "genuine liberalism" (as opposed to the "pseudo-liberalism" of corporate monopolists). Rapid economic recovery would create a European situation of strength and would make "reciprocal trade" and "intercourse between East and West" likely. Lippmann was more ambivalent toward NATO, which he believed would unnecessarily entangle "weak" states within superpower rivalry. Still, NATO represented the advance of the "communities of states" model that Lippmann and Dulles agreed were necessary to solidify the UN. Lippmann decided the Atlantic Community via NATO needed to prepare militarily for the rise of other Asian and Arab groups.[43]

Lippmann intermingled theology and politics in reflections on the Far East. He warned that China, Japan, and Southeast Asia were just as foreign to Western Christian tradition as was Russia. In his *Cold War* articles, he recommended treating Asia as "secondary" to a liberated Europe. "We have very little power in Asia," Lippmann wrote a friend in 1949, "and we must not think of ourselves as lords of creation." Democracy and free enterprise might never take root there. Rather, "a totalitarian system is normal in Asia," Lippmann concluded after travelling through India and interviewing Prime Minister Jawaharlal Nehru. He still thought India, along with Pakistan and Turkey, could be potential U.S. allies in the future but no one else. After it became clear that China would be reunited under the communist leader Mao Zedong, Lippmann invoked the "David and Goliath" Bible story to argue that the Atlantic Community needed a rapid defense buildup to resist the "armed hordes of Eurasia." He advised Sherman, the same naval commander he had advised on strengthening forces in the Mediterranean, to make Japan the center of U.S. military power in the region as a check on China and Soviet Siberia.[44]

Lippmann's musings on the Middle East were more complicated. During World War II, he had advocated for a "policy without entanglements" toward the region. The United States was not a Middle Eastern power and so would have to accommodate British and Soviet aims there. At the same time, he also observed, "we cannot stay out of the Middle East. We cannot remain there as the mere auxiliary of Britain. We cannot go in there as a third imperial power. We shall have, therefore, to enter the Middle East as the proposer and backer of a better order of life for all the peoples concerned." In a rough draft of his *Cold War* series regarding Greece and Turkey, Lippmann had concluded that "the advantage of adopting a precise Middle Eastern policy is that it can be controlled for the purpose of maintaining order. A vague global policy, which sounds like the tocsin of an ideological crusade, has no limits. It cannot be controlled. Its effects cannot be predicted. Everyone everywhere will read into it his own fears and hopes." Contesting the Soviet Union for dominance over Iran was ludicrous. It confirmed Lippmann's life message that nations like people become indentured to their stereotypes or illusions.[45]

Lippmann took a more definite interest in the Arab-Israeli conflict. Deliberately silent on anti-Semitism in America, Lippmann was outspoken in support of pacifying Palestine. He remained an anti-Zionist while adjusting his views toward the growing strength of the Zionists over their Arab neighbors. Like his CFR friends, Lippmann recognized that a Jewish state existed de facto in Palestine (that was six days before the Provisional Government of Israel declared itself one and the Soviets and Truman agreed). But Lippmann did not think Israel should be allowed to colonize its Arab neighbors. He wanted the United States to fortify its ties with Transjordan, making the Emirate its military center in the Middle East. Transjordan's King Abdullah should rule over a "Greater Palestine," working with Israel and the World Bank toward an "economic union" of Arabs and Jews.

Lippmann believed the Middle East "much too primitive" to build a successful Arab League. Questions about America's relationships with Egypt and Saudi Arabia should be dealt with separately from the Palestinian issue. However, Lippmann also encouraged the United States and Great Britain, working through the UN, to oversee a rapprochement between "pan-Arabism" and "Zionism," thus producing an interracial, interreligious, and transnational "Middle Eastern Commonwealth." Settling the Palestinian issue peacefully and diplomatically was crucial to giving the UN legitimacy as a workable universal society.[46]

The Arab–Israeli War crushed most of Lippmann's and friends' hopes for the region. Even before the declaration of Israeli statehood, however, Lippmann had encouraged Sherman to pursue a policy of disruption in the Middle East. "Our aim should be not to encourage the unity of the Arab world and of Islam," Lippmann counseled, "but to keep it divided. No dependence can be put upon the friendship and the reliability of a united Mohammedan world; a united Mohammedan world must in the end expel the western powers from all its territories, not only in the Middle East, but in North Africa. The only basis of unity in Islam is the theological and religious unity against the non-Mohammedan world." Thus Lippmann backed his way into support for Zionism—and for the Cold War writ large—by way of his fears of a Muslim jihad against the Christian West. This was not the only time Lippmann had cast the Cold War as a clash between "Islam" and "Christendom," although elsewhere he suggested the history of holy wars inspired hope for the settlement of U.S.–Soviet relations.[47]

Lippmann should be ranked among the most outspoken anti-ideologues of his generation. Yet his religious turn aligned with, if not contributed to, the binary logic of the Truman Doctrine and Cold

War. Fearing a "showdown" with the Soviets in Europe, Lippmann authorized putting the United States on a "virtual war footing" and in "possession of overwhelming power" to minimize distractions elsewhere. That demanded the same military Wilsonianism that he had been lamenting. It appears Lippmann's post-Christian impulses could hamper as much as help his penning a new American Destiny.[48]

*

"I am nobody of any public importance," Lippmann had confided in 1940, and "I am not adviser-at-large to mankind." He could not say the same ten years later. By mid-century, it was hard to find a more prominent global citizen. Lippmann had enjoyed a taste of white male state power in World War I, but too little and too brief. During World War II and the opening years of the Cold War, Lippmann won international standing and insider credentials through strenuous effort (and an excellent support staff). He would sacrifice that fame out of professional and moral duty, but not for another twenty years.[49]

Lippmann's eventual claim that he had always been a conservative seemed validated by his wartime work. After 1937, he had joined many other trans-Atlantic public intellectuals in arguing for some sort of rechristianization of the West. Only a civilized people beholden to "ancient faith" and a "great tradition" could withstand the barbarians wherever and whatever they may be. Lippmann combined that quest for cultural consensus with a dogmatic commitment against overcommitment, a one-man crusade against ideological crusading in foreign affairs. Lippmann's nostalgia for balance of power realism and isolationism placed him in line with Burke. At the same time, Lippmann espoused popular liberal ideals of full employment and free market globalization (or Americanization). In other words, Lippmann remained an incurable eclectic born of a thoroughgoing skepticism toward absolutes that he affirmed were necessary for the good life and society.

Lippmann talked less about religions after 1945, but that merely hid the fact of his agreement with Toynbee and other ex-secularists that the West was spiritually broken. During the 1930s, some Christian intellectuals on the Continent had dusted off the nineteenth-century term "post-Christian" and begun using it for culturally conservative causes. In a lecture series from 1940, published in

Civilization on Trial (1948), Toynbee had similarly repurposed the term. One of the most remarkable and disturbing developments of the twentieth century, Toynbee announced, was the emergence of a "post-Christian Western secular civilization." He was unsure whether this represented, at best, a "superfluous repetition of the pre-Christian Graeco-Roman" culture or, at worst, a "pernicious back-sliding from the path of spiritual progress." Since the 1930s, Toynbee had reversed course on the civilization-religion dialectic: Civilizations were now the "handmaids" of the "higher religions" which, in turn, all pointed to Christianity, the highest of them all. Because of the persistence of original sin, Toynbee suggested that religions' most progressive elements could only be experienced at the personal level. Nevertheless, an "immeasurable improvement" of social life could be expected under a Christian regime.[50]

But whither a post-Christian one? Lippmann agreed with Toynbee about the state of the West even if he never uttered the words post-Christian. But if Toynbee was right that a "post-Christian" culture was one "clinging to Christian practice without possessing the Christian belief," then Lippmann embodied its conflicting sides—its hopes for freedom and its fears of fracture. Lippmann, in RBNS fashion, was passing out Christian platitudes left and right while, like the SBNR, only affiliating with the tradition itself. The closest the Lippmanns ever came to church life was when they bought a spacious Tudor house across the street from the Episcopalian Washington Cathedral. In pragmatic fashion, Walter would remark to Helen "how useful a cathedral can be" to its surrounding community. Perhaps he had in mind St. John the Divine in New York that he had written about twenty years earlier.[51]

Though preoccupied with world order, Lippmann still took breaks to implore audiences to return to "the life of the spirit." By "life of the spirit," Lippmann meant "to understand and to live in the order to which man, as he is actually constituted, belongs." True freedom came through subservience to the belief that human beings had an essence. The origins of that essence were still elusive for Lippmann, however. He claimed religion was the stuff of "metaphors, parables, and poetic fantasy"—all "beyond the boundaries of common sense." The Christian's dilemma was that the "Modern Age," unlike the "Ages of Faith," limited the search for meaning and fulfillment to the field of "mundane experience." Clergy now had to win persons over to the old doctrines "without the support of a supernatural physics and a supernatural history." The older Lippmann reached out for civility in a barbaric age while his younger self—the self of *A Preface to Morals*—kept pulling him back toward spiritual disinterestedness. The result was a thin Christian humanism, an ethics shorn of metaphysics, as Toynbee might call it. Lippmann struggled with this homesickness for the remainder of his life.[52]

*

Lippmann's emphasis on conformity to a supreme order of reality (that he did not believe existed) fit well with his ongoing resistance to democratic progress. Recall his Great Depression-era premonitions to dread the disinherited masses within America. Lippmann fell in line with other RBNS managers who saw religions as irreplaceable means of social control. Biographer Barry Riccio aptly put it this way: Lippmann "was clearly more troubled by the eclipse of civic virtue than he was by the erosion of civil liberties." The most egregious example of that was when Lippmann, after touring the West Coast following the Pearl Harbor attack, hyped hysteria about a Japanese invasion. He considered the internment of 120,000 Japanese Americans—Roosevelt's war relocation program—an essential military operation conducted for their own protection.[53]

More subtly, Lippmann ignored the revival of women's rights discussions during and after the war. He lumped Amelia Earhart in with "heroes, the saints, and the seers" but denied her agency as a woman. Similarly, his "Today and Tomorrow" columns assumed that men were the first and maybe the sole sex. One chief postwar concern for Lippmann was that "young men" enjoy "equal opportunity" for college and military training. There was the sexism hiding plainly within his strong-state liberalism. Lippmann did finally acknowledge the work of his research assistant van Schaik in *U.S. Foreign Policy* and *U.S. War Aims*. On the other hand, Lippmann offered little praise for Helen. Besides guarding access to him at parties, Helen functioned as Lippmann's personal secretary, interpreter, and note-taker when they went abroad. Lippmann's benign neglect of his partner was typical of a white male republic that had been bent but not broken by depression and war.[54]

Lippmann addressed the burgeoning civil rights movement a few times but in negative and esoteric ways. While predicting that Black Americans would one day gain equal protections and opportunities, he sided with Southern Democrats in resisting Truman's 1948 and 1949 civil rights packages (he had also opposed antilynching legislation in 1938). Lippmann's point in all those cases was that protecting the filibuster was crucial to preserving the rights of "strong minorities," even segregationist ones.[55]

Lippmann passed over still another moment to fulfill his prophecy of Black liberation when eulogizing Mahatma Gandhi. Much like he had Earhart, Lippmann removed Gandhi from any recognizable geopolitical context, using New Testament terminology to explain the Indian independence leader's significance. As a "regenerate man," Gandhi offered no help regarding "the practical issues of daily life" but instead pointed others toward "what ultimate values they should give their allegiance." Lippmann's essay was a reminder of his concern that a thriving democracy should possess both robust institutions and self-directed personalities. As he explained, "it is necessary to govern mankind and it is necessary to transform men." Yet Lippmann's claim that "non-resistance, humility, poverty and chastity...can never be the laws of a secular society" was a bit absurd. Had non-violent civil disobedience not just been proven immensely practical in ending centuries of British colonialism in India? And had not Black civil rights leaders just used non-violent direct action to secure the desegregation of the U.S. armed forces?[56]

Lippmann was part of a Reform Jewish minority on the rise but remained indifferent to the oppression of women and ethnic-racial groups. The highest price he paid for his Cold War against the Truman Doctrine was a feeling of aloneness—although he could seek consolation among his ten-to-twelve million weekly readers, his salary, extensive travel, and Helen and the dogs. When Du Bois, too, attacked Truman's aggression toward the Soviet Union, he was called a communist and forced to resign from the National Association for the Advancement of Colored People (NAACP) he had co-founded. A similar fate befell Du Bois's friend, the celebrated American singer, actor, intellectual, and anti-colonialist Paul Robeson. Robeson's criticism of Marshall Plan imperialism over Africa cost him his fame, concert performance income, and passport. Lippmann never came to either of their defenses.[57]

Yet the future belonged to Robeson and Du Bois (and Helen, for that matter). Lippmann would have to learn how to get along in a revolutionary world at home and abroad. And he never would, preferring instead to puff one of the architects of the Red Scares he had fought throughout his life.

Notes

1. Walter Lippmann, "Today and Tomorrow: The Beginning of Wisdom," *New York Herald Tribune*, Dec. 25, 1941, 21; Walter Lippmann, "Today and Tomorrow: America and France," *New York Herald Tribune*, Nov. 19, 1942, 21; Walter Lippmann, "Today and Tomorrow: The Captains of Their Souls," *New York Herald Tribune*, July 31, 1943, 7; Walter Lippmann, "Today and Tomorrow: The War of Nerves," *Washington Post*, Dec. 3, 1940, 11.
2. Walter Lippmann, "Man's Image of Man," Address before the Seventeenth Annual Meeting of the American Catholic Philosophical Association, Philadelphia, Dec. 29 and 30, 1941, in *Essential Lippmann*, ed. Rossiter and Lare, 162–8.
3. See Gaston, *Imagining Judeo-Christian America*; Kevin Kruse, *One Nation Under God: How Corporate America Invented Christian America* (New York: Basic Books, 2015); and Wendy Wall, *Inventing the "American Way": The Politics of Consensus from the New Deal to the Civil Rights Movement* (New York: Oxford University Press, 2008).
4. See Walter Lippmann, Class Dinner Speech, Thirtieth Reunion of the Harvard Class of 1910, June 18, 1940, in *Essential Lippmann*, ed. Rossiter and Lare, 534–8 on "easy way" and "soft vices." See Walter Lippmann, "Today and Tomorrow: The Wind that is Blowing," *New York Herald Tribune*, Sept. 27, 1941, 13, on "un-American." For "fat" and "jitterbug age," see Walter Lippmann, "Today and Tomorrow: The Rebirth of a Nation," *Washington Post*, Mar. 28, 1942, 9. See Walter Lippmann, "Today and Tomorrow: On Painless Perfection," *New York Herald Tribune*, June 7, 1941, 13, on "free society" and "ancient faith."
5. Walter Lippmann, to Theodore Roosevelt, Jr., Jan. 10, 1942, in *Public Philosopher*, ed. Blum, 413. On "progressive education," see Walter Lippmann, "Today and Tomorrow: Youth and Age," Feb. 17, 1940, in *Essential Lippmann*, ed. Rossiter and Lare, 443. See Walter Lippmann, "Education vs. Western Civilization," Address, Annual Meeting of the American Association for the Advancement of Science, Philadelphia, Dec. 29, 1940, in *Essential Lippmann*, ed. Rossiter and Lare, 418–22, for "conserve its traditions."

6. See Lippmann, "Education vs. Western Civilization," 418–22, for "modern education" and "no common faith." For Lippmann's support for liberal arts and Great Books education, see Walter Lippmann, "Today and Tomorrow: Crisis and Reform in Education," Feb. 13, 1943, in *Essential Lippmann*, ed. Rossiter and Lare, 423; Walter Lippmann, "Today and Tomorrow: The St. Johns Program," *New York Herald Tribune*, Dec. 27, 1938, 17; and Walter Lippmann, "Today and Tomorrow: On Being Too Current," *Washington Post*, Mar. 1, 1941, 7. See Walter Lippmann, "Today and Tomorrow: To the First and Last Things," *New York Herald Tribune*, May 25, 1940, 17a, for "great inheritance."
7. Lippmann, *Stakes of Diplomacy*, 229. See Priscilla Roberts, "All the Right People: The Historiography of the American Foreign Policy Establishment," *Journal of American Studies* 26 (1992): 409–34.
8. Walter Lippmann, "Unconscious Empire," *World*, Dec. 29, 1926, 10; Walter Lippmann, "Empire: The Days of Our Nonage Are Over (1927)," in Lippmann, *Men of Destiny*, 215–22; Walter Lippmann, "Kid-Glove Diplomacy," *World*, Jan. 27, 1922, 12; Walter Lippmann, "America," *World*, July 5, 1926, 8; Walter Lippmann, "Bedazzled Suckers," *World*, Apr. 13, 1928, 10.
9. Walter Lippmann, to Hamilton Fish Armstrong, Mar. 30, 1935, in WLP, Reel 42; Walter Lippmann, to Norman P. Davis, Mar. 22, 1935, in WLP, Reel 56; Walter Lippmann, to Cordell Hull, Apr. 2, 1935, in *Public Philosopher*, ed. Blum, 330.
10. See Walter Lippmann, "Today and Tomorrow: Disentanglement in Europe," *New York Herald Tribune*, Oct. 17, 1936, 13; and Walter Lippmann, "Today and Tomorrow: The Founding of the European Union," *New York Herald Tribune*, Nov. 21, 1939, 21. On "moral authority," see Lippmann, *Interpretations, 1933–1935*, 358.
11. Walter Lippmann, "Today and Tomorrow: Reflections on Sidonius," Dec. 25, 1937, 13.
12. See Walter Lippmann, to Bruce Bliven, Mar. 11, 1938, in WLP, Reel 47, for "overwhelming." On "totally prepare," see Walter Lippmann, at Arthur Ballantine, June 8, 1940, in *Public Philosopher*, ed. Blum, 390. See Walter Lippmann, "Today and Tomorrow," *New York Herald Tribune*, Oct. 3, 1939, 17, on "keep the war."
13. Walter Lippmann, "The American Destiny," *Life*, June 5, 1939, 47, 72–3. See Walter Lippmann, to Henry A. Wallace, Nov. 26, 1942, in *Public Philosopher*, ed. Blum, 431, who calls Wallace's speech "perfect" and the best commentary produced on the war.
14. Patrick Porter, "Beyond the American Century: Walter Lippmann and American Grand Strategy, 1943–1950," *Diplomacy & Statecraft* 22 (2011): 557–77.
15. Walter Lippmann, *U.S. Foreign Policy: Shield of the Republic* (Boston: Little, Brown, 1943), viii–x, 3–10, 27, 46.

16. Lippmann, *U.S. Foreign Policy*, 108–13, 119–31. See also Walter Lippmann, "The Defense of the Atlantic World," *New Republic*, Feb. 17, 1917, which Lippmann reprinted in parts in Lippmann, *U.S. Foreign Policy*, 33–5. On varieties of Atlanticism during these years, including an essay by Steel on Lippmann's influence, see Marco Mariano, ed., *Defining the Atlantic Community: Culture, Intellectuals, and Policies in the Mid-Twentieth Century* (New York: Routledge, 2010).
17. Lippmann, *U.S. Foreign Policy*, 155, 149–52, 155–60, 168–75.
18. Lippmann, *U.S. Foreign Policy*, 155, 149–52, 155–60, 168–75.
19. Lippmann, *U.S. Foreign Policy*, 30, 44, 47, 59, 86.
20. Walter Lippmann, "The Break-Up of Illusion in 1922," *World*, Dec. 31, 1922, 10; Lippmann, *U.S. Foreign Policy*, 30, 44, 47, 59, 86; Walter Lippmann, "Today and Tomorrow: The Too Far Sighted," *Washington Post*, Dec. 9, 1943, 17. On "cosmic transcendentalism," see Walter Lippmann, to Henry Cabot Lodge, Jr., July 1, 1943, in *Public Philosopher*, ed. Blum, 441.
21. Walter Lippmann, to Jacques Maritain, July 1, 1943, in *Public Philosopher*, ed. Blum, 440. On Lippmann's earlier praise for Maritain, see Walter Lippmann, to Jacques Maritain, Nov. 14, 1939, in *Public Philosopher*, ed. Blum, 383.
22. Lippmann, to Maritain, July 1, 1943; Walter Lippmann, to John Foster Dulles, Nov. 8, 1945, in WLP, Reel 58. On "consistency," see Brown, *Through These Men*, 217.
23. Lippmann, *U.S. Foreign Policy*, 47; Lippmann, "Interview," 211–13.
24. See Brown, *Through These Men*, 215, for "One-Man State Department." Lippmann's exchanges with Kennedy, Hull, McCloy, Clark, Forrestal, and many others, including his North African memorandum, can all be found in *Public Philosopher*, ed. Blum.
25. Steel, *Walter Lippmann*, 410.
26. Walter Lippmann, *U.S. War Aims* (Boston: Little, Brown, 1944), 160, 175.
27. Lippmann, *U.S. War Aims*, 136–7, 157–9.
28. Lippmann, *U.S. War Aims*, 165–9, 189. See Steel, *Walter Lippmann*, 410–11, on Lippmann's problem with Welles.
29. Walter Lippmann, to Grenville Clark, Sept. 19, 1944, in *Public Philosopher*, ed. Blum, 453–5; Walter Lippmann, "Today and Tomorrow: The Ten Years of the U.N.," *Washington Post*, June 14, 1955, 27; Walter Lippmann, "Today and Tomorrow: The Sacred Pledge," *New York Herald Tribune*, Oct. 28, 1943, 21.
30. Walter Lippmann, "Today and Tomorrow: Toward an Economic Foreign Policy," *New York Herald Tribune*, Aug. 17, 1943, 17; Walter Lippmann, "Today and Tomorrow: The Rise of the United States," Sept. 11, 1945, in *Essential Lippmann*, ed. Rossiter and Lare, 77–80; Walter Lippmann, "Today and Tomorrow: Americanism Abroad," *Washington Post*, July 4, 1944, 5; Lippmann, *U.S. War Aims*, 154.
31. Lippmann, *U.S. War Aims*, 209–10.

32. Lippmann, *U.S. War Aims*, 171–7.
33. Walter Lippmann, "Today and Tomorrow: Discovered in Our Time," *New York Herald Tribune*, May 20, 1944, 15A.
34. Lippmann, *U.S. War Aims*, 165–7; Walter Lippmann, "Today and Tomorrow: The Great Adventure," *New York Herald Tribune*, Nov. 26, 1942, 33.
35. Walter Lippmann, to Newton Baker, Feb. 26, 1918, in *Public Philosopher*, ed. Blum, 87–8; Walter Lippmann, "Outlawing War and Outlawing Russia," *World*, Aug. 7, 1928, 10. See Walter Lippmann, to George Fielding Eliot, June 14, 1945, in *Public Philosopher*, ed. Blum, 467–8, on "no direct conflicts." For "impossibility," see Lippmann, *U.S. War Aims*, 134–5.
36. See Walter Lippmann, "Today and Tomorrow: The Rise of the United States," *New York Herald Tribune*, Sept. 11, 1945, 25, for "limited." On "absolute weapons," see Walter Lippmann, to Philip B. Stockton, Feb. 3, 1948, in *Public Philosopher*, ed. Blum, 506.
37. Steel, *Walter Lippmann*, 426–30.
38. Lippmann, *U.S. War Aims*, 149, 152, 181–2; Walter Lippmann, to Warren Austin, June 10, 1946, in *Public Philosopher*, ed. Blum, 480. See Walter Lippmann, to Dean Acheson, Oct. 1, 1946, in WLP, Reel 40, on human rights. See also Gene Zubovich, *Before the Religious Right: Liberal Protestants, Human Rights, and the Polarization of the United States* (Philadelphia: University of Pennsylvania Press, 2021).
39. For "Santa Claus," see Walter Lippmann, "Today and Tomorrow: Marshall at Harvard," *New York Herald Tribune*, June 14, 1947, 13. See also Walter Lippmann, "Today and Tomorrow: The British Problem," *New York Herald Tribune*, Feb. 11, 1947, 25.
40. On the fight with Acheson, see Lippmann, "Interview," 258. See Louis J. Halle, "Walter Lippmann: The Philosopher as Journalist," *New Republic*, Aug. 3, 1963, 20, on the State Department and Lippmann's columns. On "lonely," see Walter Lippmann, to Raymond Gram Swing, Nov. 13, 1947, in *Public Philosopher*, ed. Blum, 498.
41. Steel, *Walter Lippmann*, 489. See Walter Lippmann, "Today and Tomorrow: A Philosophy of Soviet–American Relations," *New York Herald Tribune*, Nov. 27, 1945, 25A; and Walter Lippmann, "Today and Tomorrow: The Ideological Conflict in Asia," *New York Herald Tribune*, Dec. 20, 1949, 27, for Lippmann's arguments that Russia was outside "Christendom." For his comparison to Protestant-Catholic relations, see Walter Lippmann, "Today and Tomorrow: The Petition of the Churchmen," *New York Herald Tribune*, May 4, 1948, 25.
42. Walter Lippmann, to Bernard Berenson, Mar. 1, 1949, in *Public Philosopher*, ed. Blum, 533. For "zones of power," see Walter Lippmann, to Lewis Douglas, Aug. 31, 1948, in WLP, Reel 58. See Walter Lippmann, "Today and Tomorrow: The Voice of America," *Washington Post*, May 13, 1947, 7; and Walter Lippmann, to J. William Fulbright, Apr. 3, 1947,

in *Public Philosopher*, ed. Blum, 494, on "European Union." See Steel, *Walter Lippmann*, 427, on the Soviet's charge against Lippmann.

43. On the Marshall Plan, see Lippmann, "Marshall at Harvard," 13; Walter Lippmann, "Today and Tomorrow: Socialists and Liberals," *New York Herald Tribune*, Nov. 1, 1949, 21; Walter Lippmann, "Today and Tomorrow: The Liberals Opportunity," *New York Herald Tribune*, Nov. 3, 1949, 25; and Walter Lippmann, "Today and Tomorrow: Selling It Versus Working It," *New York Herald Tribune*, Jan. 19, 1948, 17. See Steel, *Walter Lippmann*, 441, on Acheson's speech. On NATO, see Walter Lippmann, "Today and Tomorrow: The Proposed 'Defense Union'," *Washington Post*, Jan. 22, 1948, 11; and Walter Lippmann, to John Foster Dulles, Apr. 25, 1949, in *Public Philosopher*, ed. Blum, 537.

44. Lippmann, "Ideological Conflict in Asia," 27. For "lords of creation," see Walter Lippmann, to Russell C. Leffingwell, Dec. 29, 1949, in *Public Philosopher*, ed. Blum, 1949. See Walter Lippmann, to Bernard Berenson, Dec. 22, 1949, in WLP, Reel 45, for "normal." See also Walter Lippmann, "Today and Tomorrow: David and Goliath," *New York Herald Tribune*, Aug. 15, 1950, 21; and Walter Lippmann, to Forrest P. Sherman, Apr. 5, 1948, in *Public Philosopher*, ed. Blum, 508.

45. Walter Lippmann, "Today and Tomorrow: Policy without Entanglements," *New York Herald Tribune*, Dec. 14, 1943, 23. See Walter Lippmann, "Today and Tomorrow: The U.S.A. in the Middle East," *New York Herald Tribune*, Nov. 15, 1945, 25A, on working with Britain and the Soviet Union. On "cannot stay out," see Walter Lippmann, "Today and Tomorrow: The Inevitable Coming to Pass," *Washington Post*, July 6, 1946, 7. For "Middle Eastern policy," see Walter Lippmann, "Today and Tomorrow: Policy or Crusade?" *New York Herald Tribune*, Mar. 15, 1947, 13A.

46. On Israel and Transjordan, see Walter Lippmann, "Today and Tomorrow: Diplomacy in Palestine," *New York Herald Tribune*, Apr. 27, 1948, 25; Walter Lippmann, "Today and Tomorrow: Toward a Solution in Palestine," *New York Herald Tribune*, May 6, 1948, 25. See Walter Lippmann, "Today and Tomorrow: Middle Eastern Policy," June 3, 1948, 21, for the Arab League and "Commonwealth." On the UN and Palestine, see Walter Lippmann, "Today and Tomorrow: The U.N. and Palestine," *New York Herald Tribune*, May 3, 1947, 13; and Walter Lippmann, to Lewis Douglas, July 9, 1948, in *Public Philosopher*, ed. Blum, 516.

47. Lippmann, to Sherman, Apr. 5, 1948. On "Islam" versus "Christendom," see Walter Lippmann, "A Moslem Revolution," *World*, Nov. 4, 1922, 12; Lippmann, to Douglas, Aug. 31, 1948; and Walter Lippmann, "Today and Tomorrow: Mr. Bohlen on Agreements," *Washington Post*, Feb. 3, 1949, 11.

48. Lippmann, to Sherman, Apr. 5, 1948.

49. Walter Lippmann, to Alexander Woollcott, Oct. 25, 1940, in *Public Philosopher*, ed. Blum, 397.

50. Toynbee, *Civilization on Trial*, 230, 234–7, 248–52.
51. Toynbee, *Civilization on Trial*, 237. On Lippmann's comment about cathedrals, see Francis B. Sayle, Jr., "Report of the Dean to the Annual Meeting of the Cathedral Chapter," Oct. 21, 1955, in WLP, Reel 90.
52. Walter Lippmann, Address, Episcopal Theological School, Cambridge, Mass., Feb. 23, 1949, in WLP, Box 329, Folder 424.
53. Riccio, *Walter Lippmann*, 228. See Steel, *Walter Lippmann*, 393–5, for Lippmann's thoughts on Japanese American internment.
54. Walter Lippmann, "Today and Tomorrow: Amelia Earhart," *New York Herald Tribune*, July 8, 1937, in *Essential Lippmann*, ed. Rossiter and Lare, 161; Walter Lippmann, "Today and Tomorrow: Equal Opportunity for Young Men," *Washington Post*, July 28, 1942, 9. On Helen's work, see Steel, *Walter Lippmann*, 463.
55. Walter Lippmann, "Today and Tomorrow: Filibusters and the American Idea," *New York Herald Tribune*, Mar 3, 1949, 21. See Lippmann, to Berenson, Mar. 1, 1949; and Steel, *Walter Lippmann*, 551–2, on Lippmann's opposition to antilynching and Truman's civil rights package.
56. Walter Lippmann, "Today and Tomorrow: Reflections on Gandhi," *New York Herald Tribune*, Feb. 3, 1938, in *Essential Lippmann*, ed. Rossiter and Lare, 158–60.
57. Penny M. Von Eschen, *Race against Empire: Black Americans and Anticolonialism, 1937–1957* (Ithaca: Cornell University Press, 1997).

6
The Shepherd, 1949–1960

Walter Lippmann lived out his creed that human beings are a mix of great evil and great good. Once a champion of socialism and industrial democracy, Lippmann entered the Cold War thinking that labor unions were more trouble than they were worth. He either accepted or endorsed immigration restriction for most of his life—portraying Italians, the Japanese, and others as threats to national security. Lippmann had strategic reasons for pushing anti-Zionism abroad, yet he routinely abetted anti-Semitism at home, including denying asylum to Jewish refugees from Europe. Following World War I, Lippmann fell silent on civil rights for Black Americans and women. The reasons for Lippmann's liberal intolerance are not hard to uncover: He became like the men he was most attracted to, inheriting their racism, sexism, classism, and nativism along with their more noble traits. Over the course of his adult life, Lippmann demonized the dispossessed in the terms of a struggle for Western Christian "civilization" against the "barbarians," whoever and wherever they may be.

And yet few public intellectuals spoke truth to power more eloquently and to such a large audience in the American Century. The younger Lippmann had drifted in and out of middling liberalism, while his older self challenged that regime from the inside. Wedding James, Wallas, Nietzsche, and Keynes to Hamilton, Hayek, Toynbee, and Burke, Lippmann attacked the New Deal from the standpoint of a post-Christian humanism that prioritized decentralization of both the state and the economy. Lippmann's pragmatic conservativism manifested itself during World War II and the Cold War as a rejection of globalism—even as he imagined a new destiny for the United States in promoting world peace and prosperity. For all his eclecticism, Lippmann offered a faithful word to respect the limits of human knowledge and charity. It was a public theological challenge to accept that we are not gods and to get along accordingly. Lippmann remained a celebrity pastor-skeptic, or skeptic-pastor, in the vein of William James.

Throughout the 1950s, humankind's "adviser-at-large" would shepherd his country through the toils of international communism and the snares of a mass society. Those were interrelated dangers for Lippmann. America's failure to halt the red menace overseas was proof that the nation lacked moral fiber. Once again riding rough over his own pampered, privileged lifestyle, Lippmann demanded a tougher-minded citizenry and a stronger national government to care for it. The liberalism of his conservativism and the conservativism of his liberalism—and the democratic socialism running through all of it—would never be in sharper relief than during these years. Nor would his paradoxical intuition, dating back to *A Preface to Morals* and earlier, that America must embrace and yet steer clear of civil religions. Lippmann perfected his oppositional insider stance while doing his part to ensure that the straight white man's republic reigned supreme a little longer.

*

Lippmann's grilling of June and Ward Cleaver's America was fueled by a Cold War that was rapidly heating up. The decade could not have started any worse with the news that the Soviets had successfully detonated their own atomic bomb and China had been reunited under Chairman Mao Zedong. The Truman administration militarized its leadership of the free world through NATO. The specter of a united communist East, however, led many to wonder if an even bolder collectivism was needed. North Korea's invasion of South Korea in June of 1950 provided the excuse to build up preponderant power to fight America's enemies everywhere. President Eisenhower's team, which included Secretary of State John Foster Dulles, rejected containment as a strategy of defeat. They instead contemplated the liberation of communist-controlled lands. But one thing Eisenhower's and Truman's men could all agree upon: Making weapons of small and mass destruction was good for the economy. The newly formed Pentagon, CIA, and National Security Council (NSC)—all components of the National Security Act (1947)—kept millions of Americans working in the defense sector and sent billions of dollars of military aid and hardware around the world. The second Red Scare caused the nation to stop worrying and to love the world's most extravagant military-industrial complex.

Addressing a planet that had an expiration date, Lippmann positioned himself somewhere between a hawk and a dove. He had been advocating for American military hegemony long enough to be considered a jingoist. Yet when Truman sent a 1.5-billion-dollar military aid bill to Congress on the same day that he signed NATO into law, Lippmann went ballistic, echoing his friend Senator Vandenberg's charge that the president was now the "number one war lord of the earth." Lippmann himself called the bill a "shocking example of utter disregard for our constitutional traditions and for the very processes of law." The "Big Money" spent on defense was because the administration wanted to wage all kinds of wars at once. As the decade wore on, Lippmann became convinced that America's global policemanship was the main barrier keeping Europe and the world from reconciliation. His county's national security might be awesome, but "its influence for good was declining."[1]

If only Truman had heeded Lippmann's warning about Asia. Lippmann had argued in *The Cold War* that China and its region were "secondary" to U.S. interests. He lamented that more had not been done for South Korea to deter invasion by the North, but he was also quick to declare the Korean War an American "defeat." A fortuitous defeat, even a "salvation," Lippmann wrote, as it would force countrymen to abandon globalism. Lippmann asked Truman to quit Japan as well to lessen tensions between the West and the "Chinese-Soviet masses." Treating Asia as the "instrument" of American foreign policy hurt Western "prestige." It also made it impossible for the East to achieve the "self-respect" necessary for modernization. While Lippmann initially supported French efforts to recolonize Vietnam, he recommended abandoning Southeast Asia and solidifying Nehru's government in India. "Disentanglement" from China and the East was vital.[2]

Lippmann took his One-Man State Department on an apology tour of British universities in 1952. His lectures updated *The Cold War*, in which Lippmann had been critical of British anti-communism. Now he placed the blame for global anarchy squarely upon Truman. Still, Lippmann was confident that America's "detour into moment, but his mental state never improved under Eisenhower and Dulles. To Lippmann, the greatest presidents were teachers, a role Eisenhower held no interest in playing. Lippmann had once thought the general an unqualified "dream boy" who might be able to heal and unite the country. Instead, Eisenhower settled for being an ineffectual executive who refused to lead Congress and his party. He was a "constitutional monarch, who reigns but does not govern." Furthermore, Lippmann believed that Eisenhower was too reliant on political appointees borrowed from America's largest corporations. Lacking the inclination for strategic thought, the Eisenhower–Dulles "liberation" of communist-controlled areas "will butter no parsnips." Lippmann had voted for Eisenhower in 1952 but lamented the administration's "militarized diplomacy" in the run-up to the 1956 elections.[6]

Lippmann's disparaging of Dulles combined political and theological critique per usual. As members of the CFR brotherhood, the two had agreed on a lot before Korea. Yet Lippmann became one of Dulles's harshest detractors once the latter partnered with Eisenhower. Lippmann juxtaposed his "quiet diplomacy" with Dulles's "loud-mouthed" variant. But it was more style than substance Lippmann was upset about. He used the occasion of Dulles's address to Protestant leaders to roast the Secretary's "pretense to know and to speak for the universal order of things." As Lippmann elaborated,

> There is no surer way for a leader in the free world to repel free men than to let it seem that in our foreign policies we make the assumption of infallibility, that what finally emerges from the vast bureaucracy which forms these policies, is hedged with divinity, and that only the blind, the ignorant and the wicked can disagree with whatever the policy finally happens to be.... The tendency to transform our mundane and secular matters ... into religious and moral dogmas is an old and a bad habit of the human race. Freedom has one of its deepest roots in the realization that the business of states is the business of fallible and altogether human persons, that tariffs and budgets and military establishments and what to do in Lebanon and Cyprus and the rest, cannot be deduced directly and neatly and obviously from the moral principles of any religion. The spirit of freedom is an emanation of the human experience in which men have learned to distrust politicians who, lacking humility, are too sure of themselves, and pretend to have some special kind of inspiration.

universalism" was at an end and that his countrymen were ready to work through the Atlantic Community to evacuate and reunify Germany. Lippmann used the occasion to denounce Wilsonianism in the strongest possible terms. "The Wilsonian ideology is American fundamentalism made into a universal doctrine," he complained. Wilsonianism was a "crusading doctrine," simultaneously the creature and creator of imperial overreach. It was "an impossible foundation" for U.S. diplomacy.[3]

Lippmann's trust that America had gotten over globalism was shattered by the Eisenhower–Dulles escapades in the Middle East. Lippmann appreciated the administration's refusal to support Zionism in Palestine. Yet, for his theory of regionalism, Lippmann opposed Dulles's efforts to enlist the Middle East in a Western-led anticommunist league. Lippmann had advised against including Iran and Turkey in his "little NATO," but he completely rejected the Southeast Asia Treaty Organization (SEATO) hastily assembled following the French defeat in Vietnam in 1954. At a dinner party, Lippmann tried in vain to convince Dulles that a SEATO that included Pakistan and only one southeast Asian nation (Thailand) would fail. Lippmann agreed with Eisenhower and Dulles that the Suez crisis of 1956 should never have happened. But, once started, Lippmann hoped Israel, Britain, and France (against American wishes) would disarm the "typical aggressor-dictator" of Egypt, the Arab nationalist Gamal Abdel Nasser.[4]

After Suez, Lippmann retreated once more to "disentanglement," warning against sending troops into Lebanon. The Eisenhower Doctrine of shutting Russia entirely out of the Middle East was impossible given its proximity. Instead, the administration should make as its goal the "neutralization" of Lebanon—and Korea, China, and all of Africa while they were at it. In so many words, Lippmann endorsed coexistence with the Soviet Union while anticipating the rise of the Non-Aligned Movement (NAM) launched in 1961. His foreign policy counsel continued to defy easy cataloguing. At the same time, his concentration on nation building over worldmaking stayed consistent.[5]

Writing in 1950 to the great-nephew of Teddy Roosevelt, shortly after the start of the Korean War, Lippmann had admitted, "I am rather gloomy about the quality of men in charge of our destiny." Truman and Acheson had been the cause of his dejection at that

Lippmann's column was a dig at Dulles the moralist. It was also one more affirmation of Lippmann's Jamesian mistrust of doctrines, now more than half a century old. That ever-wavering wariness put Lippmann on the outs as well as the ins of the country's Protestant power elite.[7]

*

The older Lippmann was not all doom and gloom in America's age of anxiety. He sometimes joined public intellectuals who believed the United States happily had escaped the iron logics of history to build a Jeffersonian Empire of Liberty. As Lippmann explained to a friend, "no other country in the history of the world where so many people, so diverse in their origins and in their interests, have on so vast a territory governed themselves so long and preserved their freedom." Lippmann decided that Madison had been right all along about the new world's ability to control factions: "We have developed out of our experience a process by which the conflicts and diversities of sections, of classes and sects are assuaged and mollified, are purged and cooled, so that the nation can live with them and the government be carried on." Yet Lippmann also criticized the "fatty degeneration" of Truman's national security state in libertarian fashion. "It is the inevitable, unavoidable, incurable tendency of all modern governments to expand," he admonished, "and the need to contract and to reduce them is therefore never finished."[8]

But for his occasional optimism, Lippmann believed the nation was enduring a "crisis of leadership." "We're in the grip of great forces that we dimly understand," he confided to Nevins. Reading history had helped in other times, but the present just felt so unprecedented. Staring into the abyss of an undifferentiated Great Society, Lippmann worried his 1920s premonition of government by "crowds" was coming to fruition. "Our public seems, for the time being, incapable of any moderate, considered, discriminating view of any international question," he complained to Kennan. Returning to his Catholic phase, Lippmann decided that Americans had unlearned their founders' "higher law" and so were incapable of self-government. Lippmann had once rejected Bryan's majoritarian principles because they had threatened the independence of experts like himself. Now he argued that majoritarianism was the gateway to totalitarianism.[9]

Lippmann's frustrations with mass society were the occasion of his last and most eclectic major work, *The Public Philosophy* (1955). Lippmann told Berenson his book was "a discussion of the sudden and steep decline of the Western Society immediately upon the achievement of universal suffrage and the democratic control of war and peace." Apparently, Lippmann never forgave women for the Harding presidency. Still, the leadership crisis he identified was the unmanly management of foreign affairs. Truman–Acheson and Eisenhower–Dulles had been too beholden to public opinion. Their refusal to articulate, delimit, and pursue American interests abroad had led to Quixotic crusades into Asia and the Middle East. Their tender-mindedness had encouraged the proto-fascism of General Douglas "go it alone" MacArthur in Korea and the demagoguery of anticommunist Senator Joseph McCarthy, who Lippmann claimed was planting the "seeds of totalitarianism."[10]

Eisenhower's unwillingness to reign in McCarthy had been the final straw. Lippmann reminded readers that the social fabrics "rest not on law and not on force, but on a certain indispensable faith and confidence, mixed with some affection and much charity, each person for his fellow men. Without that a free society will disintegrate into a mere horde of frightened, angry, suspicious and suspected separate egos, and the last defenses will have fallen against the rise and the invasion of the barbarians and of the tyrannies they bring with them." The revival of Red Scare Christian Americanism caused Lippmann once again to publish or perish.[11]

As a preface to *The Public Philosophy*, Lippmann offered his homespun personalism—the "higher law" of the inviolability of the human spirit—as a rebuttal to McCarthy's right-wing populism. The country must find suprahistorical common ground if it was to stay together. His fierce urgency for Hamiltonianism strangely-not-surprisingly manifested itself in a turn toward monarchy. Reporting on the coronation of Queen Elizabeth II in 1953, Lippmann wrote,

> In every good society there must be a common center, known to be legitimate, to which the loyalty and the public love of all men are bound. That center of allegiance may be incarnate in an actual person or, as in a republic, it may be disembodied and have its being in the idea of the constitution and its ideal meaning. But always and everywhere, if a government is to be good, a center of men's allegiance must

be recognized that is above the diversities and conflicts of their interests, and that is invulnerable to the pressure of party, faction, class, race, and sect.

The older Lippmann's royalism was an extension of his conviction, expressed in 1938 while abroad, that "a civilization must have a religion." His notes on that subject had become "The Image of Man" and *The Good Society*. Both then served as base texts for the new book (the intended sequel to *A Preface to Morals* only twenty-six years in the making).[12]

Yet at its core, *The Public Philosophy* was a Christian humanist updating of *Public Opinion*. Lippmann's argument was familiar: "A mass cannot govern." He dated the "decline of the West" to 1917. That was when (per Wallas) the Great Society had revealed that it was too complex for democratic omnicompetence—although Lippmann's singling out of "large mass electorates" also betrayed his irritation with women's suffrage. Whatever the cause of the disorder, though, it was evident that the Western democracies were "reacting to events and they were not governing them." For Lippmann, a revival of the Rooseveltan state must follow upon the demythologization of the "sovereign people." "No more than the kings before them should the people be hedged with divinity," he challenged readers. The modern ideal of the "emancipated and sovereign people," derived from Rousseau, was the "Christian heresy" of Jacobinism (and Marxism and Leninism), the belief that heaven could be established on earth. Lippmann doubled down on Toynbee's fears of the proletarian mass that was "in" but not "of" Western civilization. Writing again as pastor and theologian besides journalist and culture critic, Lippmann renewed the secularization-totalitarianism linkage first popularized during the 1930s. "The masses that Hitler was planning to dominate," Lippmann threatened, "are the modern men who find in freedom from the constraints of the ancestral order an intolerable loss of guidance and of support."[13]

Given his comments about Hitler (and MacArthur and McCarthy), it might have been a surprise to find Lippmann calling for a stronger executive to captivate the unruly masses. That was a break from *Public Opinion*. There, he had considered disenchantment a blessing that would inspire disinterested experts to take statecraft into their own tough-minded hands. Now, Lippmann complained that "the growing incapacity of the large majority of the democratic peoples to believe in intangible realities... has stripped the government of that imponderable authority which is derived from tradition, immemorial usage, consecration, veneration, prescription, prestige, heredity, hierarchy." Lippmann joined famed anti-secularists like Jesuit theologian John Courtney Murray in decrying the political evils of a "secular and agnostic people"—he elided his self-identification as an agnostic during his recent interviews with Nevins. The prevalence of "public agnosticism," or the "practical neutrality in ultimate issues," meant that statesmen could not trust their subjects. Leaders should not consider themselves beholden to a public opinion that, even if it could be organized, would still be morally bankrupt. To save mass American democracy, Lippmann invested the executive branch with the centripetal force of divine right monarchy. The problem was not that Eisenhower conducted himself as a king. It was that he was not a very good one.[14]

But Lippmann also reunited the personal with the political whenever he talked about the fight for "traditions of civility" against the "rising tide of barbarity." "Traditions of civility" was a repeated phrase in Lippmann's book lifted from Sir Ernest Barker's *Traditions of Civility* (1948). Borrowing liberally from Barker, Lippmann tracked a special revelation about human dignity from the Stoics and Romans, to the church fathers and Aquinas, to the Renaissance and Reformation, and on to the English civil war and the American Revolution. Nodding to Washington and the founders, Lippmann invoked "the public interest," by which he meant "what men would choose if they saw clearly, thought rationally, acted disinterestedly and benevolently." Lippmann ended his work talking about the Chinese "Mandate of Heaven" as still one more expression of an extrahistorical reality that should shape human affairs. Lippmann tried to set up Nietzsche, via the popular existentialist writer Jean-Paul Sartre, as his chief foil. God might be dead, but Sartre's rejection of an "objective order" and "public world to which we belong" undermined faith in humanity and gave sanction to a "war of all men against all men."[15]

No doubt Lippmann intended his message about respecting Barker's "traditions of civility" for an elite audience. His altar call to rise above Sartre's "quagmire of moral impressionism" and to embrace "rational inquiry" demanded an individual response nonetheless. Readers could assume that Lippmann was concerned about the "good society," yes, but also the "good man in society." The world's most famous scrivener still would prefer not to choose between the SBNR he was and the RBNS he thought he had to be.[16]

*

Reactions to *The Public Philosophy* were mixed. Sociologist David Riesman, whose *The Lonely Crowd* (1950) had popularized the mass society catchphrase, the "other-directed personality," was a long-time Lippmann devotee and appreciated the new work. Yet most other left-of-center associates refused to accept Lippmann's self-characterization as a "liberal democrat." That included Niebuhr, who questioned whether Lippmann's "cure is not more dangerous than the disease." Philosopher Mortimer Adler, a Great Books champion, chided Lippmann for stressing executive powers over less coercive social controls. According to another friend, "Mr. Lippmann's outlook ... betrays in his book the unreality of the world in which a small handful of American conservatives live. There is a charm about it, like the shimmering vision of a distant dream country—but it is not our country." Lippmann was so deflated by the lukewarm reception of his pretended and pretentious Summa Theologica that he had to be hospitalized for nervous exhaustion.[17]

Traditionalists other than Adler loved Lippmann's work. *The Conservative Mind* (1953) author Russell Kirk, a darling of Buckley, Jr.'s *National Review*, praised Lippmann for endorsing "natural law" thinking (Lippmann had relied on Barker and the philosopher Leo Strauss). Similarly, considering their concerns about the future of "post-Christian Western civilization," Catholic and Protestant church leaders endorsed Lippmann, including Episcopal Bishop Angus Dunn who tutored Walter on theology. Lippmann and his colleague Thompson did not agree on much, but they both thought that Americans needed to reprioritize God and the humanities over the social sciences. Lippmann's longstanding pen pal Berenson, echoing Santayana's "socialist aristocracy," wrote that there was no hope for the West "unless we return to a graduated, pyramidal, i. e., hierarchical and even oligarchical society." Lippmann's top choice for the American presidency, General de Gaulle, suggested how much he agreed with Berenson.[18]

Still, Lippmann never became as anti-democratic as friends and foes made him out to be. He also never became so sure of himself. On his mental health collapse, Lippmann told a lifelong confidant, Judge Learned Hand, that he was tired of "trying to swim so long against the currents of public opinion.... Sometimes I wish I had a profession, like law or medicine or chemistry, which has a recognizable subject matter and methods—perhaps that is what set me off looking for a public philosophy." Recall that, later in life, Lippmann would muse about the aesthetics—the "precision" and "elegance"— of being a mathematician. His love–hate relationship with indeterminacy was ongoing.[19]

It was thus inevitable that Lippmann would fail to forge an inclusive moralism for the flailing American republic. That defeat was most noticeable in Lippmann's discussion of natural law that Kirk had acclaimed. Lippmann recommended the concept repeatedly to correspondents and throughout *The Public Philosophy*. Judge Hand noticed— in the letter that set off Lippmann's soul-searching—just how unnatural that was for his friend. Indeed, "natural law" remained so pliable in Lippmann's pragmatic hands as to render the idea of a cohesive public philosophy meaningless. He was not asking (unlike Murray and Adler) for a "neo-medieval restoration" or "romantic return to feudalism, folk-dancing and handicrafts. We cannot rub out the modern age, we cannot roll back the history that has made us what we are."[20]

But then how to move forward into the past? Lippmann's observation that "the new generation is faced with the task of re-discovering and re-inventing and relearning, by trial and error, most of what the guardians of a society need to know" subordinated Barker's "traditions of civility" to empirical verification. Elsewhere, while defending his position to a professor of international law, Lippmann admitted that "rational procedure" alone could cut through a society's "diversities of belief." In other words, Lippmann expressed faith in the pragmatic method for ascertaining truth, not in truth itself. His incapacity to make any theological or ethical principle absolute, or even to identify conditions in which they could be made so, self-sabotaged his natural law talk from the start. Natural law was merely the MORE he wrongly thought he had earned the right to believe in.[21]

Lippmann's Christian humanism could only ever be a post-Christian humanism. This was further evident in the fact that

The Public Philosophy advocated for and against civil religions simultaneously. As we have seen, Lippmann had been against civil religions before he was for them. At some level, he had always recognized that "right and wrong are not transitory" but are "inherent in the nature of things." Yet that was as far as Lippmann ever moved toward confession of belief in the supernatural. He never joined a church. He told one biographer he could only "respect" those who trusted in divine revelation ("I believe in man's progressive discovery by using his own resources," Lippmann countered). Following Dunn and pop theologian Paul Tillich, Lippmann held anthropomorphic perceptions of God as optional at best. In quintessentially post-Christian fashion, Lippmann conceded that the Ten Commandments were not of divine origin. He then added that "a fiction is not necessarily a falsehood" if it produced the desired result of getting humanity to reverence contractual obligations. But ultimately, Lippmann said he preferred the "universal rational order" of Justinian and Roman law to anything Moses or Jesus ever said. His severed connection to Jewish tradition persisted, as did his tenuous affiliation with Christianity to mask that ethnic homelessness.[22]

Yet while agreeing that an objective moral order really did exist, Lippmann equivocated over its sociopolitical value. Quoting James's *A Pluralistic Universe* (1910)—an anti-natural law text if ever there was one—Lippmann confessed,

> There is no final resting point.... Words like liberty, equality, fraternity, justice, have various meanings which reflect the variability of the flux of things. The different meanings are rather like different clothes, each good for a season, for certain weather and for a time of day, none good for all times. In the infinite change and diversity of the actual world, our conceptual definitions are never exactly and finally the whole truth.... In this actual world of diversity and change, how do we find the right rule?

Good question. Lippmann's answer (recalling his reflections on Gandhi) would have pleased the mentor he loved the most:

> In the immediate, urgent, and particular issues of daily life the major prophets, the seers and the sages, have remarkably little to offer by way of practical advice and specific guidance. The deposit of wisdom in the Bible and in the classic books does not contain a systematic and

> comprehensive statement of moral principles from which it is possible to deduce with clarity and certainty specific answers to concrete questions. He who goes to this wisdom looking for guidance of this sort will be disappointed.... There is a hiatus between the highest wisdom and the actual perplexities with which men must deal. An encyclopedia of all that the prophets and the philosophers have taught will not tell a man clearly and definitely how to make laws, how to govern a state, how to educate his children—how, in fact, to decide the problems that the priest encounters in the confessional, the doctor with his patients, the lawyer with his clients, the judge with the litigants, the man of affairs in his business.... The recorded sayings of Jesus and the Apostles do not contain a comprehensive body of laws and of precepts for the ordering of men's lives.... All this is so obvious that, manifestly, these ideas, which we find in all high religion, cannot be treated as public rules of human conduct. They are, however, related to human conduct. For they affect the nature of man, in that the vision of ourselves transformed can modify our appetites and our passions.... The regenerate man, says Saint Paul, is not conformed to this world, but is transformed in the renewing of his mind.... They can, as Confucius said, follow what their hearts desire without transgressing what is right.

Here was Lippmann's anti-preface to moralizing. Given his makeshift dualism between "high" and "public" religion—his "two realms" theory—Lippmann could advance a private philosophy only. There was no place for theological conceptions of the nation collectively shared. Elsewhere, Lippmann compared the Cold War to the conflict between "Christendom" and "militant Islam," concluding that no "universal moral order" was in sight.[23]

Lippmann, following Catholic teaching, imagined a cooperative relationship between church and state, including public funding for religious schools. But he also wanted them to remain separate. Lippmann believed that public education needed to restore the "central tradition of the classical and Christian world" yet applauded the Supreme Court for cancelling "surreptitious and denatured religion" in schools. "There is little room for freedom under the absolute power of a totalitarian church which dominates the secular force of the government," Lippmann advised, "and none under a totalitarian state which has absorbed the spiritual powers into the secular." In the end, *The Public Philosophy* was about the necessity and the impossibility of a moral majority.[24]

Some of Lippmann's general readership saw through his façade. One of them, Dorothea Fulkerson, responded, "no philosopher can decide what 'the public philosophy' must consist of, nor ordain that faith in God shall be universal in order that all conflict cease." Fulkerson was tired of what she saw as the new conservative push for certainty. She professed instead that man "is a finite being with an infinite capacity for growth." She rebuked Lippmann's retreat to monarchism: The problem was not that democracy had been tried and found wanting but rather that its leaders lacked confidence in their peoples. For Fulkerson, the good life was endless pilgrimage lived in nonconformity to immutable verities. She noted, "we struggle manfully towards the Promised Land, and when we arrive there we find that yet other unexplored lands (more beautiful than the one we have found?) lie beyond the mountains." The truly rational inquirer "seeks the truth in all points-of-view."[25]

Fulkerson was a fellow Jamesian agnostic calling Lippmann back into the pluralist fold. She did not have to try that hard. The best that Lippmann could do with any mode of civility—natural or supernatural—was affiliate without affirming it. In a revealing, most likely autobiographical, admission from *The Public Philosophy*, Lippmann stated, "a man who has humility will have acquired in the last reaches of his beliefs the saving doubt of his own certainty. Though he produces wealth and uses it, and though he resists evil, he will have little acquisitiveness and possessiveness, he will have no final attachment to things, he will have no strong lust for power or for vengeance. He cannot and he will not be perfect. But in some measure he will be pulled toward perfection." Lippmann was not above plagiarizing himself: In this instance, retooling his "disinterested man" of *A Preface to Morals* in a book that was supposed to be about recommitment to suprahistorical truths. The passage was a reminder that, no matter how much the older Lippmann publicly sounded like the pastor of the RBNS, privately he retained the "saving doubt" of his younger SBNR self. That ceaseless struggle between Lippmann's two post-Christian persuasions was what produced some of the most insightful, unfinished homilies on twentieth-century American politics, culture, and diplomacy.

*

Lippmann might have tried to stop redeeming the world after the disappointment of *The Public Philosophy*, but the world was not done rescuing him from irrelevance. It looked to Lippmann for answers more than ever, and he provided them in efficiently eclectic fashion. Foremost on his mind was developing a Mean between the extremes of the American anticommunist left and right. Reflecting on Soviet advances in rockets and space exploration, Lippmann grumbled about the corrosive effects of mass consumerism: "With prosperity acting as a narcotic, with Philistinism and McCarthyism rampant, our public life has been increasingly doped and without purpose." Lippmann was reveling in conservative cultural criticism at the same moment that his thinking on national politics was at its most liberal. That was one more apparent contradiction only if we allow ourselves to be beguiled by the liberal-conservative binary of the long culture wars.[26]

As Lippmann later testified, he never ran with Buckley, Jr. and the *National Review*. He never endorsed their global anticommunism nor supported the "totalitarian bureaucracy" (Buckley's words) of the military-industrial complex except when he did. Lippmann was the frontrunner and face of a cohort of heterodox conservatives, also known as "liberal conservatives" and "conservative socialists." Two in particular—the popular scholar Peter Viereck, author of *Conservatism Revisited: The Revolt against Ideology* (1949, 1962); and the Bancroft prize-winning historian Clinton Rossiter, writer of *Conservatism in America* (1956)—found Lippmann an affable friend and ally. Rossiter and assistants poured over Lippmann's thousands of writings to produce *The Essential Lippmann* (1965). After naming him "perhaps the most important American political thinker of the twentieth century," Rossiter observed, "it is, indeed, the unresolved tension in his own mind between tough-minded liberalism and warm-hearted conservatism that makes him one of the most appealing of the modern American thinkers." Lippmann would praise Viereck's updating of *Conservativism Revisited* before the 1964 elections. He would also back Viereck's rendering of Buckley Republicans as "subversive gangster soapboxers [and] traditional agitators of the lunatic-fringe right."[27]

Viereck and Rossiter followed Lippmann in roasting the *National Review*'s pet ideologist, Arizona Senator and presidential hopeful Barry Goldwater. They considered him, in Lippmann's words, "radically reactionary." The liberal conservatives thereby won the respect of liberal anticommunists like Niebuhr, economist John Kenneth Galbraith, and the historian Arthur Schlesinger, Jr. "In Goldwater we have a demagogue who dreams of arousing the rich against the poor," Lippmann remarked of the New Right's corporate populism. "His feet are not on the ground. His head is in some kind of private cloud." Lippmann was alarmed by Goldwater's embrace of the "Southern strategy" of luring segregationists to the Republican party (Lippmann had borrowed that term from an unknown source).[28]

Lippmann's feud with Goldwater and the New Right traversed foreign and domestic policy. Lippmann had blessed so many Cold War actions while never becoming a Cold Warrior. He had gone out of his way in the 1930s to insist that communism was an "alien stereotype" that could never take hold in the United States. He continued to do so into the 1950s and 1960s. "The so-called socialism which is supposed to be creeping up on us is in fact nothing more than the work of making life safe and decent for a mass society collected in great cities," Lippmann protested. Modernity was expensive, but it was worth it. Lippmann's chief worry was that the bipartisan national security state was too amorous of guns and was not willing to spend more on butter.[29]

In fact, no self-identifying conservative of this era was more committed to increasing public expenditures than Lippmann. His alignment with Galbraith, a fellow Keynesian and author of *The Affluent Society* (1958), was critical. They each held the federal government responsible to make urban centers great again—to stimulate human flourishing throughout the country—as well as to maintain a large defense establishment. That meant more public dollars going to schools and universities, highway construction, health care, conservation efforts, and inner-city renewal. Lippmann had little patience for the tax revolt propagated by both parties, which he equated with a hedonist trend toward "private self-indulgence" over "public responsibilities." Lippmann also favored dusting off Roosevelt's "big stick" (i.e., trustbusting) to manage the "giant business" and "giant labor" of Eisenhower's corporate commonwealth. The national imperative must be to produce better kitchens and everything else than the Soviet and Chinese command economies. "In the real world," Lippmann alerted readers, "we are up against great mass societies of powerfully disciplined people, and unless we can restore and concentrate our own energies to outdo them, it will not matter at all how many adjectives we hurl at them in the battle of words."[30]

The movement for Black civil rights during the Cold War tested Lippmann's desire to "outdo" communism. Recall his earlier secret support for Harvard's quota system. Lippmann's liberalism, like that of the Roosevelts, could not tolerate social disorders. Thus, he had resisted antilynching legislation, Truman's civil rights initiatives, and anything else that threatened the Southern racial hierarchy. Lippmann interacted with few persons of color at cocktail and dinner parties, and his political home was with pro-segregationist Democratic Senators like Byrd of Virginia and J. William Fulbright of Arkansas. Not surprisingly, then, Lippmann joined other white moderates in considering *Brown vs. Board of Education* (1954) a mistake for imposing desegregation upon an unwilling people—and so risking "social convulsions." Lippmann softened *Brown*'s blow by arguing that the educational standards of every American youth needed to be raised. He also insisted, well into the 1960s, that colleges and graduate programs should be integrated first where it would supposedly be easier. Lippmann did hope that Southerners would accept the Supreme Court's decision without too much trouble and was caught off guard by the "massive resistance" campaign led by Byrd among others. He supported federal intervention at Little Rock High School in 1957 but only to resolve what he saw as a national embarrassment and international crisis. He maintained that "integration is a problem in persuasion and consent, which cannot be solved by injunction and soldiers."[31]

That was not the first time Lippmann held the color line, nor would it be his last. All the same, Lippmann recognized that segregation was a "legal caste system" intent on keeping Black Americans divided and submissive. Recalling his "race parallelism" from Red Scare Chicago, Lippmann assumed that the surest way to end white supremacy was through Black self-determination. That was why he preferred promoting voter rights over enforcing school integration. Lippmann applauded the passage of the 1957 Civil Rights Act, popular among Northern white liberals as well as Black Southern activists, because he believed it was a clear case of federal jurisdiction over the states. He also hoped expanding the Black electorate would allow their communities to achieve social equality through the exercise of countervailing political power. It was a logic as close to Malcolm X as it was to Martin Luther King, Jr. (and Lippmann's friend Galbraith, for that matter). Still, Lippmann would back Fulbright and other conservative Democrats for positions in the Kennedy and Johnson administrations. His silence in the face of mounting white backlash to civil rights advance would be deafening.[32]

*

Lippmann's seventieth birthday in 1959 became an occasion for several loud celebrations of the journalist's life and work. Dulles was dead, Soviet premier Khrushchev had just completed a goodwill tour of the United States and UN, and the Cold War seemed to be cooling off. Criticisms of *The Public Philosophy* notwithstanding, Lippmann's performance as a "lonely" oppositional insider was finally rewarded with a fame equal to his giant salary. The National Press Club held a meeting in his honor and gave the sage a stage to explain what it meant to be an opinion columnist in a democracy. A few months later, Lippmann (who hated television) was asked to appear on the CBS network. The program was so well received that Lippmann was signed to a five-year contract.[33]

Lippmann was also presented with a festschrift, *Walter Lippmann and His Times* (1959). The contributors—ranging from Binger, Kennan, and other old friends; to peers like the *New York Times*'s James Reston; and to the fellow travelers Niebuhr, Schlesinger, Jr., and the French sociologist and philosopher Raymond Aron—were a veritable who's who of Cold War liberalism. Their honor suggested that Lippmann belonged among the academic elite. Yet not all of the tributes were positive. Reprising his review of *The Public Philosophy*, Niebuhr concurred with Lippmann that "democracy requires an aristocracy for an adequate foreign policy as it requires an aristocracy of knowledgeable and wise leaders in every realm of policy." He also begged Lippmann to surrender the eccentricity of the natural law theorist. Schlesinger, Jr., repeated Niebuhr's concerns. Quoting Lippmann himself, Schlesinger, Jr., said the columnist had chosen Santayana (idealism) over James (pragmatism) in the end. Yet in a wink at his friend's Jamesian-Keynesianism, Schlesinger, Jr., lauded Lippmann as "a wonderful example of the Compensated Mind, seeking through continuous intervention to restore our society to the paths of decency and rationality."[34]

Lippmann friends and family had another reason to party: He had just won his first Pulitzer prize for an extended interview with Khrushchev in 1958. Thanks to Helen's notetaking, translating, and comradery, Lippmann would win a second Pulitzer after another meeting with the Soviet Premier in 1961 (the one described in this book's preface). Not bound to a formal transcript, Lippmann was free to bend Khrushchev's words to his own purposes. Together, their message for the United States was to chill out. According to Lippmann, the Premier had promised that, regarding Cold War hot spots like China, Vietnam, Germany, and Korea, there would be "no change of frontiers by military force." Instead, the Soviets feared a U.S. first strike from Europe or Turkey would halt their peaceful conquests. The trick, Lippmann editorialized, was how America could maintain military supremacy minus a global "scare campaign" to sell it. Lippmann, through Khrushchev, or vice versa, emphasized that, while a "showdown" over Germany was inevitable, it did not have to be a "military showdown." Venturing into the cosmic, the two diagnosed the "American psychosis" manufactured by Dulles and the "militarists." Both feared that the United States was begging for "religious war in which the contending positions are absolute." Lippmann the iconoclast added that "there never has been a universal state or a universal religion."[35]

But that did not stop Lippmann from trying to lift America up as a model for the non-communist world. His real fear of the Soviet Union was the "force of their example" throughout the majority world. Communism was a "secular religion," and Khrushchev was a "true believer" who embodied his countrymen's "relentless determination" and "unqualified faith" in international communism. The Soviets were not interested in "world conquest," but they did want to exercise their powers "as the guardian against American interference with the predestined world revolution." It was thus critical that the United States outlive their Russian and Chinese rivals. Lippmann had been talking about "American destiny" to develop "backward" peoples since World War II. His calls to increase public outlays in education, health care, and cities were central to that mission. "The only real alternative to communism is a liberal and progressive society," Lippmann counseled.

Lippmann and Khrushchev were skeptical that the United States could export democracy to "feudal" and "tribal" countries (Lippmann described them elsewhere as "old, crowded, politically primitive"). American modernization was "unique," but Lippmann still thought it was "imitable," notably endeavors like the TVA. He challenged readers to set a good example of growth in "material progress" and "civil liberty" while promoting them elsewhere through aid and investment. He reiterated anti-imperialist warnings from years earlier about how enlisting "The Unaligned" in an anticommunist front would backfire. Instead, the United States needed to cultivate a new Wallace-type partnership with NAM countries rooted in mutual respect.[36]

Lippmann's Khrushchev interviews returned him to the realistic Wilsonianism of his Cold War columns and even further back to *The Stakes of Diplomacy*. His constantly contrarian body of work on foreign affairs had anticipated Cold War modernization theories as espoused by the CFR, the Kennedy administration, and Walt Rostow's *The Stages of Economic Growth* (1960). Lippmann knew Rostow and cautioned him in 1956 about trying to confront communism everywhere. Rostow and Kennedy did not listen, and their coupling of TVA-style projects with military abundance in Vietnam would corroborate Lippmann's anti-global global Americanism (more on that in the next chapter). Lippmann remained a devoted critic of imperial hubris and overreach until his death.[37]

*

Yet too few knew or cared at the time that one of the most revered Americans in all the world kept women locked in his attic. A trinity of female assistants labored daily in the upper room of the Lippmann house in a makeshift reference library. One of the assistants admitted, "the pressure is terrific when he is around." That was revealed in 1952 when author John Mason Brown was granted rare access into Helen's and Walter's lives. Each weekday morning and afternoon, Lippmann's secretary Jean Wehner and research associate Barbara Donald (who had replaced van Schaik in 1948 and was herself succeeded by Elizabeth Farmer in 1959) waited upstairs "under strict instructions not to disturb [Lippmann] until he buzzes for them." They were aided by Charlotte Wallace, the Lippmanns' social secretary who had worked for Helen in government administration during World War II. As we have seen, Lippmann rarely acknowledged female contributions to his success. That was especially the case with Donald, who not only assembled his research and read new books for him, but also conducted research at the Library of Congress, attended press conferences, and interviewed congressmen and other public officials. The neglect was intentional, part of belonging to a well-paid white straight male aristocracy that extended far beyond the nation's capital.[38]

Brown bore witness to the weirdness of the Lippmann household at some level. His defense of Lippmann was subtly a critique: "The charge that [Lippmann] only sees the 'right people' overlooks his temperament, background, and the special nature of the role he has made his own," Brown explained. "He sees the people he enjoys, the people who stimulate him, the people he needs to see for professional reasons—in other words, the people who are right for him. That does not mean they are politically to the right. He only hopes they will talk well, and does not mind if they live well, too."[39]

Several years later, one historian would be much less sparing in his denunciation of Lippmann, writing, "while he held the conduct of other people to a very high standard indeed, mankind's self-appointed conscience was himself guilty of conscienceless acts." By all accounts, Lippmann was generous in relationships and dearly loving toward Helen. Despite (or due to) his identification as a conservative, for over thirty years Lippmann backed many robust welfare policies against the fake news that they were slipping the country into socialism. Lippmann also stood against universal nationalism no matter what party was in charge. He was a Wilsonian critic of military Wilsonianism, always looking for a moral equivalent to the Cold War, even if he ended up supporting most foreign interventions until Vietnam. What was most conscienceless about Lippmann was his use of religions to delegitimize women, minorities, and the working classes seeking the same civil rights and liberties that he had for so long (if precariously as a Jew) enjoyed. Lippmann's certain blindness on matters of race, sex, and class were typical of the New England pragmatism and Rooseveltan strong-state tradition that had made him and that he had made.[40]

Lippmann's pilgrimage from post-Christian secularist to post-Christian humanist continued into the 1960s amidst national and world insurgency. He would occupy the Kennedy and Johnson White Houses while feeding the youth revolt against American empire. Lippmann's life and career would end in defiance of the liberalism he had led through so many wildernesses.

Notes

1. Walter Lippmann, "Today and Tomorrow: The Big Money," *New York Herald Tribune*, Mar. 10, 1952, in *Essential Lippmann*, ed. Rossiter and Lare, 345–7; Walter Lippmann, "Today and Tomorrow: Three Weak Governments," *New York Herald Tribune*, Oct. 27, 1949, 29. On "war lord," see Steel, *Walter Lippmann*, 460–1; and Walter Lippmann, to Arthur Vandenberg, Aug. 8, 1949, in *Public Philosopher*, ed. Blum, 542–3. See Walter Lippmann, to Dorothy Thompson, Jan. 13, 1954, in WLP, Reel 94, for the negative effects of U.S. military presence.
2. Walter Lippmann, "Today and Tomorrow: Withdrawal and Reexamination," *New York Herald Tribune*, Dec. 11, 1950, 21; Walter Lippmann, "Today and Tomorrow: Some Self-Examination," *New York Herald Tribune*, Jan. 22, 1952, 21; Walter Lippmann, "Today and Tomorrow: Disentanglement," *New York Herald Tribune*, Apr. 21, 1955, 18.
3. Walter Lippmann, *Isolation and Alliances* (Boston: Little, Brown, 1952), 23–6, 35–6, 42, 51–2.
4. On SEATO and the Dulles conversation, see Steel, *Walter Lippmann*, 503–4. See Walter Lippmann, "Today and Tomorrow: Disaster in the Middle East," *New York Herald Tribune*, Nov. 1, 1956, 21, on the Suez crisis.
5. For Lebanon, China, Korea, and Africa, see Walter Lippmann, "Today and Tomorrow: Disentanglement," *New York Herald Tribune*, July 10, 1958, 16; Walter Lippmann, "Today and Tomorrow: The Marines in the Lebanon," *New York Herald Tribune*, July 17, 1958, 14; and Walter Lippmann, "Today and Tomorrow: Senator Mansfield's Proposal," Sept. 1, 1960, 16.
6. On "gloomy," see Walter Lippmann, to Joseph Alsop, July 19, 1950, in *Public Philosopher*, ed. Blum, 554. See Walter Lippmann, "Today and Tomorrow: The President and the People," *New York Herald Tribune*, Mar. 7, 1961, in *Essential Lippmann*, ed. Rossiter and Lare, 273, on teachers. See Lippmann, to Douglas, July 9, 1948; Walter Lippmann, "Today and Tomorrow: Candidate and Leader," *New York Herald Tribune*, July 10, 1956, in *Essential Lippmann*, ed. Rossiter and Lare, 271–2; Walter Lippmann, "Today and Tomorrow: Taft and the President," *New York Herald Tribune*, Aug. 4, 1953, 19; Walter Lippmann, "Today and

Tomorrow: The McElroy Affair," *New York Herald Tribune*, Mar. 3, 1959, in *Essential Lippmann*, ed. Rossiter and Lare, 316–17, on Eisenhower. For Lippmann's thoughts on the liberation strategy, see Walter Lippmann, "Today and Tomorrow: Containment and Liberation," *New York Herald Tribune*, Sept. 9, 1952, 25; Walter Lippmann, "Today and Tomorrow: The Declaration on Captive Peoples," *New York Herald Tribune*, Feb. 24, 1953, 21. See Walter Lippmann, to George Ball, Nov. 25, 1955, in WLP, Reel 44, on "militarized diplomacy."

7. Walter Lippmann, "Today and Tomorrow: Quiet Diplomacy, for Now, is Hope of the World," *New York Herald Tribune*, Jan. 26, 1961, 16; Walter Lippmann, "Today and Tomorrow: Dulles and the Churchmen," *New York Herald Tribune*, Nov. 27, 1958, 18.

8. Walter Lippmann, "Today and Tomorrow: The Election Explained," *New York Herald Tribune*, Nov. 3, 1952, in *Essential Lippmann*, ed. Rossiter and Lare, 303–4; Walter Lippmann, "Today and Tomorrow: Morale and Discipline," *New York Herald Tribune*, Dec. 2, 1952, in *Essential Lippmann*, ed. Rossiter and Lare, 53.

9. Walter Lippmann, "Interview," 233; Walter Lippmann, to George Kennan, Aug. 24, 1953, in *Public Philosopher*, ed. Blum, 573. See Walter Lippmann, "Today and Tomorrow: The Isolationist Tide," *New York Herald Tribune*, Dec. 19, 1950, 29, on the "crisis of leadership." On majoritarianism and totalitarianism, see Walter Lippmann, "Today and Tomorrow: The American Idea," *New York Herald Tribune*, Feb. 22, 1954, in *Essential Lippmann*, ed. Rossiter and Lare, 5–6. The 1954 essay was taken from a 1947 address Lippmann delivered at the unveiling of Washington's statue at the Washington Cathedral.

10. Walter Lippmann, to Bernard Berenson, Aug. 23, 1954, in *Public Philosopher*, ed. Blum, 578. On MacArthur, see Lippmann, *Isolation and Alliances*, 43–4.

11. On McCarthy, see Walter Lippmann, "Today and Tomorrow: Nightmare in Washington," *New York Herald Tribune*, May 3, 1954, 14; and Walter Lippmann, "Today and Tomorrow: Acheson and McCarthy," *New York Herald Tribune*, May 2, 1950, 21.

12. Walter Lippmann, "Today and Tomorrow: The Coronation of a Queen," *New York Herald Tribune*, June 2, 1953, in *Essential Lippmann*, ed. Rossiter and Lare, 204–5; Lippmann, "Men and Ideas."

13. Walter Lippmann, *Essays in the Public Philosophy* (Boston: Little, Brown, 1955), 4, 10–14, 40, 71–2, 96, 111–12, 179. Lippmann's book has always been called *The Public Philosophy* for short.

14. Lippmann, *Public Philosophy*, 46–57, 78, 96–7, 100, 113.

15. Lippmann, *Public Philosophy*, 3, 42, 97–8, 104–8, 177–81.

16. Lippmann, *Public Philosophy*, 3, 42, 97–8, 104–8, 177–81. See Brown, *Through These Men*, 227, for "good man."

17. Lippmann, *Public Philosophy*, 13; David Riesman, to Walter Lippmann, Apr. 18, 1953, in WLP, Reel 88; Reinhold Niebuhr, "A Matter of

Popular Will," *New York Times Book Review*, Feb. 20, 1955, 3; Mortimer Adler, to Walter Lippmann, Aug. 24, 1954, in WLP, Reel 40; Francis Biddle, "Lippmann and Reality," *New Republic*, Nov. 14, 1955, 13. On Lippmann's hospitalization, see Steel, *Walter Lippmann*, 493–4.

18. Russell Kirk, to Walter Lippmann, Mar. 7, 1955, in WLP, Reel 149; Angus Dunn, to Walter Lippmann, Feb. 6, 1955, in WLP, Reel 58; Dorothy Thompson, to Walter Lippmann, Feb. 14, 1955, in WLP, Reel 94. See Steel, *Walter Lippmann*, 494–5, for the Berenson and de Gaulle letters. On "post-Christian," see "Sheen Tells Collegians World 'Divorces' God," *New York Herald Tribune*, Nov. 10, 1958, 21.
19. Walter Lippmann, to Learned Hand, Mar. 12, 1955, in WLP, Reel 65.
20. Lippmann, to Berenson, Aug. 23, 1954; Lippmann, *Public Philosophy*, 136; Learned Hand, to Walter Lippmann, Mar. 7, 1955, in WLP, Reel 65. See Riccio, *Walter Lippmann*, 182–8, for critique of his use of natural law by contemporaries. Riccio concludes that natural law was, for Lippmann, a "useful prop" (188).
21. Lippmann, *Public Philosophy*, 136; Walter Lippmann, to Quincy Wright, Jan. 25, 1955, in *Public Philosopher*, ed. Blum, 580.
22. Lippmann, *Public Philosophy*, 108, 164–6, 168–9. On "right and wrong," see Walter Lippmann, quoted in Weingast, *Walter Lippmann*, 107 (the quotation is from a conversation Weingast had with Lippmann in 1946). For Lippmann never joining a church and his thoughts on revelation, see Wellborn, *Twentieth-Century Pilgrimage*, 134–6, which are based on letters Lippmann sent in March of 1964.
23. Lippmann, *Public Philosophy*, 144–5, 147–52; Walter Lippmann, "Today and Tomorrow: The Second Inaugural," *Washington Post*, Jan. 24, 1957, A19.
24. Lippmann, *Public Philosophy*, 154–5. On "central tradition" and "denatured religion," see Walter Lippmann, "Today and Tomorrow: The Prayer Cases," *Washington Post*, June 20, 1963, A21. Lippmann appeared to change his mind on the school issue. See Walter Lippmann, "Today and Tomorrow: The Religious Peace," *Washington Post*, Mar. 14, 1961, A13; and Walter Lippmann, "Today and Tomorrow: On Aid to Religious Schools," *Washington Post*, Apr. 15, 1965, A21.
25. Dorothea Fulkerson, to Walter Lippmann, Apr. 24, 1955, in WLP, Reel 150. Fulkerson's letter was a part of Lippmann's "public opinion" collection. She did not leave any clues as to her location or career.
26. Walter Lippmann, "Today and Tomorrow: The Portent of the Moon," *New York Herald Tribune*, Oct. 10, 1957, in *Essential Lippmann*, ed. Rossiter and Lare, 68.
27. Clinton Rossiter and James Lare, "Introduction," in *Essential Lippmann*, ed. Rossiter and Lare, xi, xx; Peter Viereck, to Walter Lippmann, Aug. 20, 1964; Walter Lippmann, to Peter Viereck, Oct. 1, 1964, both in WLP, Reel 96. See also Jennifer Burns, "Liberalism and the Conservative Imagination," in *Liberalism for a New Century*, edited Neil Jumonville and Kevin Mattson (Berkeley: University of North Carolina Press, 2007), 58–72.

28. Walter Lippmann, to Barry Goldwater, Nov. 22, 1958, in WLP, Reel 64; Walter Lippmann, "Today and Tomorrow," *New York Herald Tribune*, Sept. 22, 1964, A15.

29. Walter Lippmann, "Today and Tomorrow: Big Money," *New York Herald Tribune*, Jan. 2, 1962, in *Essential Lippmann*, ed. Rossiter and Lare, 348.

30. John Kenneth Galbraith, to Walter Lippmann, Apr. 24, 1950; Walter Lippmann, to John Kenneth Galbraith, Apr. 27, 1950, both in WLP, Reel 63. On increasing public expenditures, see Walter Lippmann, "America Must Grow," *Saturday Evening Post*, Nov. 5, 1960, in *Essential Lippmann*, ed. Rossiter and Lare, 330–1; Walter Lippmann, "Today and Tomorrow: The Size of the Problem," *New York Herald Tribune*, Mar. 8, 1960, in *Essential Lippmann*, ed. Rossiter and Lare, 365–7; Walter Lippmann, "Today and Tomorrow: The Incoming Tide," *New York Herald Tribune*, Nov. 20, 1958, in *Essential Lippmann*, ed. Rossiter and Lare, 362–3. See Walter Lippmann, "Today and Tomorrow: Public Need and Private Pleasure," *New York Herald Tribune*, Sept. 5, 1957, in *Essential Lippmann*, ed. Rossiter and Lare, 361–2, on taxes. For "big stick," see Walter Lippmann, "Today and Tomorrow: Fiasco in Steel," *New York Herald Tribune*, Oct. 13, 1959, in *Essential Lippmann*, ed. Rossiter and Lare, 357. For "great mass societies," see Walter Lippmann, "Today and Tomorrow: Crucial Internal Question," *New York Herald Tribune*, Dec. 11, 1958, in *Essential Lippmann*, ed. Rossiter and Lare, 365.

31. On *Brown*, see Walter Lippmann, "Today and Tomorrow: The Mounting Crisis in Education," *New York Herald Tribune*, May 20, 1954, 20; Walter Lippmann, "The Two School Systems," *New York Herald Tribune*, June 2, 1955, 22; Walter Lippmann, "Today and Tomorrow: The Third Year," *New York Herald Tribune*, Sep. 4, 1956, 16; Walter Lippmann, "Today and Tomorrow: Nullification in Mississippi," *New York Herald Tribune*, Sept. 27, 1962, 26; Walter Lippmann, "Today and Tomorrow: Mississippi and After," *New York Herald Tribune*, Oct. 4, 1962, 26. On Little Rock and integration, see Walter Lippmann, "Today and Tomorrow: The Army at Little Rock," *New York Herald Tribune*, Oct. 1, 1957, 24.

32. Walter Lippmann, "Today and Tomorrow: The Mounting Crisis in Education," *New York Herald Tribune*, May 20, 1954, 20; Walter Lippmann, "Today and Tomorrow: Voting and Integration," *New York Herald Tribune*, July 11, 1957, 18; Walter Lippmann, "Today and Tomorrow: A Strong Bill," *New York Herald Tribune*, Aug. 8, 1957, 14.

33. Steel, *Walter Lippmann*, 511–20.

34. Reinhold Niebuhr, "The Democratic Elite and American Foreign Policy," in *Walter Lippmann and His Times*, ed. Childs and Reston, 173, 187; Arthur Schlesinger, Jr., "Walter Lippmann: The Intellectual v. Politics," in *Walter Lippmann and His Times*, ed. Childs and Reston, 190, 224.

35. Walter Lippmann, *The Communist World and Ours* (Boston: Little, Brown, 1958), 12, 14, 28–9, 30–1, 37–40, 51; Walter Lippmann, *The Coming Tests with Russia* (Boston: Little, Brown, 1961), 24, 27.

36. Lippmann, *Communist World and Ours*, 24, 37, 41–55; Lippmann, *Coming Tests with Russia*, 16, 28–9, 35–7; Walter Lippmann, "Today and Tomorrow: Unique and Imitable," *New York Herald Tribune*, Jan. 26, 1956, 18; Walter Lippmann, "Today and Tomorrow: The Unaligned," *Washington Post*, Nov. 30, 1961, A27. On "secular religion," see Walter Lippmann, "Today and Tomorrow: Peking and Moscow," *Washington Post*, Apr. 10, 1962, A17.
37. Walter Lippmann, to Walt Rostow, Sept. 26, 1956, in WLP, Reel 89. On Rostow, Vietnam, and modernization theory, see David Ekbladh, *The Great American Mission: Modernization and the Construction of an American World Order* (Princeton: Princeton University Press, 2011), 100, 182–3, who mentions Lippmann's support.
38. Brown, *Through These Men*, 203–6; Steel, *Walter Lippmann*, 499–500.
39. Brown, *Through These Men*, 205–6.
40. Kenneth S. Lynn, "Versions of Walter Lippmann," *Commentary* 70 (Oct. 1980): 65.

7
The Heretic, 1960–1974

"There is no denying the general truth that life in the modern world is far from being the good life." That was Lippmann's lament to Donna Reichel in 1969, an undergraduate at the University of Maryland at College Park. Reichel was part of the "New Left," distinguished by its base in universities as opposed to the labor unions of the "Old Left." Over the course of the 1960s, the New Left had fought for Black civil rights and against urban poverty. They had also led massive demonstrations against the Vietnam War. After their preferred dove, the Democratic Senator Eugene McCarthy, lost his primary—and his party lost to Nixon and the Republicans in the 1968 election—Reichel and friends wondered if what they called "the system" could be saved.[1]

The New Left hoped Lippmann would be sympathetic to their desire to level the military-industrial complex. They were no doubt disappointed by his reply:

> In the advanced nations in the modern age, the old conceptions of revolution—the overthrow and the replacement of an establishing governing class—is, I believe, antiquated. It belongs to the horse-and-buggy age, to the time before the great technological achievements, which have produced, among other things, an affluent majority, which is able and ready to put down the activist rebels of the minorities. In a way, I believe that society can be improved and reformed but not transformed by disruption of the established institutions, in which and on which and through which all of us have to live.

The really older Lippmann maintained that domination was so entrenched within Great Societies that it was impossible to name let alone uproot (it appears he had been reading Jacques Ellul's antimodernist classic, *The Technological Society*, first published in 1954). Since his Harvard days, Lippmann had advocated for more organic ways of life than Megalopolis could afford. Yet his rebuff to Reichel was typical of his anti-radicalism forged during the Progressive era and Great Depression. It also masked the ways that Lippmann had busied himself in retirement by helping to destroy the Cold War liberal order, most notably by disrespecting Democrats and then promoting Richard Nixon (the subject of this final chapter).[2]

The skeptic Lippmann had never found a system to love, so until 1968 he had mostly loved the strong-state liberalism he had been with since his House of Truth and *New Republic* days. Liberalism had provided security and status for homeless Jews like himself. In turn, they had been expected to defend liberalism's privileging of toughminded white Christian males of Northern European descent. That was no problem for Lippmann since he had valorized such men since boyhood.

Over the years, Lippmann's greatest weapon against Reichel's radical liberalism had been his silence: He had simply ignored, in print and on television, The President's Commission on the Status of Women (1961–63), Betty Friedan's *The Feminine Mystique* (1963), the National Organization of Women (1966), the ERA, and most other originating moments of women's liberation. Lippmann was once pressed by the historian and international correspondent Mary Blume for his opinion on the women's movement, to which he admitted, "there have been so many liberation movements. I'd flunk out on that question. I haven't had any particular contact with it. I hadn't really thought that women were a deprived part of mankind. There is a great deal of discrimination in jobs, but that's a fairly simple problem to settle." Privately, Lippmann complained that "we are living in days when our public life has been corrupted" due to bad schools, advertising, and "family breakdown"—code for increasing female independence. In one of the final interviews of his life, Lippmann reminded Steel his biographer, "I wrote a book back in the beginning of the century about the dissolution of the ancestral order," referencing *A Preface to Morals*. "Clearly, the ancestral order of the family, for instance, has been much more affected by the contraceptive pill than it has by anybody's speeches or by the war."[3]

*

Lippmann's suggestion that birth control was a worse disaster than Vietnam was one more conscienceless act in a life full of them. The older Lippmann was still capable of surprise, however. Take his apology for Black revolution. Massive resistance to integration at Little Rock and elsewhere had shown Lippmann that American moral standing in the world required bolder commitments to civil rights. Like most white liberals, Lippmann was dragged along by the course of events, still preferring university over elementary school desegregation. But by the early 1960s, he was recommending the comprehensive antiracist measures that became the 1964 Civil Rights Act. The war-like conditions of the South demanded a "national movement to enforce national laws" that protected Black Americans. That change should be "led and directed by the national government," Lippmann informed readers—that was just before the police riot against the Children's Crusade in Birmingham in 1963. It was imperative that the country "recover the confidence of the Negroes in the good faith of the whites." Lippmann invoked jurist Blackstone and "the central truths of Christendom" in arguing that private property rights were never absolute. They could be violated in order to overcome the "public humiliation" of segregation. While most of Lippmann's CBS interviews concerned foreign policy, he briefly suggested that the Civil Rights Act was needed to promote the "internal peace of this country."[4]

When that peace came too little, too late, Lippmann issued an atypical statement. Between 1965 and 1968, most major American cities experienced uprisings in response to police brutality and other systemic racial injustices. Black nationalism and pan-Africanism split the civil rights movement, leading to demands for "Black Power" to achieve by collective grassroots action what white liberals could not. Though calling for a "politics of consensus" as late as 1966, Lippmann defended Black Power advocates. He predicted that the recommendations coming out of the "Kerner Report" (1968) on the urban revolts—which claimed that "our nation is moving toward two societies, one black, one white—separate and unequal"—would not work. In light of the tax revolt of "white flight" suburbanites led by Goldwater and Ronald Reagan Republicans, Lippmann claimed that white Americans would never tolerate higher taxes to aid cities that were more and more predominantly Black. Thus, civil rights leaders had no choice but to pioneer new forms of interest-group mobilization. "That is the constructive and creative element in the irrationality and wildness of black power," Lippmann argued. "Ugly as are some of its manifestations, the growing feeling among the Negroes that they must help themselves is one of the bright spots in a somber picture."[5]

Lippmann's characterization of groups like the Black Panthers was racist. It was also a return to his "race parallelism" of the first Red Scare. At that time, Lippmann had assumed that Black solidarity and self-determination ("pride and self-respect") must precede successful experiments in racial integration. His refusal to join in simple condemnation of Black Power was tribute to his continuing independence of thought—if not also to his incurable eclecticism and maybe hypocrisy. Lippmann never softened toward women's liberationists, though.

*

Lippmann was clearly disillusioned with Cold War liberal America by the time of Reichel's letter. It was a despair matched only by the joy he had felt at the beginning of the decade. Then, it had seemed the Kennedy and Johnson administrations would renew strong-state liberalism following the drift of the Eisenhower years. Throughout 1960, Lippmann argued that the nation needed an "Innovator," in the "Roosevelt–Wilson-Roosevelt" vein, to meet the Soviet challenge. Outliving international communism meant that "we change many of our cherished dogmas and harden ourselves to a sterner way of life." It was a Nietzschean–Jamesian sermon Lippmann had delivered so many times before but never to such a receptive audience. With two Pulitzers behind him, Lippmann took "Today and Tomorrow" to the *Washington Post* in 1962, and he began to write regularly for *Newsweek*. He, Helen, and the poodles never seemed more fortunate nor needed.[6]

Thanks to his connections and world renown—and indebted to his new research assistant, Elizabeth Farmer, who had worked on the Kennedy campaign—Lippmann was finally invited back into the White House. Lippmann rediscovered himself there while consulting on cabinet and foreign service picks among old Harvard friends like Schlesinger, Jr., and Galbraith. At one point, Kennedy considered Lippmann for an ambassadorship, a position he might have accepted. Though that never happened, Lippmann still interacted with the president regularly in unofficial and official capacities. Almost every night he and Helen mingled with Kennedy's "whiz kids" at dinners and parties. The Kennedy family, like most of Washington, realized it was best to stay on Lippmann's good side.[7]

It is unclear the extent to which Lippmann went rogue when, in a "Today and Tomorrow" column during the Cuban crisis, he pushed the idea of a missile dismantlement swap with Khrushchev (Turkey for Cuba). The Kennedys were evidently stunned by Lippmann's olive branch, but some in his administration might have encouraged him to pen it. In any case, the Soviets warmly embraced Lippmann's offer and made it the basis of their demands. Lippmann thus complicated the Cuban missile crisis but also played an indirect role in its resolution and the ensuing movement toward détente. His "One-Man State Department" was precisely that, and even more so as the Kennedy White House passed to Johnson.[8]

Both presidents courted Lippmann for good press, but that was a costly decision. Each would have to learn a point made at the beginning of this book: Lippmann was no sycophant. He used Kennedy and Johnson to advance his conservative liberal vision just as he had tried to bend the Roosevelts and Wilson to his will to power. He turned on all of them when they did not come through. Lippmann became critical of Kennedy for not being the teacher the nation needed, particularly on civil rights and the welfare state. He was happier to see Johnson at the helm to make Camelot a reality.

On Johnson's announcement of the Great Society reform package, Lippmann told CBS viewers:

> The Great Society is a result of a revolution that's occurred, a silent and beneficent revolution that's occurred in our generation, under which, we have learned, not perfectly because it's very difficult—it's a new art—we have learned how to control, regulate, and promote the production of wealth in an advanced industrial society. We are able to produce more wealth by putting on taxes, interest rates, and all the budgetary arrangements that we use, and make the thing grow, and we finance the new developments, education and everything that we talk about in the Great Society, the beautifying of cities, and everything of that sort out of the taxes on the increase of wealth that we're able to produce.

Lippmann did not believe the Great Society "revolution" was the New Deal revisited. It was not redistributing static wealth. It was maximizing monetary, moral, and social capital throughout all sectors of American life by means of enlightened fiscal policy. Fitting that Johnson's reform program was almost named "The Good Society," intentionally after Lippmann's 1937 book, as it embodied the pro-capitalist, white male breadwinner Keynesianism that Lippmann had championed for so long. The "Great Society" branding paid only quiet tribute to its originator Wallas and to his student-friend Lippmann who had steered the slogan through world war, affluence, depression, world war, and affluence again.[9]

The Great Society would fail in Lippmann's estimation—undone, not by Buckley's small-state conservatives, but by the Democrats' foreign follies. The Bay of Pigs had renewed Lippmann's conviction that military disentanglement was a necessary first step toward winning the Cold War. Lippmann rejected attempts to overthrow Castro as un-American and unnatural ("like a cow that tried to fly"). He deplored the CIA's "dirty tricks" and called for curtailment of the agency's ability to wage shadow war. Lippmann was more predisposed toward Kennedy's Alliance for Progress, a massive developmental aid package for Central and South America.[10]

In public and behind closed doors, Lippmann reviewed his foreign policy life lessons: A country should not make promises or threats it did not have the power to fulfill; the U.S. military was not built for long-term occupations; and ideology inevitably corrupted diplomacy. "Our security and well-being are not involved in Southeast Asia or Korea and never have been," Lippmann warned about the rising tide of anti-Americanism there. "If it is said that this is isolationism, I would say yes. It is isolationism if the study of our own vital interests and the realization of the limitations of our power is isolationism. It is isolationism as compared with the globalism which became fashionable after the Second World War." For Lippmann, it was time once again to prefer "cool examination" to "hot ideologies" and to what he called "scatteration."[11]

Lippmann was asked by CBS in 1965 if the rumors were true that he was an isolationist. He reacted,

> Well, I don't think these words mean anything, or at least I don't care whether anybody uses them. I don't care about the word isolationism, and I don't care about the word appeasement. I'm interested in the

rights and needs and responsibilities of the United States. We are not the policeman of mankind. We are not able to run the world, and we shouldn't pretend that we can. Let us tend to our own business, which is great enough as it is. It's very great. We have neglected our own affairs. Our education is inadequate, our cities are badly built, our social arrangements are unsatisfactory. We can't wait another generation. Unless we can surmount this crisis, and work and get going onto the path of settlement in Asia, and a settlement in Europe, all of these plans of the Great Society here at home, all the plans for the rebuilding of backward countries in other continents will all be put on the shelf, because war interrupts everything like that.

Lippmann's bombshell recalled Roosevelt's similar letter to Europe in 1933 (which Lippmann had opposed then). The older Lippmann hated playing with dominoes, notably with the kind that could topple his country's precarious stability. As he had put it in an earlier interview, "I do not like warlike old men."[12]

*

Lippmann did not support escalation in Vietnam except when he did. He had initially backed French efforts to retake the country following World War II. He had abandoned them as foolish after the French defeat in 1954. The sooner the United States "outlawed" military solutions to the problems of "weak states," the better. Heavily influenced by de Gaulle, Lippmann preached reunification and neutralization of Vietnam under the Christian anticommunist leader of the South, Ngo Dinh Diem. On television, Lippmann invoked Korea as a cautionary tale about avoiding land wars in Asia. He advised that, while the Soviets had no immediate interests in the region, Chinese communist control of Southeast Asia was a question of "when" and not "if." America could be a "good neighbor" to Asia, but it was still a "daughter of Europe" with whom it shared a "common ancestry, a common heritage, a common culture, the same religions, the same basic jurisprudence, and the vast philosophical and artistic treasury of Western civilization." Notice that religions continued to shape Lippmann's geopolitical binary between East and West.[13]

Lippmann believed the United States needed to get its own neighborhood in order. That meant settling the balance of power with the Soviets as a prerequisite to consolidating European unity and the

Atlantic Community. Advisers should remain in Vietnam long enough to ensure a tidy withdrawal of Western forces. Still, no number of modernization projects could transform the country into an "American outpost." Lippmann dismissed talk of extending the Great Society to Asia as "globaloney" (a term coined by Republican representative Clare Boothe Luce in 1943). Behind closed doors, Lippmann relayed messages from de Gaulle that a military solution in Vietnam was impossible. Per Lippmann's custom of accepting Cold War policies but not Cold War ideologies, he sanctioned Johnson's initial bombing campaign of Northern Vietnam as useful for forcing Ho Chi Minh to the negotiating table.[14]

When the bombings became Operation Rolling Thunder—and U.S. helicopters, bases, and troops started establishing outposts— Lippmann broke hard with the administration. The policy was "all stick and no carrot," Lippmann explained to Johnson privately on why the Vietcong would not discuss a settlement. He urged the president's team to go on a "peace offensive" akin to Wilson's Fourteen Points. When the *Washington Post* apologized for Johnson, Lippmann took his own newspaper to task:

> A mature great power will make measured and limited use of its power. It will eschew the theory of a global and universal duty which not only commits it to unending wars of intervention but intoxicates its thinking with the illusion that it is a crusader for righteousness, that each war is a war to end all war.... If we examine this idea thoroughly, we shall see that it is nothing but the old isolationism of our innocence in a new form. Then we thought we had to preserve our purity by withdrawal from the ugliness of great power politics. Now we sometimes talk as if we could preserve our purity only by policing the globe. But in the real world we shall have to learn to live as a great power which defends itself and makes its way among other great powers.

Twenty-five years (if not fifty years) later, Lippmann was still trying to convince Washington to "get rid of the globalism." Nevertheless, Lippmann remained cautiously optimistic that the "warlike old men" were confined to the Pentagon. He trusted that Johnson's team would take his advice to approach Hanoi with an offer of unconditional cease-fire.[15]

When a cease-fire did not happen, Lippmann complained to friends that he had been duped. He described the student antiwar movement as "self-defeating" and "pathetic" yet also understandable given the vacuum of responsible leadership in the country. He even began learning from antiwar protestors and foreign correspondents. Lippmann impugned American exceptionalism to friends unabashedly, chiding Schlesinger, "the search for security and the assembling of an empire are two sides of the same coin." He was even harsher in print. "It is panic-mongering to flagellate ourselves into paroxysms of anguish and shame at the prospect of negotiating settlements which end our entanglements in East Asia," Lippmann charged in 1965. "The time has come to stop beating our heads against stone walls under the illusion that we have been appointed policeman to the human race." A year later, Lippmann would accuse Johnson of suffering from the "messianic megalomania which is the Manila madness." The President's team were trying to "kill mosquitoes with tanks and build a Great Society with B-52s." In turn, it was putting the United States on a "collision course" with the Chinese and Soviets and making it difficult to protect "weak countries" when and where it really mattered. Lippmann argued that America was becoming a "bastard empire which relies on superior force to achieve its purposes and is no longer an example of the wisdom and humanity of a free society." The upshot of Vietnam was simple: "The American promise has been betrayed and abandoned."[16]

The older Lippmann soon found himself homeless once more, cast out by young and old alike. The eighty-year-old had become hip to the New Left's anti-imperialism. He shared its frustration that the Great Society was being neglected (which was why Reichel had written him in the first place). Lippmann foretold that the collapse of Great Society programming would fall heaviest upon those Black Americans who had been counting on participation in the country's urban revival. At the same time, student radicals had disrupted Cold War liberals' white, straight, and male normalcy too much for Lippmann's liking. However, even with all he held in common with Kennedy's and Johnson's men—including a commitment to an American hegemon engaged in the peaceful penetration of "backward" peoples—Lippmann's refutation of military Wilsonianism and the politicians peddling it led to a "war on Walter Lippmann." He never reentered the White House after April of 1965. He was effectively shunned out of the Beltway.[17]

Lippmann ended his journalistic career a self-described "neo-isolationist" opposed to the "foolish globalism" of the Democrats. "Nobody is wise enough or clever enough or strong enough to arrange it all for the world," he explained to Steel in 1971. Lippmann recommended that U.S. policymakers let majority world revolutions play themselves out. As he had warned the whiz kids six years earlier about their ambitions to liberate communist-controlled territory, "they little know the hydra who think that the hydra has only one head and that it can be cut off."[18]

*

Lippmann entered retirement during a "minor Dark Age." At least that was how he characterized his fears to Steel about growing populations, pollution, and promiscuity. He and Helen left Washington, D.C., in April 1967 and moved back to New York. Walter ceased "Today and Tomorrow" in May, although he continued to write occasionally until 1971. If Walter felt excommunicated from the nation's capital, he found New York more violent and less fun than he had remembered. He and Helen still went out to plays and parties but absent the former friendships, conversations, and intrigue. The older Lippmann now could get into all the clubs his younger self could not—and without the Lamonts' backing. However, Lippmann often ended up dining among strangers. The American Establishment no longer worried what he might say about them, so they no longer sought him out.[19]

In his loneliness, Lippmann started one more book that he never finished, "The Ungovernability of Man." It was a patchwork tapestry of his greatest hit pieces. Amidst the disorderly drafts—the symbol and cost of his open mind—Lippmann reported that he had been worrying about "Ungovernability" ever since Harvard and befriending Wallas, which was true. Lippmann never settled on a single argument for the new work, but unsurprisingly he repeated the words "revolution" and "order" the most.[20]

The broken form of Lippmann's manuscript betrayed his sense that an age of fracture was upon America in the world. Lippmann charged that "rationality," the hallmark of a 500-year-old "modernity," had dissolved the "ancestral order," including the moral force of neighborhoods, families, and churches. He asserted that liberal egalitarian democracy—an offspring of an earlier Christian humanism—was living on borrowed time. It could not be made efficacious in ever-more-complex Great Societies. Having revisited *Public Opinion* and *A Preface to Morals*, Lippmann then replayed *The Good Society* and *The Public Philosophy*: The West needed "an ordered moral, political, religious consensus which the preponderant mass of men accept and obey and enforce." In a *New Republic* essay from a few years earlier, though, Lippmann had claimed that only universities and their "universal company of scholars," not churches and priests, could resolve the West's crisis of authority. His characteristic yes/no to civil religions had grown more erratic.[21]

Lippmann blamed humanity's crossing of the "Ungovernability" Rubicon on two sources: The breakup of the European empires after World War II and (from Ellul) the emergence of "new technology" that weakened the integrity of nation states. "The new world is cold, uncaring, strange, mechanical, and ruthless," Lippmann concluded—echoing his lament to Reichel. Lippmann's autopsy of the "very rich and very unhappy" 1960s might tempt historians to place him in the "neoconservative" camp alongside other disillusioned Jewish intellectuals within the Democratic Party. It would not be the first time Lippmann was ranked among Tired Radicals.[22]

But Lippmann never became a neoconservative. He remained a keen-eyed optimist standing against the proliferation of "prophecies of doom" about environmental change and over-population. As a post-Christian, post-socialist, liberal conservative or conservative liberal humanist, Lippmann resumed shouting (to no one listening but Steel) that men were not gods yet were still tasked with doing God's will of organizing a humane republic. In fact, Lippmann offered one of his most precise declarations of principles amongst his manuscript's wreckage, "The Four Components of Civility." Those included commitments to "no unaccountable power," to the innate dignity or "inviolability" of persons, to "excellence" in all private and public labor, and to the "golden rule" of Jesus. The last one anticipated Stephen Carter's 1998 classic *Civility*.[23]

Lippmann was disturbed as never before by the banal brutality of "technological men." He renewed his pre-1960s charge to build cities back better. He also waxed nostalgic for the town hall America that had been the Progressive endgame dating back to Addams and

Dewey. "Ungovernability of Man" was Lippmann at his most eclectic, oscillating between hard observations about living big and modern and soft pleas for thinking small and disinterested.[24]

*

The hard Lippmann won out in practical politics. He proclaimed shortly before the 1968 elections that "Nixon's the only one" who could govern the ungovernable. Lippmann had initially backed the antiwar Democrats Robert Kennedy and Eugene McCarthy. But after Kennedy was assassinated, the Chicago Democratic Party Convention collapsed in chaos, and McCarthy lost the nomination, Lippmann went all in for the Red Scare Republican that had once sent him fleeing the party. His endorsement was the insult he returned to Johnson liberals for the injuries he thought they had inflicted upon him for his opposition to Vietnam. Lippmann predicted that Democrats would need to find or invent a common enemy if they were ever to reunite in the future.[25]

Referencing Nixon, Lippmann went cosmic one last time: "His role in American history has been that of the man who had to liquidate, diffuse, deflate the exaggeration of the romantic period of American imperialism and American inflation. Inflation of promises, inflation of hopes, the Great Society, American supremacy—all that had to be deflated because it was all beyond our power and beyond the nature of things." The neo-isolationist Lippmann was most attracted to Nixon's efforts to ease Cold War tensions. He believed the Republican would return America to the balance-of-power realism that Lippmann had been preaching for decades. Furthermore, Lippmann considered Nixon a kindred Keynesian who would roll back the excesses of strong-state liberalism but not the welfare state itself. Lippmann repeated his observation from earlier that white people would not suffer higher taxes to fund Black community support— though he never said if he was one of those white people.[26]

More subtly, Lippmann was drawn to Republicans' "law and order" messaging for a post-democratic America. Streamlining "Ungovernability of Man" as well as *The Public Philosophy* and *Public Opinion*, Lippmann portrayed the United States as a "mass society" that had grown too complex, too selfish, and too permissive for self-governance. The country must transition to either a dictatorship or a parliamentary system. It was in this context that Lippmann first revealed that he had always been a Burkean conservative at war with the Jacobins—the New Left as well as Johnson and McGovern—who supposedly preached human perfectibility. Lippmann now doubted that the "ancestral order of the family" could be saved apart from a restoration of "authority and the belief in something" (notice that the best this self-termed agnostic could offer readers at the end of his life was "belief in something").[27]

Lippmann warned that rejections of Jacobinism throughout history, such as McGovern's defeat, could take the form of fascism. Nonetheless, he was hopeful that Nixon and the Republicans would know when and how to curb their anti-liberal enthusiasm. When pressed elsewhere by Steel about the Watergate scandal, Lippmann concluded, "The President of the United States is like a King with all the powers and limitations inherent in a King."[28]

*

The monarchist Lippmann would not live to witness the Reagan counterrevolution against the strong-state liberalism that Nixon and Goldwater had made way for. Lippmann suffered his first seizure in the spring of 1973, and his mental and physical health declined gradually thereafter. He was cared for mainly by his former ward Jane, as Helen laid plans to move to Europe indefinitely. "She was a tormented person," Steel concluded of Helen's actions, "torn by her feeling for Walter, and by the consuming resentment she also felt, even if she could not admit it to herself... the subordination that formerly seemed natural appeared a needless sacrifice." Helen died suddenly of a heart attack in early 1974. Walter would pass away in December of that year, also from a heart attack.[29]

Shortly before his death, Lippmann was honored with New York's Bronze Medallion, a distinguished award for "exceptional citizenship and outstanding achievement." The ceremony was presided over by the city's first Jewish mayor, Abraham Beame. At one point, Lippmann confided to Beame, "my ancestors, like yours, were immigrants." It was a rare moment in which Lippmann admitted to his foreignness and hinted at his Jewish ancestry. He had spent a lifetime hiding his ethnicity through attachments to powerful white men like Wilson, the Roosevelts, and the Kennedys; through strenuous service to the American warfare-welfare state; and through pragmatic affiliation with Western Christianity. Lippmann remained a post-Christian pundit to the end, finding religions useful for meeting personal and social needs while never himself encountering a God he could believe in. His MORE would be the assemblage of books, articles, and addresses—all those "prefaces" and "inquiries"—that we still mull over today to discover something about our world and ourselves.[30]

Notes

1. Walter Lippmann, to Donna M. Reichel, Dec. 15, 1969, in *Public Philosopher*, ed. Blum, 617–18.
2. Lippmann, to Reichel, Dec. 15, 1969.
3. Walter Lippmann, to Donald McDonald, Dec. 1, 1967, in WLP, Reel 77; Blume, "Walter Lippmann at 80," B3; "Walter Lippmann at 83," C4. On the 1960s as a struggle over the racial and gender limitations of liberalism, see Robert O. Self, *All in the Family: The Realignment of American Democracy since the 1960s* (New York: Hill and Wang, 2012).
4. "Lippmann and Eric Sevareid," CBS interview, Apr. 8, 1964, in *Conversations with Walter Lippmann*, ed. Edward Weeks (Boston: Little, Brown, 1965), 192–3. On "national movement," see Walter Lippmann, "Today and Tomorrow: The Negroes and the Nation," *Washington Post*, May 28, 1963, A19. On property rights, see Walter Lippmann, "The Negroes' Grievances," *Newsweek*, Sept. 16, 1963, 21. See also Walter Lippmann, "Today and Tomorrow: The Civil Rights Bill in Sight," *Washington Post*, June 11, 1964, A23.
5. Walter Lippmann, "The Race Report," *Newsweek*, Mar. 25, 1968, 19. On "consensus" and "taxes," see Walter Lippmann, "Today and Tomorrow: Broken Promise," *Washington Post*, July 12, 1966, A13.
6. Walter Lippmann, "The Country is Waiting for Another Innovator," *Life*, June 20, 1960, in *Essential Lippmann*, ed. Rossiter and Lare, 70–4.
7. Steel, *Walter Lippmann*, 521–84.
8. On Lippmann's involvement in the Cuban missile crisis, see Matthew A. Wasniewski, "Walter Lippmann, Strategic Internationalism, the Cold War, and Vietnam, 1943–1967" (PhD, University of Maryland, College Park, 2004), 176–235.
9. "Lippmann and Eric Sevaried," CBS interview, Feb. 22, 1965, in *Conversations with Walter Lippmann*, ed. Weeks, 220–1. The Princeton historian Eric Goldman had suggested the name "The Good Society" after Lippmann's book. Johnson's advisors instead chose "The Great Society," evidently unaware of its use by Wallas and Lippmann. See Robert Dallek, *Flawed Giant: Lyndon Johnson and His Times, 1961–1973* (New York: Oxford University Press, 1998), 81.

10. Lippmann, *Coming Tests*, 33–4; Walter Lippmann, "Today and Tomorrow: Intelligence and Dirty Tricks," *Washington Post*, Feb. 23, 1967, A21. On Lippmann's support for development, see Walter Lippmann, "Today and Tomorrow: Shock Treatment," *Washington Post*, May 19, 1959, A21.
11. Walter Lippmann, "Today and Tomorrow: Globalism and Anti-Americanism," *Washington Post*, Dec. 29, 1964, A17.
12. "Lippmann and Eric Sevaried," 231–2; "Lippmann and Howard K. Smith," CBS interview, June 15, 1961, in *Conversations with Walter Lippmann*, ed. Weeks, 70.
13. "Lippmann and Eric Sevaried," 199–207. See Walter Lippmann, "Today and Tomorrow: The Military Cut," *Washington Post*, Jan. 11, 1955, 11, on the fallacy of military solutions in Asia. For "daughter," see Walter Lippmann, "Today and Tomorrow: Historical Note," *Washington Post*, Nov. 24, 1966, A21.
14. "Lippmann and Eric Sevaried," 199–207. On the Atlantic Community, see Walter Lippmann, "Today and Tomorrow: Atlantic Partnership," *Washington Post*, July 10, 1962, A11. See Walter Lippmann, "Today and Tomorrow: Politics and the Eggheads," *Washington Post*, Apr 26, 1966, A17, on "globaloney."
15. Walter Lippmann, "Today and Tomorrow: The Unfinished Debate," *Washington Post*, Apr. 27, 1965, A17. On Lippmann's White House meetings and recommendations for a "peace offensive" and "unconditional cease-fire," see Steel, *Walter Lippmann*, 560–3, which relies heavily on Farmer's notes in Steel's possession.
16. Walter Lippmann, "Today and Tomorrow: On the Student Demonstrations," *Washington Post*, Oct. 26, 1965, A17; Walter Lippmann, to Arthur Schlesinger, Jr., Sept. 25, 1967, in WLP, Reel 90. On "time," see Walter Lippmann, "Today and Tomorrow: The Johnson Beginning," *Washington Post*, Feb. 2, 1965, A11. See Walter Lippmann, "Today and Tomorrow: Manila Madness," *Washington Post*, Nov. 7, 1966, A23, on "megalomania." For "mosquitoes," see Walter Lippmann, "Today and Tomorrow: War Shrouds U.S. Role in Asia," *Washington Post*, Jan. 19, 1967, A21. On "collision course," see Walter Lippmann, "Today and Tomorrow: A Collision Course," *Washington Post*, May 23, 1967, A17. See Walter Lippmann, "The American Empire," *Newsweek*, Oct. 9, 1967, 21, for "bastard empire" and "promise."
17. Ronald Steel, "The World We're In: An Interview with Walter Lippmann," *New Republic*, Nov. 13, 1971, 20–1. See Steel, *Walter Lippmann*, 578–9, for the turn against Lippmann. See Walter Lippmann, "The Negro's Hopes are a War Casualty," *Washington Post*, Aug. 20, 1967, B1, on race, Vietnam, and the Great Society.
18. Steel, "The World We're In," 21; Walter Lippmann, "Today and Tomorrow: On the Way to the Brink," *Washington Post*, Mar. 30, 1965, A13.
19. Steel, "The World We're In," 21. See Steel, *Walter Lippmann*, 580–4.

20. Walter Lippmann, "The Ungovernability of Man," undated, unpaginated manuscript, in WLP, Box 223, Folders 326–7. The folders contain numerous handwritten and typed drafts of chapters, book introductions, prospectuses, addresses, and articles dated between 1969 and the summer of 1970 in no particular order.
21. Lippmann, "Ungovernability of Man"; Walter Lippmann, "The University," *New Republic*, May 28, 1966, 17–20.
22. Lippmann, "Ungovernability of Man."
23. Lippmann, "Ungovernability of Man."
24. Lippmann, "Ungovernability of Man."
25. Walter Lippmann, "Nixon's the Only One," *Washington Post*, Oct. 6, 1968, B2.
26. "Walter Lippmann at 83," C1, C4; Steel, "Walter Lippmann," 16–17. See also Steel, "World We're In," 20–1; and "Lippmann on American Destiny," *Washington Post*, Apr. 1, 1973, C1, C4, which focus more on foreign affairs.
27. "Walter Lippmann at 83," C1, C4; Steel, "Walter Lippmann," 16–17.
28. "Walter Lippmann at 83," C1, C4; Steel, "Walter Lippmann," 16–17.
29. Steel, *Walter Lippmann*, 594–9.
30. Walter Lippmann, quoted in Steel, *Walter Lippmann*, 598.

Epilogue
Saint Walter

> Let us be saints then, if we can, whether or not we succeed visibly and temporarily.
>
> William James, 1902[1]

Ronald Steel understood much but also forgave much about the man that won him a National Book Award and the Bancroft Prize for best book in American history. He offered the following summation while introducing Lippmann's *The Public Philosophy*:

> Those inner convictions—a belief in the dignity of man, in the essential contrariness of human nature, in the need to strive for the best despite the odds, in the promise of American democracy—were the mark of a humanist, a skeptic, and a man of enormous integrity. But Lippmann responded to events like a pragmatist; he did not form patterns like a philosopher. He was more like William James than he imagined, and less like Santayana than he preferred to believe. He could analyze situations with finesse and give off brilliant flashes of illumination. Yet when he tried to use those powers to mold a coherent philosophy, he stumbled.

Lippmann was a lot like William James. He was a public intellectual of remarkable productivity, profound insight, and rhetorical flourish. He was a culture critic beholden to few powerful men, even the ones he loved. Lippmann was not, however, a person of "enormous integrity." He was a professional chameleon with so much to say because he thought he had so much to hide.[2]

What impressed one reviewer of Steel's biography was how closed Lippmann's open mind could be. Edward Said, a founder of post-colonialism and "Orientalist" studies, commended Steel for recreating the American Establishment that Lippmann had frequented as an insider-outsider. Lippmann had found a home among America's power elite, Said claimed, because of his skill at rationalizing "the appearance, and actually more than that, the conviction, of realism." But that realism had cost him and the country greatly. Lippmann's "general aura of coldness, distance, and emotional inadequacy" was part of the problem. It was also that Lippmann "stripped the self of its ties to community, family and personal loyalty, in order to enhance the claims of a 'national' interest." Lippmann, in Said's estimation,

> was the journalist of consolidation. For him, what mattered was the status quo: he elaborated it, he was tempted by and he succumbed to it, he sacrificed his humanity to it. Childless, shedding and acquiring friends and attitudes with alarming frequency and poise, allowing his writing only very rarely to express the uncertainty and human frailty that Steel convinces us he often felt, Lippmann articulated the 'national interest' as if only his insider's view was responsibly serious. Hence his ultimate public influence and his ultimate superficiality as a commentator on the world.

Consolidation of other people's ideas—Nietzsche's, James's, Wallas's, Keynes's, Toynbee's, Gilson's, Barker's, Ellul's—really was Lippmann's life's work. Said concluded that Lippmann "exemplifies his country's choice of the style of reassuring authority over any concrete message or social vision."[3]

Neither Steel nor Said captured the whole of Walter Lippmann because no one can. That is true of any biography but especially one of a constant contrarian. The story I have told here challenges narratives of Lippmann as a solely spiritless commentator. Lippmann should be remembered as a public theologian and pastor, too. He cared so much about politics and diplomacy because he was trying to answer philosophical and religious questions about living well with and in spite of others. He "went cosmic" a lot more often than was recognized in his time or since.

Said was right to marvel at how inhumane Lippmann could be. Lippmann rarely if ever confronted the straight white male positionality of strong-state liberalism. But Said was wrong to suggest that everything solid Lippmann wrote about modernity melted into air.

Lippmann could be a lavish critic of civil religions when he was not promoting them. He thought they seduced Americans away from honest assessments of their power and into disastrous campaigns promising satisfaction in this life. Every generation needs someone reminding them that human beings are mortals, not gods, and Walter Lippmann was that for the twentieth century. If we still need Niebuhr, then we are missing Lippmann even more so.

*

Lippmann could not fully bear his agnosticism toward absolutes, which led him to become a post-Christian model of and for his era. There is no evidence that Lippmann read the "Death of God" scholars who curated post-Christianity after Toynbee and Bayne. Still, Lippmann's corpus, like Nietzsche's, had heralded their coming. In *The Death of God* (1961), French theologian Gabriel Vahanian explained that the "post-Christian era" was marked by a "levelling down" of existence. Transcendental habits of imagining God had become untenable, thereby constricting all quests for the good life and society to material realms. Westerners could no longer accept the old-time religions even if they wanted to. Yet, as Toynbee, Lippmann, and Bayne had insisted earlier, this was an ironic fate: Christianity had produced post-Christianity which, in turn, had made Christianity "alien" to an age of big science, technology, and cities. Vahanian believed every moment of history was "post-Christian" in that it was impossible to incarnate a God in any system or institution. Nevertheless, he decided that an irreversible rupture between the natural and supernatural had finally occurred. Much as Lippmann had argued in *A Preface to Morals*, Vahanian concluded that modern man had a "cultural incapacity" for Christianity.[4]

Post-Christianity arrived in the United States amidst the Christian nationalist revival of the 1950s. Vahanian joined Bayne and others in criticizing pop conceptions of the divine as a "Cosmic Pal" and "livin' doll." Whenever people "try God," it meant that Christianity had lost the culture war. Echoing Will Herberg's *Protestant, Catholic, Jew* (1955), Vahanian attacked "civic religion" and the "threefold religion of democracy." That disease had been there much earlier, though, if we recall Small's American Religion or Croly's "Religion of Humanity"—or Lippmann's State religion, for that matter. Vahanian reset the post-Christian timeline even further back. He suggested that the Declaration of Independence had encouraged "idolatrous concern about secular matters." Americans had killed God and there was no bringing it back to life. Individuals might still encounter the "Wholly Other," but Vahanian left no hope for Christianity as a social ethic.[5]

Vahanian would have enjoyed spending time with the younger Lippmann but not so much the older one. The younger Lippmann would have agreed with Vahanian that Eliot, Maritain, and the later Toynbee were fools to cast Christianity as the fulfillment of universal religion and society. Vahanian would have seen in Lippmann's iconoclasm the Protestant endgame of "secularity," the devotion to keeping temporal affairs temporal, as opposed to the "secularism" of Christian nationalism, with its idolatrous sacralization of the profane. Yet Vahanian might have missed that Lippmann had always believed civilizations needed religions. When Lippmann turned to Toynbee and Catholic intellectuals in the 1930s, he was making explicit a desire for order—personal, professional, political—that had been there from his Sachs and Harvard days. The older Lippmann, like Vahanian, recognized the radical immanence of the American religion, calling it a "religion without a theology," a "benign morality," and a "residual ideology" held over from an earlier Christian age. Lippmann just chose to believe parts of the big lie, or at least tried to convince others that they needed to believe them.[6]

Since the 1960s, several writers have continued Vahanian's attacks on post-Christianity. Contemporary usages were taken up by the ecumenical missionary Leslie Newbigin in books such as *Honest Religion for Secular Man* (1966). Since 1980, conservative Catholic and evangelical writers have co-opted the term "post-Christian" and employed it in their wars on secularity. Their works include Harry Blamires's *The Post-Christian Mind: Exposing Its Destructive Agenda* (1999), and Gene Edward Veith, Jr.'s, *Post-Christian* (2020). Lamenting (like the older Lippmann) "family breakdown" as the "largest single social disaster" to hit the West, one conservative wrote in the *National Review*, "a post-Christian society is not merely a society in which agnosticism or atheism is the prevailing fundamental belief. It is a society rooted in the history, culture, and practices of Christianity but in which the religious beliefs of Christianity have been either rejected or, worse, forgotten. In other words a post-Christian society is a particular sort of

Christian society.... Though much of what Christianity taught is forgotten, even unknown, by modern Europeans and Americans, they nonetheless act on its teachings every day." The Barna Group, an evangelical polling agency, has since identified the "most post-Christian Cities in America," although they interchanged the terms "post-Christian" and "secularized."[7]

There have been other attempts to give post-Christianity more weight but to little avail. Harold Bloom's *The American Religion: The Emergence of the Post-Christian Nation* (1992) followed Vahanian in suggesting that the United States had never been Christian. Whereas Vahanian had feared how Christianity was being used to manufacture Cold War consent, Bloom's point was that Americans were too individualistic, too anti-intellectual, and too anti-institutional to express Christianity's corporate dimensions. Bloom mentioned the word "post-Christian" only a few times in his text yet asserted, "there are tens of millions of Americans whose obsessive idea of spiritual freedom violates the normative basis of historical Christianity, though they are incapable of realizing how little they share of what was once considered Christian doctrine." More recently, Christopher James built upon Barna in his investigation into Seattle as a "post-Christian" clearinghouse. James defines post-Christian as a society characterized by "low levels of Christian church affiliation and participation." Yet Seattle's Nones are hardly that. "Their spirituality may be a patchwork," James concluded, "but the scraps of cloth at hand for many are well worn and patently Christian." The remainder of his book is advice on how to make the most of America's residual ideology.[8]

The term post-Christian has become ubiquitous since Lippmann's day, yet its analytical value remains elusive. Is it possible to grow it into a scholarly concept out of its pejorative origins? I am not sure, but any words used to describe the intellectual revolutions of the early twentieth century—secularization, dechristianized, post-Protestant, disenchantment, Protestant secular, disestablishment, crisis of faith, death of Christendom, and so on—will also be what Lippmann called stereotypes.

I have intended "post-Christian" to denote an imaginary, common among the Progressives and their pragmatist successors like Lippmann, that assumed the utility of Christian ideas, ethics, and institutions to promote mental health and social order. Lippmann embodied post-Christianity as he developed an affiliation with Christian traditions but never felt bound to or by them. Though he fellow-traveled with Christian lefts and rights throughout his life, he was always closer to someone like anthropologist and rival influencer Margaret Mead, a self-described "post-agnostic."[9] Lippmann promulgated post-Christianity whenever he called audiences to rediscover religions as crucial to personal integrity and a civil society. Lippmann's political and diplomatic counsels were framed by his post-Christian feeling that, because the "God" of Christendom was dead, everyone had to figure out how to get along without it. Post-Christianity was forever a hope-fear for Lippmann, more rhetorical than actual and ultimately unrealized.

Lippmann's status as a secularist Jew turned Western post-Christian traditionalist was a pretension meant to solve private and public disruptions. That repositioning implicated him in battles against "barbaric" women, racial and ethnic minorities, immigrant working classes, and at times the Majority World. The pictures in Walter Lippmann's head could be incredibly cruel ones. It is tempting to leave him behind as a vestige of heterosexual white male liberal conservativism or conservative liberalism. Yet that would be a mistake, as Lippmann offered so much guidance about how and why to live beyond Christian America's very long Red Scare.

*

Our binary political culture still pits democracy against socialism, Jefferson against Hamilton, freedom against authority, and the SBNR against the RBNS. Granted, the SBNR has drawn more attention because it has appeared to be the victor. Since the 2000s, all organized religions have faced and are facing some degree of decline. Disorderly spirituality is the new normal and has always been part of being American (as Bloom and Vahanian argued). At the same time, the less-discussed RBNS thrives amid anti-institutional religious individualism. Christian nationalism, with its conviction that democratic republics cannot survive absent loyalty to an organized religious ideology and establishment, remains a powerful force in American public life. In both instances, the RBNS and the SBNR cross over into politics, reminding of how the two-party media system determines personal and group well-being as much as any community of worship.[10]

Lippmann had been laboring to reconcile the RBNS and the SBNR before anyone knew they were at war. Just because he never used those terms does not mean he was not contending with them throughout his life. The younger Lippmann had been an SBNR stalwart, proclaiming the end of Christianity and urging followers to embrace a Spartan spirit of disinterestedness. In those same years, he foresaw a new religion of the State, or "democratic collectivism," to reincorporate the disinherited, disenchanted masses. That State religion evolved into Lippmann's amalgamation of socialism–liberalism–conservativism–humanism. His older self, meanwhile, went all in with the lonely RBNS crowd, demanding mass consent to "the higher law" and "traditions of civility" while reimagining (Republican) presidents as kings. Yet Lippmann was still optimistic that some individuals could become inner-directed saints despite civilizational collapse. They could act as checks on State overreach.

The older and younger Lippmanns navigated the SBNR–RBNS divide by never deciding between them. They determined, however consciously and always episodically, that large urban-industrial societies required both self-made persons (the SBNR) and robust mechanisms of government (the RBNS) committed to balancing liberty, opportunity, security, and order. Lippmann never supported Christian nationalism any more than he applauded the demise of churches, mosques, and synagogues. His story shows us that we are better off working through our differences rather than ignoring or destroying them. In his best moments, Lippmann was on a pilgrimage to uncover democracy's best practices. If his mission to prove that opposites really do attract seemed impossible, his message stayed clear: Keep trying.

Do we need a new Walter Lippmann today? Every few years, someone says so. Most recently, Lippmann was featured in Robert Putnam's and Shaylyn Romney Garrett's *The Upswing: How America Came Together a Century Ago and How We Can Do It Again* (2020). In a final chapter entitled "Drift and Mastery," the two sociologists invoke Lippmann (and Teddy Roosevelt) to support their call for a new Progressive coalition. Obviously, I would hate it if we stopped reading works by and about Lippmann. We need his cautions against ideological crusades now more than ever.[11]

Yet wanting a new Lippmann misses several facts. We already have so many Lippmanns today—op-ed columnist David Brooks chief among them. Brooks, remarkably like Lippmann, is a liberal conservative of Jewish decent yet attracted to Christianity as a means for improving social capital (Brooks described himself in 2019 as "a wandering Jew and a very confused Christian").[12] The "needing Lippmann" question also elides who Lippmann was. It is not just that he was a liberal willing to sacrifice the basic liberal rights of others to hold on to his precarious position as a Jew in an anti-Semitic age. It was also his lifelong sense that his generation was stuck between a deceased Christian-Jeffersonian world and a tough-minded Beloved Community yet to be born.

To live "post"—"post-Christian," "post-secular," "post-racial," "post-gender," "post-industrial," "post-truth"—is no fun. It means we do not yet know what we will be or should be. But the chief Lippmann sermon, the pragmatist's main lesson, is to lean forward while conserving the best that the past had to offer. "The modern conservative," Lippmann preached, "has to work in unprecedented ways for an undefined future. He has to create the new forms in which the enduring truths and values can be carried on in a world that is being radically transformed." Wherever we end up, we should see that skepticism can be productive of a greater self and republic—even if each remain a bit incurably eclectic.[13]

Notes

1. James, *Varieties of Religious Experience*, 316.
2. Steel, *Walter Lippmann*, 490.
3. Edward Said, "Grey Eminence," *London Review of Books*, Mar. 5, 1981, 7.
4. Gabriel Vahanian, *The Death of God: The Culture of Our Post-Christian Era* (New York: George Braziller, 1961), 6, 8, 37, 131, 137, 140, 144, 149.
5. Vahanian, *Death of God*, 49, 53–5, 75, 78, 125, 191, 196, 199, 203.
6. Vahanian, *Death of God*, 60–78, 154–62; Lippmann, "Ungovernability of Man."
7. John O'Sullivan, "Our Post-Christian Society," *National Review*, Dec. 14, 2013, at https://www.nationalreview.com/2013/12/our-post-christian-society-john-osullivan/ (last accessed 11/1/21); Barna, "The Most Post-Christian Societies in America: 2019," June 5, 2019, at https://www.barna.com/research/post-christian-cities-2019/ (last accessed (2/4/21). To qualify as "post-Christian," respondents had to meet nine or more of

the following sixteen criteria: Do not believe in God; Identify as atheist or agnostic; Disagree that faith is important in their lives; Have not prayed to God (in the last week); Have never made a commitment to Jesus; Disagree the Bible is accurate; Have not donated money to a church (in the last year); Have not attended a Christian church (in the last 6 months); Agree that Jesus committed sins; Do not feel a responsibility to "share their faith"; Have not read the Bible (in the last week); Have not volunteered at church (in the last week); Have not attended Sunday school (in the last week); Have not attended religious small group (in the last week); Bible engagement scale: low (have not read the Bible in the past week and disagree strongly or somewhat that the Bible is accurate); Not Born Again.

8. Harold Bloom, *The American Religion: The Emergence of the Post-Christian Nation* (New York: Simon and Schuster, 1992), 45, 263; Christopher James, *Church Planting in Post-Christian Soil* (New York: Oxford University Press, 2017), 1, 23–9.
9. Elesha J. Coffman, *Margaret Mead: A Twentieth-Century Faith* (New York: Oxford University Press, 2021), 53–4.
10. On this point, see Michele F. Margolis, *From Politics to the Pews: How Partisanship and the Political Environment Shape Religious Identity* (Chicago: University of Chicago Press, 2018).
11. Alexander Heffner, "Where's the Next Walter Lippmann?" *Washington Post*, Aug. 15, 2011, at https://www.washingtonpost.com/blogs/political-bookworm/post/wheres-the-next-walter-lippmann/2011/08/15/gIQAv2CfHJ_blog.html (last accessed 2/9/21); Robert Putnam, with Shaylyn Romney Garrett, *The Upswing: How America Came Together a Century Ago and How We Can Do It Again* (New York: Simon and Schuster, 2020), 317–18.
12. David Brooks, quoted in Sarah Pulliam Bailey, "Is David Brooks a Christian or a Jew?" *Washington Post*, May 3, 2019, at https://www.washingtonpost.com/religion/2019/04/29/is-david-brooks-christian-or-jew-his-latest-book-traces-his-faith-his-second-marriage/ (last accessed 9/23/22).
13. Walter Lippmann, "Today and Tomorrow: 'A Virtual Despair'," *Washington Post*, Aug. 4, 1964, A13.

Selected Bibliography

Archival Collections

The Walter Lippmann Papers (MS 326). Manuscripts and Archives, Sterling Memorial Library, Yale University.

The Robert O. Anthony Collection of Walter Lippmann (MS 766). Manuscripts and Archives, Sterling Memorial Library, Yale University.

Newspapers and Journals

New Republic
New York Herald Tribune
New York *World*
Newsweek
Washington Post

Lippmann Books and Edited Collections

Lippmann, Walter. *A Preface to Politics*. 1913. Reprint, Ann Arbor: University of Michigan Press, 1962.

Lippmann, Walter. *Drift and Mastery*. New York: Mitchell Kennerley, 1914.

Lippmann, Walter. *The Stakes of Diplomacy*. New York: Henry Holt, 1915.

Lippmann, Walter. "Introductory Note." *The Chicago Race Riots, July 1919* by Carl Sandburg, iii–iv. New York: Harcourt, Brace, and Howe, 1919.

Lippmann, Walter. *Liberty and the News*. New York: Harcourt, Brace, 1920.

Lippmann, Walter. *Public Opinion*. 1922. Reprint, Lexington: Pantianos Classics, 2019.

Lippmann, Walter. *Men of Destiny*. New York: Macmillan, 1927.

Lippmann, Walter. *American Inquisitors*. 1928. Reprint, New Brunswick: Transaction, 1993.

Lippmann, Walter. *A Preface to Morals*. 1929. Reprint, New York: Time Incorporated, 1964. Lippmann, Walter. *Interpretations, 1931–32*. Edited by Allan Nevins. New York: Macmillan, 1932.

Lippmann, Walter. *The Method of Freedom*. New York: Macmillan, 1934.

Lippmann, Walter. *The New Imperative*. New York: Macmillan, 1935.

Lippmann, Walter. *Interpretations, 1931–32*. Edited by Allan Nevins. New York: Macmillan, 1932.

Lippmann, Walter. *Interpretations, 1933–1935*. Edited by Allan Nevins. New York: Macmillan, 1936.

Lippmann, Walter. *An Inquiry into the Principles of the Good Society*. Boston: Little, Brown, 1937.

Lippmann, Walter. *U.S. Foreign Policy: Shield of the Republic.* Boston: Little, Brown, 1943.

Lippmann, Walter. *The Cold War: A Study in U.S. Foreign Policy.* New York: Harper and Brothers, 1947.

Lippmann, Walter. *Isolation and Alliances.* Boston: Little, Brown, 1952.

Lippmann, Walter. *The Communist World and Ours.* Boston: Little, Brown, 1958.

Lippmann, Walter. *The Coming Tests with Russia.* Boston: Little, Brown, 1961.

Lippmann, Walter. *The Essential Lippmann: A Political Philosophy for Liberal Democracy.* Edited by Clinton Rossiter and James Lare. New York: Vintage, 1963.

Lippmann, Walter. *Conversations with Walter Lippmann.* Edited by Edward Weeks. Boston: Little, Brown, 1965.

Lippmann, Walter. *Force and Ideas: The Early Writings.* Edited by Arthur Schlesinger, Jr. New Brunswick: Transaction, 1970.

Lippmann, Walter. *Public Philosopher: Selected Letters of Walter Lippmann.* Edited by John Morton Blum. New York: Ticknor and Fields, 1985.

General Sources

Addams, Jane. *Democracy and Social Ethics.* New York: Macmillan, 1907.

Addams, Jane. *Twenty Years at Hull House.* New York: Macmillan, 1910.

Allen, David John. "Every Citizen a Statesman: Building a Democracy for Foreign Policy in the American Century." PhD diss., Columbia University, 2019.

Arnold-Forster, Tom. "Democracy and Expertise in the Lippmann–Terman Controversy." *Modern Intellectual History* 16 (Aug. 2019): 561–92.

Baltzell, E. Digby, *The Protestant Establishment: Aristocracy and Caste in America.* New York: Random House, 1964.

Barna. "The Most Post-Christian Societies in America: 2019." June 5, 2019. Accessed February 4, 2021. https://www.barna.com/research/post-christian-cities-2019/.

Bayne, Stephen F. *The Optional God.* 1953. Reprint, Wilton, Conn.: Morehouse-Barlow, 1980.

Bergin, Angus. *The Great Persuasion: Reinventing Free Markets since the Depression.* Cambridge: Harvard University Press, 2015.

Betts, George Herbert. *The Beliefs of 700 Ministers.* New York: Abingdon, 1929.

Binger, Carl. "A Child of the Enlightenment." In *Walter Lippmann and His Times*, edited by Marquis Childs and James Reston, 21–36. New York: Harcourt, Brace, 1959.

Bloom, Harold. *The American Religion: The Emergence of the Post-Christian Nation.* New York: Simon and Schuster, 1992.

Blume, Mary. "Walter Lippmann at 80: The Hopeful Skeptic," *Washington Post*, May 31, 1970, B3.

Bourne, Randolph. "Trans-national America." *Atlantic Monthly* 118 (July 1916): 86–97.

Brown, John Mason. *Through These Men: Some Aspects of Our Passing History*. New York: Harper and Brothers, 1952.

Burge, Ryan P. *The Nones: Where They Came From, Who They Are, and Where They Are Going*. Minneapolis: Fortress Press, 2021.

Burnidge, Cara Lea. *A Peaceful Conquest: Woodrow Wilson, Religion, and the New World Order*. Chicago: University of Chicago Press, 2016.

Burns, Jennifer. "Liberalism and the Conservative Imagination." In *Liberalism for a New Century*, edited by Neil Jumonville and Kevin Mattson, 58–72. Berkeley: University of North Carolina Press, 2007.

Childs, Marquis "Introduction: The Conscience of a Critic." In *Walter Lippmann and His Times*, edited by Marquis Childs and James Reston, 1–20. New York: Harcourt, Brace, 1959.

Coffman, Elesha J. *Margaret Mead: A Twentieth-Century Faith*. New York: Oxford University Press, 2021.

Cotkin, George. *William James: Public Philosopher*. Baltimore: Johns Hopkins University Press, 1990.

Croly, Herbert. *The Promise of American Life*. New York: Macmillan, 1909.

Curtis, Susan. *A Consuming Faith: The Social Gospel and Modern American Culture*. Baltimore: Johns Hopkins University Press, 1991.

Dallek, Robert. *Flawed Giant: Lyndon Johnson and His Times, 1961–1973*. New York: Oxford University Press, 1998.

Dewey, John. *Democracy and Education*. New York: Macmillan, 1916.

Dewey, John. *Reconstruction in Philosophy*. New York: Henry Holt, 1920.

Dewey, John. "The American Intellectual Frontier," *New Republic*, May 10, 1922, 303–4.

Dewey, John. "Public Opinion," *New Republic*, May 3, 1922, 286–8.

Dewey, John. *The Public and Its Problems*. New York: Henry Holt, 1927.

Dinnerstein, Leonard. "Jews and the New Deal." *American Jewish History* 72, no. 4 (June 1983): 461–76.

Edwards, Mark. *The Right of the Protestant Left: God's Totalitarianism*. New York: Palgrave Macmillan, 2012.

Eisenach, Eldon J. *The Lost Promise of Progressivism*. University Press of Kansas, 1994.

Ekbladh, David. *The Great American Mission: Modernization and the Construction of an American World Order*. Princeton: Princeton University Press, 2011.

Eliot, T. S. Preface to *After Strange Gods: A Primer of Modern Heresy*. London: Faber and Faber, 1934.

Erlandson, Sven. *Spiritual but Not Religious: A Call to Religious Revolution in America*. Bloomington: IUniverse, 2000.

Fisher, Linford D. *The Indian Great Awakening: Religion and the Shaping of Native Cultures in Early America*. New York: Oxford University Press, 2012.

Follett, Mary Parker. *The New State: Group Organization the Solution of Popular Government*. New York: Longmans, Green, 1918.

Forcey, Charles. *The Crossroads of Liberalism: Croly, Weyl, Lippmann, and the Progressive Era, 1900–1925*. New York: Oxford University Press, 1961.

Fosdick, Harry Emerson. *As I See Religion*. New York: Harper and Brothers, 1932.

Fuller, Robert C. *Spiritual, but Not Religious: Understanding Unchurched America*. New York: Oxford University Press, 2001.

Gaston, K. Healan. "Then as Now, Why Niebuhr?" *Modern Intellectual History* 11 (November 2014): 761–71.

Gaston, K. Healan. *Imagining Judeo-Christian America: Religion, Secularism and the Redefinition of Democracy*. Chicago: University of Chicago Press, 2019.

Gelfand, Lawrence E. *The Inquiry: American Preparations for Peace, 1917–1919*. New Haven: Yale University Press, 1963.

Gerstle, Gary. *American Crucible: Race and Nation in the Twentieth Century*. 2002. Reprint, Princeton: Princeton University Press, 2017.

Goodwin, Craufurd D. *Walter Lippmann: Public Economist*. Cambridge: Harvard University Press, 2014.

Gorski, Philip. *American Covenant: A History of Civil Religion from the Puritans to the Present*. Princeton: Princeton University Press, 2019.

Grabiner, Judith V. and Peter D. Miller. "Effects of the Scopes Trial: Was It a Victory for Evolutionists?" *Science* 185 (September 6, 1974): 832–7.

Halle, Louis J. "Walter Lippmann: The Philosopher as Journalist." *New Republic*, Aug. 3, 1963, 16.

Handy, Robert T. *A Christian America: Protestant Hopes and Historical Realities*. 2nd ed. New York: Oxford University Press, 1984.

Hedstrom, Matthew S. *The Rise of Liberal Religion: Book Culture and American Spirituality in the Twentieth Century*. New York: Oxford University Press, 2012.

Henry, Patrick. "'And I Don't Care What It Is': The Tradition-History of a Civil Religion Proof-Text." *Journal of the American Academy of Religion* 49, no.1 (March 1981): 35–47.

Herman, Paul. "'Our Post-Christian Age': Historicist-Inspired Diagnoses of Modernity, 1935–1970." In *Post-Everything: An Intellectual History of Post Concepts*, edited by Paul Herman and Adrian van Veldhuizen, 17–39. Manchester: Manchester University Press, 2021.

Hoeveler, Jr., J. David. *The New Humanism: A Critique of Modern America, 1900–1940*. Charlottesville: University Press of Virginia, 1977.

Hollinger, David. *Christianity's American Fate: How Religion Became More Conservative and Society More Secular*. Princeton: Princeton University Press, 2022.

Horton, Walter. *Theism and the Modern Mood*. New York: Harper and Brothers, 1930.

Imhoff, Sarah. "My Sons Have Defeated Me: Walter Lippmann, Felix Adler, and Secular Moral Authority." *Journal of Religion* 92 (October 2012): 536–50.

James, Christopher. *Church Planting in Post-Christian Soil*. New York: Oxford University Press, 2017.

James, William. *The Varieties of Religious Experience*. 1902. Reprint, New York: Signet Classic, 1983.

James, William. *Pragmatism: A New Name for Some Old Ways of Thinking*. 1907. Reprint, New York: Dover, 1995.

Selected Bibliography

James, William. "The Moral Equivalent of War." In *The Moral Equivalent of War and Other Essays*, edited by John K. Roth, 4–14. New York: Harper, 1971.

Jenkins, Philip. *The Great and Holy War: How World War I Became a Religious Crusade*. New York: HarperOne, 2014.

Katznelson, Ira. *Fear Itself: The New Deal and the Origins of Our Time*. New York: Liverlight, 2014.

King, Charles. *Gods of the Upper Air: How a Circle of Renegade Anthropologists Reinvented Race, Sex, and Gender in the Twentieth Century*. New York: Doubleday, 2019.

Kittelstrom, Amy. *The Religion of Democracy: Seven Liberals and the American Moral Tradition*. New York: Penguin, 2016.

Kloppenberg, James T. *Uncertain Victory: Social Democracy and Progressivism in European and American Thought, 1870–1920*. New York: Oxford University Press, 1988.

Kruse, Kevin. *One Nation Under God: How Corporate America Invented Christian America*. New York: Basic Books, 2015.

Krutch, Joseph Wood. *The Modern Temper: A Study and a Confession*. New York: Harcourt, Brace, 1929.

Lacey, Robert J. *Pragmatic Conservativism: Edmund Burke and His American Heirs*. New York: Palgrave Macmillan, 2016.

Lewis, David Levering. *W. E. B. Du Bois: A Biography, 1868–1963*. New York: Henry Holt, 2009.

Luekens, Craig. "4 Reasons Why I'm Religious, But Not Spiritual." *Huffpost* (Feb. 16, 2016). Accessed February 2, 2023. https://www.huffpost.com/entry/4-reasons-why-im-religiou_b_9240166.

Luhan, Mabel Dodge. *Movers and Shakers*. New York: Harcourt, Brace, 1936.

Lynn, Kenneth S. "Versions of Walter Lippmann." *Commentary* 70 (October 1980): 65–9.

Margolis, Michele F. *From Politics to the Pews: How Partisanship and the Political Environment Shape Religious Identity*. Chicago: University of Chicago Press, 2018.

Mariano, Marco, ed. *Defining the Atlantic Community: Culture, Intellectuals, and Policies in the Mid-Twentieth Century*. New York: Routledge, 2010.

McCarter, Jeremy. *Young Radicals: In the War for American Ideals*. New York: Random House, 2017.

McDuffie, Erik S. "Chicago, Garveyism, and the History of the Diasporic Midwest." *African and Black Diaspora* 8, no. 2 (April 2015): 129–45.

Mercier, Louis J. A. "Walter Lippmann's Evolution." *Commonweal*, August 4, 1939, 348–50.

Mislin, David. *Saving Faith: Making Religious Pluralism an American Value at the Dawn of the Secular Age*. Ithaca: Cornell University Press, 2015.

Morrow, Felix. "Faith on Easy Terms." *Commonweal*, October 16, 1929, 604–5.

Morrow, Felix. "Religion and the Good Life," *Menorah Journal* 18 (February 1930): 86–7.

Mowry, George. *Theodore Roosevelt and the Progressive Movement.* Madison: University of Wisconsin Press, 1946.

Nevins, Allan. "Walter Lippmann and the *World.*" In *Walter Lippmann and His Times*, edited by Marquis Childs and James Reston, 60–82. New York: Harcourt, Brace, 1959.

Nichols, Christopher McKnight. *Promise and Peril: America at the Dawn of a Global Age.* Cambridge: Harvard University Press, 2011.

Niebuhr, Reinhold. "Review of *A Preface to Morals.*" *World Tomorrow* 12 (July 1929): 313–14.

Niebuhr, Reinhold. "A Matter of Popular Will." *New York Times Book Review*, February 20, 1955, 3.

Niebuhr, Reinhold. "The Democratic Elite and American Foreign Policy." In *Walter Lippmann and His Times*, edited by Marquis Childs and James Reston, 168–88. New York: Harcourt, Brace, 1959.

O'Sullivan, John. "Our Post-Christian Society," *National Review*, December 14, 2013. Accessed November 1, 2021. https://www.nationalreview.com/2013/12/our-post-christian-society-john-osullivan/.

Parsons, William B, ed. *Being Spiritual but Not Religious: Past, Present, Future(s).* New York: Routledge, 2018.

Putnam, Robert and Shaylyn Romney Garrett. *The Upswing: How America Came Together a Century Ago and How We Can Do It Again.* New York: Simon and Schuster, 2020.

Riccio, Barry D. *Walter Lippmann: Odyssey of a Liberal.* New Brunswick, N. J.: Transaction, 1994.

Ross, Dorothy. *The Origins of American Social Science.* New York: Cambridge University Press, 1992.

Ross, Edward A. *Sin and Society: An Analysis of Latter-Day Iniquity.* Boston: Houghton, Mifflin, 1907.

Rotunda, Ronald D. "The 'Liberal' Label: Roosevelt's Capture of a Symbol." *Public Policy* 17 (1968): 377–408.

Rubinstein, Annette T. "Disinterestedness as Ideal and as Technique." *The Journal of Philosophy* 28, no. 17 (August 1931): 461–6.

Said, Edward. "Grey Eminence." *London Review of Books,* March 5, 1981, 7.

Sanger, Margaret. *Margaret Sanger: An Autobiography.* New York: W. W. Norton, 1938.

Santayana, George. *Reason in Society.* New York: Charles Scribner, 1905.

Schlesinger, Jr., Arthur. "Walter Lippmann: The Intellectual v. Politics." In *Walter Lippmann and His Times*, edited by Marquis Childs and James Reston, 189–225. New York: Harcourt, Brace, 1959.

Schultz, Kevin M. *Tri-Faith America: How Catholics and Jews Held America to Its Protestant Promise.* New York: Oxford University Press, 2011.

Schulzinger, Robert D. *The Wise Men of Foreign Affairs: The History of the Council on Foreign Relations.* New York: Columbia University Press, 1984.

Self, Robert O. *All in the Family: The Realignment of American Democracy since the 1960s.* New York: Hill and Wang, 2012.

Shotwell, James T. *Intelligence and Politics*. New York: Century, 1921.

Shotwell, James T. *The Religious Revolution of Today*. Boston; Houghton Mifflin, 1913.

Simmons, J. Aaron. "Religious, but Not Spiritual: A Constructive Proposal." *Religions* 12 (June 2021). Accessed Sept. 5, 2022. https://www.mdpi.com/2077-1444/12/6/433.

Small, Albion. "The Bonds of Nationality." *American Journal of Sociology* 20, no. 5 (1915): 629–83.

Smith, Warren Allen. "Authors and Humanism." *The Humanist* 11 (October 1951): 199.

Snyder, Brad. *The House of Truth: A Washington Political Salon and the Foundations of American Liberalism*. New York: Oxford University Press, 2017.

Stansell, Christine. *American Moderns: Bohemian New York and the Creation of a New Century*. Rev. ed. Princeton: Princeton University Press, 2009.

Steel, Ronald. "Walter Lippmann: An Interview with Ronald Steel," *New Republic*, April 14, 1973, 16–17.

Steel, Ronald. "Walter Lippmann at 83: An Interview with Ronald Steel," *Washington Post*, March 25, 1973, C4.

Steel, Ronald. *Walter Lippmann and the American Century*. Boston: Little, Brown, 1980.

Steel, Ronald. "The World We're In: An Interview with Walter Lippmann," *New Republic*, Nov. 13, 1971, 20–1.

Stephanson, Anders. "Cold War Degree Zero." In *Uncertain Empire: American History and the Idea of the Cold War*, edited by Joel Isaac and Duncan Bell, 19–50. New York: Oxford University Press, 2012.

Sullivan, Andrew. "Keynes on Burke." *Atlantic*, February 1 2007. Accessed October 28, 2020. https://www.theatlantic.com/daily-dish/archive/2007/02/keynes-on-burke/231119/.

Sutton, Matthew. *American Apocalypse: A History of Modern Evangelicalism*. Cambridge: Harvard University Press, 2014.

Taylor, Charles. *A Secular Age*. Cambridge: Belknap Press, 2007.

Toynbee, Arnold. *Civilization on Trial*. New York: Oxford University Press, 1948.

Turner, James. *Without God, Without Creed: The Origins of Unbelief in America*. Baltimore: John Hopkins University Press, 1986.

Turpin, Andrea L. *A New Moral Vision: Gender, Religion, and the Changing Purposes of Higher Education, 1837–1917*. Ithaca: Cornell University Press, 2016.

Vahanian, Gabriel. *The Death of God: The Culture of Our Post-Christian Era*. New York: George Braziller, 1961.

Von Eschen, Penny M. *Race against Empire: Black Americans and Anticolonialism, 1937–1957*. Ithaca: Cornell University Press, 1997.

Wall, Wendy. *Inventing the "American Way": The Politics of Consensus from the New Deal to the Civil Rights Movement*. New York: Oxford University Press, 2008.

Wallas, Graham. *The Great Society*. New York: Macmillan, 1914.

Wasniewski, Matthew A. "Walter Lippmann, Strategic Internationalism, the Cold War, and Vietnam, 1943–1967." PhD diss., University of Maryland, College Park, 2004.

Watts, Sarah. *Rough Rider in the White House: Theodore Roosevelt and the Politics of Desire*. Chicago: University of Chicago Press, 2003.

Weingast, David Elliott. *Walter Lippmann: A Study in Personal Journalism*. Westport, Conn.: Greenwood, 1949.

Wellborn, Charles. *Twentieth Century Pilgrimage: Walter Lippmann and the Public Philosophy*. Baton Rouge: Louisiana State University Press, 1969.

Westcott, Brooke Foss. *The Gospel of the Resurrection: Thoughts on Its Relation to Reason and History*. London: Macmillan, 1884.

Whitehead, Andrew L. and Samuel L. Perry. *Taking America Back for God: Christian Nationalism in the United States*. New York: Oxford University Press, 2020.

Williams, Rhys H., Raymond Haberski, Jr., and Philip Goff, eds. *Civil Religion Today: Religion and the American Nation in the Twenty-First Century*. New York: New York University Press, 2021.

Zubovich, Gene. *Before the Religious Right: Liberal Protestants, Human Rights, and the Polarization of the United States*. Philadelphia: University of Pennsylvania Press, 2021.

Zweigenhaft Richard L. and G. William Domhoff. *Jews in the Protestant Establishment*. New York: Praeger, 1982.

Index

For the benefit of digital users, indexed terms that span two pages (e.g., 52–53) may, on occasion, appear on only one of those pages.

Acheson, Dean 146, 149, 165–6, 168
Addams, Jane 21, 79–81, 86, 198–9
Adler, Mortimer J. 171–2
Africa 108, 151, 155–6, 165
Agnosticism 19, 21–2, 50, 56, 68, 169–70, 175
Albertson, Ralph 30–1, 44
"America First" movement 72, 75, 118, 134–6
"American Century, The" (1941) 136–8, 143
"American Destiny, The" (1940) 136, 143–5, 151–2
American Establishment, The 133–4, 140–1, 145–6, 197, 204–5
American Inquisitors (1928) 52–3, 78
"American Religion, The" (1915) 23–4, 107, 131, 206–7
Anti-Semitism 32–5, 45, 62, 66, 73–6, 88–90, 106–9, 130–1, 162
Armstrong, Hamilton Fish 113–14, 134–5
Asia 2, 101, 135, 138, 141–4, 148–50, 163–7, 193–7
Atlantic Community v, 2, 4, 71–3, 137–8, 140–3, 148–50, 164–5, 194–5

Baker, Newton 73, 76, 91, 107–8, 112
Barker, Ernest (Sir) 170–2
Bayne, Stephen (Bishop) 7–8, 206
Berenson, Bernard 75–6, 168, 171
Binger, Carl 20, 35, 179–80
Black Power 85, 178–9, 190–1, 196
Blume, Mary 189
Boaz, Franz 83
Bohemians 30–2, 46, 69, 116
Bourne, Randolph 46, 83, 88
Bowman, Isaiah 73–5
Brandeis, Louis D. (Justice) 31–2, 88

Brooks, David 211
Bryan, William Jennings 51–3, 77–8, 168
Buckley, Jr., William F. 99, 124, 171, 176–7
Buell, Raymond Leslie 81–2
Burke, Edmund 8–9, 99, 107, 111–12, 116, 124, 131–2, 152, 162–3
Byrd, Harry Flood, Jr. (Senator) 86, 115–16, 178

Catholicism 3, 21–3, 30, 53, 55, 57, 84, 100, 105–6, 114, 120–2, 130–3, 138–40, 167, 171, 174, 207
China 138, 142, 149–50, 163–4, 170, 177–8, 180, 194
Christendom 4, 6–7, 10–11, 123–4, 131, 143–4, 148, 151, 174, 190
Christian Americanism 3–4, 11, 35, 75, 100, 121–3, 143–5, 168, 206–7, 209–10
Christianity 5, 8, 12, 21–2, 25, 35, 39–45, 57, 68, 91, 100–1, 103, 105, 114–15, 120–3, 130–3, 140–1, 143, 145, 152–4, 162, 172–3, 197–8, 200–1. *see also* post-Christian
Civil religions vi, 3–7, 10, 23–4, 29–30, 46–9, 54, 64–5, 72–3, 100, 114–15, 130–3, 138–41, 143–5, 152–4, 167–75, 197–8, 205–6, 210
Civil rights movements 9–10, 66–9, 83–90, 100–1, 154–6, 162, 178–9, 181–2, 189–91
Clark, Mark (General) 140–1
Cold War, The 1–4, 146–52, 163–81, 191–200
Cold War, The (1947) 1–7, 42–3, 147–50, 164–5
Cold War liberalism. *see* liberalism
Collier, John 84–5

Index

Council on Foreign Relations (CFR) 82, 104–5, 114, 134–5, 141, 166, 181
Croly, Herbert 23–4, 29–30, 32, 47–8, 69–70, 79, 107, 114–15, 206–7
Cuba 192–3

Darrow, Clarence 52, 77–8
Davis, Norman P. 118, 134–5
"Death of God," 7, 27, 39, 46, 206–8
Death of God, The (1961) 206–8
Democratic Party 107–24, 134–5, 191–6, 198–200
Dewey, John 8–9, 51–2, 79–83, 114–15, 198–9
"Disentanglement," 135, 164–5, 193
Dodge, Mabel 30–2, 69–70
Donald, Barbara 181–2
Drift and Mastery (1915) 47, 68–9, 86
Du Bois, W. E. B. 24, 84–5, 155–6
Dulles, John Foster 140–1, 149, 163–8, 179–80
Dunn, Angus (Bishop) 171–3

Eastman, Max 30–2, 66
Eisenhower, Dwight D. 7–8, 140–1, 163–70, 177–8
Eliot, T. S. 24, 107–8, 131, 207
Ellul, Jacques 188–9, 198
Elsas, Lucile ("Lucy") 28–9, 33–4, 44–5, 54
Emanu-El (Temple) 20, 33
England. *see* Great Britain
Europe 2–3, 19–20, 33, 71, 73–5, 87, 90–1, 99–103, 105, 107–8, 115, 130–1, 134–5, 137–8, 143–6, 148–52, 164, 180, 189, 193–5, 200
European Union 135

Fabian Society 29–30, 66, 116
Farmer, Elizabeth 181–2, 191–2
Federal Council of Churches (FCC) 50, 56, 86, 114, 123, 140
Feminism 6, 42, 66–9, 86–7, 104, 123, 154, 168–9, 181–2, 188–9
Follett, Mary Parker 79–81
Foreign Affairs 1, 82, 113–14
Foreign Policy Association (FPA) 82, 86
Fosdick, Harry Emerson 39–40, 50–1, 56
"Fourteen Points, The" (1918) 63, 73–4, 195

Frankfurter, Felix (Justice) 31–2, 57–8, 69–70, 73–5, 87–8, 106
Freud, Sigmund 26–7, 39–40, 46–7, 67, 104
Fulbright, J. William (Senator) 178–9
Fundamentalism 4, 39–40, 44, 50–3, 77–9, 122–3, 131, 207–8

Galbraith, John Kenneth 176–9, 191–2
De Gaulle, Charles (General) 140–1, 171, 194–5
Germany 2, 106, 141–2, 145–9, 164–5, 180
Gilson, Etienne 114–15
Goldwater, Barry 99, 124, 176–7, 190–1, 200
Good Society, The (1937) 116–23, 169, 192–3, 197–8
Great Britain 2, 71–3, 136–8, 141–2, 165
Great Depression, The 101–24, 131–2, 134–5, 189
Great Society, The (1914) 67–8
"Great Society," v, 9–10, 41, 63, 70–1, 79–80, 90–1, 100–1, 109–11, 116, 119, 132–3, 135, 167, 169, 188–9, 192–6, 199

Hamilton, Alexander 8–9, 11–12, 69–70, 72, 102–3, 112, 114, 122, 135, 168, 209–10
Hand, Learned (Judge) 172
Harding, Warren G. 75, 87, 168
Harvard University 20–30, 43–5, 64–5, 70–1, 83, 88–90, 101, 131–2, 178, 188–9, 197, 207
Hayek, Friedrich von 8–9, 116–19
Hitler, Adolf 106, 134–6, 144, 169
Holmes, Oliver Wendell, Jr. (Justice) 31–2
Hoover, Herbert 31–2, 84, 107, 109
House, Edward M. (Colonel) 73–5
House of Truth 31–3, 72–3, 84, 88, 107, 115–16, 189
Humanism 39, 47–50, 55, 101, 107–8, 130–3, 137, 139, 162–3, 172–3, 197–8, 204

"Image of Man, The" (manuscript) 114–15, 117, 120, 169
"Inquiry, The" 73–6, 88
Islam 5, 123–4, 151–2, 174

Index 223

James, William 8–11, 24–7, 29–30, 39–41, 46–9, 52–4, 56, 63–4, 66–7, 77, 79–80, 83–5, 91, 111–12, 115, 117, 132–3, 137, 140, 162–3, 167, 173, 175, 179–80, 204
Jefferson, Thomas 11, 63, 69, 77–8, 100, 123, 167, 209–10
Johnson, Lyndon Baines v, 178–9, 191–7, 199–200
Judaism 5–9, 12, 20, 23, 32–5, 41–3, 45, 53, 55, 62, 73–5, 88–90, 105–9, 114–15, 150–2, 155–6, 172–3, 182–3, 189, 198, 200–1, 209, 211
Judeo-Christian 7–8, 108, 131–2

Kallen, Horace 83, 88
Kennan, George v, 1–4, 148, 167, 179–80
Kennedy, John F. 123, 178–9, 181, 183, 191–2
Kennedy, Joseph P. (Senator) 140–1
Keynes, John Maynard (Lord) 8–9, 111–12, 116, 137
Keynesianism 111–12, 116, 119, 135, 144–5, 149, 177–8, 199
Khrushchev, Nikita (Premier) v, 179–81, 192
Kirk, Russell 171–2
Korean War 163–7, 193
Krutch, Joseph Wood 49–50, 55
Ku Klux Klan (KKK) 76, 84–5, 87–8, 105–6, 108–9, 134

Lamont, Thomas 101, 123
Lewis, Sinclair 39, 49–50
Liberalism 9–10, 32, 47–8, 69–71, 90–1, 107–24, 130, 132, 137, 144–5, 149, 162–3, 176–9, 183, 189, 191–3, 195–200, 209
Libertarianism 84, 115–19
Liberty and the News (1920) 76
Lippmann, Faye (Albertson) 30–1, 39, 44, 62, 76, 87, 91, 113–14
Lippmann, Helen (Byrne) v, 35, 39, 57, 113–14, 117, 133, 140–1, 146, 153–6, 180–2, 191, 197, 200
Lippmann, Walter
  and "America First," 72, 75, 134–6
  on Africa 108, 155–6, 165

  as an agnostic 19–20, 35, 56, 68, 77–8, 136, 147–8, 169–70, 175, 208–9
  on the Atlantic Community v, 2, 4, 71–3, 137–8, 140–3, 148–50, 164–5, 194–5
  and bohemianism 30–2, 35, 46–7, 69
  anti-urbanism of 40–1, 63–4, 75–6, 188–9, 197–9
  on Asia 2, 101, 135, 138, 141–4, 148–50, 163–7, 193–7
  and Catholicism 3, 21–3, 30, 45–6, 53, 55, 57, 84, 100, 105–6, 114, 120–2, 130–3, 138–40, 167, 171, 174, 207
  celebrity of v, 1, 84, 90–1, 101–3, 133, 140–1, 152, 155–6, 179–82, 191–2, 204–5
  on Christendom 4, 6–7, 10–11, 123–4, 131, 143–4, 148, 151, 174, 190
  on civil religions vi, 3–7, 10, 23–4, 29–30, 46–9, 54, 64–5, 72–3, 100, 114–15, 130–3, 138–41, 143–5, 152–4, 167–75, 197–8, 205–6, 210
  on civil rights 9–10, 66–9, 83–90, 100–1, 154–6, 162, 178–9, 181–2, 189–91
  and uses of "civilization," 71–2, 105–6, 109, 131–6, 139–40, 148, 162, 194
  on the Cold War 1–4, 146–52, 163–81, 191–200
  on communism 3, 101, 103, 109, 138, 146–52, 163–82, 191–7
  as a conservative 10, 41–3, 47, 57–8, 90–1, 99–124, 132, 163, 176–9, 197–200, 211
  as a critic and proponent of Christian nationalism 3–4, 11, 35, 75, 100, 121–3, 143–5, 168, 206–7, 209–10
  daily routine of 41–2, 102–3, 123, 133, 181–2, 197
  on democracy 3, 29–30, 62–5, 76–83, 109–11, 122–3, 130–3, 144–5, 154–6, 167–75, 197–200
  as a Democrat 107–24, 134–5, 191–6, 198–200
  and "disentanglement," 135, 164–5, 193
  education of 20–30, 102, 207
  on Europe 2–3, 19–20, 33, 71, 73–5, 87, 90–1, 99–103, 105, 107–8, 115, 130–1, 134–5, 137–8, 143–6, 148–52, 164, 180, 189, 193–5, 200

Lippmann, Walter (*cont.*)
  on executive over legislative
    theory 69–71, 107–11, 115–19,
    163–75, 191
  on fascism 84, 101, 103, 105–6, 109,
    118, 136, 168–9, 200
  on feminism 6, 42, 66–9, 86–7, 104,
    123, 154, 168–9, 181–2, 188–9
  on the founding fathers 8–9, 11–12,
    69–70, 72, 77–8, 100, 102–3,
    109–15, 120, 122, 132, 135, 167–8,
    170, 209–10
  on Fundamentalism 4, 39–40, 44, 48,
    50–3, 77–9, 131, 207–8
  and the Great Depression 101–24,
    131–2, 134–5, 189
  at Harvard University 20–30
  as a humanist 39, 47–50, 55, 101,
    107–8, 130–3, 137, 139, 162–3,
    172–3, 197–8, 204
  on immigration 20, 87–8, 108–9
  on imperialism 2–3, 34, 72–4, 84, 108,
    134–5, 137–40, 144–5, 147–52,
    164–5, 193–7, 199
  influences of 8–9, 24–7, 29–30, 35,
    66–8, 104–5, 111–15, 133–4, 137,
    162–3, 169–73, 188–9, 205
  and Judaism 5–9, 12, 20, 23, 32–5,
    41–3, 45, 53, 55, 62, 73–5, 88–90,
    105–9, 114–15, 150–2, 155–6,
    172–3, 182–3, 189, 198, 200–1,
    209, 211
  and Keynesianism 111–12, 116, 119,
    135, 144–5, 149, 177–8, 199
  and liberalism 9–10, 32, 47–8, 69–71,
    90–1, 107–24, 130, 132, 137, 144–5,
    149, 162–3, 176–9, 183, 189, 191–3,
    195–200, 209
  as a libertarian 84, 115–19, 149
  and love of art and nature 19–20,
    24–5, 27–8, 33–4, 91, 121
  and the "manufacture of consent,"
    63, 76
  marriages of 30–1, 33, 39, 62, 73, 91,
    113–14, 117, 123, 133, 200–1
  on the Middle East 2, 150–2, 165–6, 168
  and Modernism 21–2, 39–40, 50, 64,
    77, 105–6
  on modernization theory 54, 72–3,
    119, 136, 144–5, 181, 193

  as a monarchist 168–70, 200
  and natural law 8, 24, 54, 114–15,
    120–3, 130–3, 168–75, 179–80
  as a neo-isolationist 3, 100–1, 137–41,
    193–4, 199
  and the New Deal 107–24, 132,
    144–5, 162–3, 192
  and New York City 19–20, 30–2, 49,
    53, 66, 73, 77, 84, 102, 123, 135–6,
    197, 200–1
  as an opinion columnist v, 1, 49, 62,
    84, 101–3, 140–1, 152, 179–81,
    191, 197
  on organized labor 32, 57–8, 67, 69,
    80–2, 112–13, 135, 144–5
  personality of 12, 27–8, 31, 44, 123–4,
    140, 172, 181–2, 204–6
  and "positionality," 6, 83, 87, 162–3,
    205–6
  as a post-Christian vi, 6–12, 21–4, 35,
    39–40, 43–5, 53–4, 65–6, 82–4, 90,
    99–100, 111–12, 123, 130–3, 139,
    151–4, 162–3, 171–3, 175, 183, 198,
    200–1, 206–9
  as a Pragmatist 24–7, 29–30, 40–1,
    79–83, 99–111, 132–3, 152, 172–5,
    182, 200–1, 204
  as a Progressive 9–10, 21–4, 48, 63,
    69–72, 115–16, 189, 198–9
  and Protestantism 39–40, 50, 53, 56,
    77, 107–8, 122–3, 140, 166–7
  as a realist 1–3, 72–3, 100–1, 133–52,
    163–8, 193–7, 199
  as Religious but Not Spiritual
    (RBNS) 10–12, 19, 66, 105–6, 109,
    121–2, 132–3, 139–40, 153–4,
    170–1, 175, 209–10
  as a Republican 57–8, 75, 86, 101–2,
    115–16, 136, 176–7, 188–91,
    199–200, 210
  on the Roosevelts v, 9, 20, 23,
    25, 69–71, 101, 104, 107–13,
    115–17, 131–6, 169, 177–8, 183,
    191–2
  on the Scopes Trial 51–3, 77–9
  as a secularist 5, 8, 39–58, 64–5, 73,
    77–9, 84, 105, 132–3, 166–7, 171,
    174, 207
  and secularization theory 8, 39–41,
    43–4, 47, 54, 89–90

and socialism 10, 30–1, 33–5, 44–5, 66–9, 76, 90–1, 102, 110–12, 149, 163, 177
and South America 84, 134, 193
on "stereotypes," v, 5, 63, 76, 83–4, 109, 208
as Spiritual but Not Religious (SBNR) 10–12, 19, 28, 33–4, 42, 47, 51, 66, 100, 105–6, 109, 121, 132–3, 139–40, 153, 170–1, 175, 209–10
as theorist of the Great Society v, 9–10, 41, 63, 70–1, 79–80, 90–1, 100–1, 109–11, 116, 119, 132–3, 135, 167, 169, 188–9, 192–6, 199
as a "Tired Radical," 12, 58, 75–7, 91, 102, 198
and the Vietnam War 165, 180–1, 188–9, 194–200
and Washington D. C. 31–2, 73, 123, 133, 191, 197
wealth of 6, 19–20, 30, 41–2, 49, 89–91, 101–3, 133, 155–6
and William James 8–11, 24–7, 29–30, 39–41, 46–9, 52–4, 56, 63–4, 66–7, 77, 79–80, 83–5, 91, 111–12, 115, 117, 132–3, 137, 140, 162–3, 167, 173, 175, 179–80, 204
as a Wilsonian 44, 71–5, 100–1, 133–7, 141–5, 147, 151–2, 164–5, 181–2, 196
in World War I 48–9, 63, 71–6, 82, 195
in World War II 2, 133–46, 198
on Zionism 5, 32–3, 88–90, 150–1, 165
Luce, Henry 136–8, 143, 145

MacArthur, Douglas (General) 168
Madison, James 102–3, 110–11, 113–14, 167
Mahan, Alfred T. (Captain) 72, 133–4
Maritain, Jacques 131, 139–40, 207
Marshall Plan 149
Mather, Jane 39, 42, 200
McCarthy, Joseph P. 168, 176
McGovern, George 99, 199–200
Mead, Margaret 83, 208–9
Mencken, H. L. 39, 51–3, 77–8
Middle East 2, 150–2, 165–6, 168

Modernism 21–2, 39–40, 50, 64, 77, 105–6
Mont Pelerin Society 118–19
Murray, John Courtney 169–70, 172
Muste, A. J. 81–2

National Conference on Christians and Jews (NCCJ) 50, 56, 108
Natural law theory 114–15, 120–3, 130–3, 168–75, 179–80
Nevins, Allan 19, 57, 140, 144–5, 167, 169–70
Neo-liberalism 118–19. *See also* Libertarianism
New Deal, The 107–24, 144–5
New Left 188–9, 196, 199–200
New Republic v, 32, 46–9, 69–72, 82, 99, 112, 115–16, 118, 189, 197–8
New Right. *see* Republican Party
New York Herald Tribune v, 101–2, 108–9, 113
New York Times 2, 76, 179–80
Niebuhr, Reinhold 5, 8–9, 56, 63–4, 104, 114, 145, 171, 176–7, 179–80, 205–6
Nietzsche, Friedrich 8–11, 27, 43–7, 54, 62, 69–70, 84–5, 104, 115, 137, 147, 170, 191, 206
Nixon, Richard 9, 99, 188–9, 199–200
Non-Aligned Movement (NAM) 165, 181
"Nones," 5–7, 41–2, 100, 132–3, 208
North Atlantic Treaty Organization (NATO) 149, 164–5

Optional God, The (1953) 7–8

Phantom Public, The (1925) 79, 87
Post-Christian 6–12, 21–4, 151–4, 206–9
Post Christum (1935) 7
Pragmatism 24–7, 79–83
Preface to Morals, A (1929) v, 4, 7, 39–58, 62, 64–5, 77, 79, 87, 90–1, 99–100, 105–6, 120, 132–3, 137, 147, 163, 169, 175, 189, 197–8, 206
Preface to Politics, A (1913) 45–7, 67, 70
Progressivism 9–10, 21–4, 69–70
Progressive Party 21, 69–70
Protestant Establishment, The (1964) 35

Protestantism 39–40, 50, 53, 56, 77, 107–8, 122–3, 140, 166–7
Public Opinion (1922) v, 62–5, 76–8, 81, 90–1, 99–100, 119, 147, 169–70, 197–200
Public Philosophy, The (1955) 168–76, 197–200, 204

Reed, Jack 30–1, 66
Reichel, Donna 188–9, 198
"Religion of Humanity," 23–4, 47–8, 69, 107, 115, 206–7
Religious but Not Spiritual (RBNS) 10–12, 209–10
Republican Party 69, 74–5, 86, 115–16, 199–200, 210
Robeson, Paul 155–6
Roosevelt, Franklin Delano v, 1–2, 69, 101, 107–13, 115–17, 135–6, 140, 154, 191–2
Roosevelt, Theodore (Teddy) v, 9, 20–1, 23, 25, 69–71, 104, 131–2, 136, 165–6, 177–8, 191–2, 210
Rossiter, Clinton 176
Rostow, Walt 181
Royce, Josiah 25, 83, 115
Rubinstein, Annette 55, 57–8
Russia. *see* Soviet Union

Sacco and Vanzetti trial 87–8
Said, Edward 204–6
Sanger, Margaret 30–1, 86
Santayana, George 24–5, 28, 39–42, 65, 91, 115, 171, 179–80, 204
Sartre, Jean-Paul 170–1
Schaik, Frances van 123, 154, 182
Scopes trial 51–3, 77–9
Secularism 5, 8, 39–58, 64–5, 73, 77–8, 84, 105, 132–3, 166–7, 171, 174, 207. *see also* post-Christianity
Secularization 8, 39–41, 43–4, 47, 54, 89–90
Shotwell, James T. 43–4, 73
Small, Albion 23–4, 29–30, 107, 131, 206–7
Smith, Adam 9, 117–18
Smith, Al 84, 86–7, 105–6
Socialism 10, 30–1, 33–5, 44–5, 66–9, 76, 90–1, 102, 110–12, 149, 163, 177

South America 84, 134, 193
Soviet Union 1–3, 74, 76, 137, 143–52, 163–81, 191–2
Spiritual but Not Religious (SBNR) 10–12, 42, 47, 51, 209–10
Stakes of Diplomacy, The (1915) 72–4, 133–4, 181
Steel, Ronald vi, 31, 33, 99, 141, 148, 197–8, 200, 204–6
Stereotypes v, 5, 63
Strong-state liberalism. *see* Liberalism

Tennessee Valley Authority (TVA) 119, 181
Thompson, Dorothy 101, 108–9, 171
Tillich, Paul 172–3
"Today and Tomorrow" (column) v, 1, 101–2, 119, 130, 143–4, 154, 191–2, 197
Toynbee, Arnold J. 7–8, 104–5, 121, 124, 130–1, 137–8, 152–3, 169, 206–7
Traditions of Civility (1948) 8, 170–2
Truman, Harry S. 1–2, 146–9, 155–6, 163–8
Truman Doctrine 1–3, 147–52, 163–5

"Ungovernability of Man, The" (manuscript) 197–200
United Nations (UN) 138, 142–3, 147, 179
U. S. Foreign Policy (1943) v, 137–41
U. S. War Aims (1945) 141–5

Vahanian, Gabriel 206–8
Varieties of Religious Experience, The (1902) 25–6
Viereck, Peter 176
Vietnam War 165, 180–1, 188–9, 194–200

Wallace, Charlotte 181–2
Wallace, Henry 136, 145–6
Wallas, Graham 9–10, 29–30, 40, 63, 66–8, 79, 91, 111, 116–17, 137, 169, 192–3
Walter Lippmann and the American Century (1980) v
Walton, Lester 86, 91
Washington Post v, 99, 191, 195
Wehner, Jean 181–2
Weyl, Walter 32, 47–8, 58, 69

Whitehead, Alfred North 104
Willkie, Wendell 135–6, 140
Wilson, Woodrow v, 23, 48, 51–2, 63, 71–5, 109, 133, 141–5, 147, 181, 191–2
Women's Liberation 189. *see also* Feminism

World (New York) v, 19, 49–50, 52, 57–8, 84, 88–91, 101, 105–6
World War I 1–2, 48–9, 63, 71–5, 84–5, 111, 133–4, 137–8, 195
World War II 2, 133–46, 198

Zionism 5, 32–3, 88–90, 150–1, 165